THE ORGANIC TRADITION

an anthology of Writings on
ORGANIC FARMING,
1900-1950

Edited by
PHILIP CONFORD

with a foreword by
Jeremy Seabrook

GREEN BOOKS

This book is dedicated to
Mrs Penelope Massingham,
widow of HJM

First published in 1988 by
GREEN BOOKS
Ford House, Hartland, Bideford, Devon EX39 6EE

Cover design by Thomas Keenes and Simon Willby
Woodcut by Thomas Bewick

Typeset by MRR, Chard, Somerset,

Printed by Robert Hartnoll (1985) Ltd
Victoria Square, Bodmin, Cornwall

British Library Cataloguing in Publication Data

The Organic Tradition
1. Crops. Organic cultivation
I. Conford, Philip
631.5'84

ISBN 1-870098-09-9

CONTENTS

ACKNOWLEDGEMENTS

I would like to express my grateful thanks to the following publishers:

B.T. Batsford Ltd, for permission to re-print extracts from *England and the Farmer* (ed. H.J. Massingham).

Faber and Faber Ltd, for permission to re-print extracts from *The Autobiography of William Cobbett* (ed. W. Reitzel), *The Clifton Park System of Farming* by R.H. Elliot, *Farming and Gardening for Health or Disease* by Sir Albert Howard, *The Rape of the Earth* by G.V. Jacks and R.O. Whyte, *The Way of the Land* by Sir George Stapledon, and *Food, Farming and the Future* by Friend Sykes.

John Murray (Publishers) Ltd, for permission to re-print extracts from *Soil and Civilization* by Edward Hyams.

Oxford University Press, for permission to re-print extracts from *An Agricultural Testament* by Sir Albert Howard.

Thanks are also due to Lady Eve Balfour, for permission to re-print extracts from *The Living Soil,* and to reproduce her portrait (p.132); to the Society of Authors, as the literary representative of the Estate of H.J. Massingham, for permission to re-print extracts from *The Faith of a Fieldsman, Men of Earth, Remembrance, This Plot of Earth* and *The Wisdom of the Fields;* to Mr Robert Waller, for permission to re-print extracts from *Human Ecology* by Sir George Stapledon, and from *Prophet of the New Age;* to A.P. Watt Ltd, on behalf of Irene Collis, for permission to re-print extracts from *The Triumph of the Tree* by John Stewart Collis.

Acknowledgement is given for the photographs, although for some it was not possible to trace the owners.

I would also like to thank everybody who has helped me in the preparation of this anthology, and particularly Miss Clare Likeman, of Chichester College of Technology, for enabling me to make extensive use of her library's facilities, and her assistant Miss Christina Thomas who has been cheerfully indefatigable in hunting down innumerable books on compost and manure; Mrs Penelope Massingham, for allowing me to dedicate the anthology to her; Bob Waller, for background information and hospitality; Melanie Conford, for help with the Introduction; and Elizabeth Saxby of Green Books, for help in the anthology's preparation.

Finally my thanks are due to Jeremy Seabrook for agreeing to write the Foreword, and to Satish Kumar for suggesting the project.

Philip Conford

FOREWORD

Philip Conford's anthology shows to what extent so many of the concerns that the green movement has made its own in recent years are not new. It demonstrates that green sensibility is no alien implant in our culture, but is simply the reappearance in contemporary guise of a long tradition of sustainable agriculture, of respect for the earth, of reverence for the life-giving cycle of organic farming. That this tradition should have been marginalized and scorned by those who have a vested interest in the promotion of agri-business and chemicalized food-production has been an inestimable loss, particularly at the very time when it is most needed as a model and source of inspiration in the world. The revalidation of the organic tradition is both overdue and exciting: overdue, because it reveals that so many of what are regarded as urgent contemporary issues are, in fact, deeply rooted within our own culture in Britain, and indeed, have been discussed in ways that are immediately relevant to today for well over a century; and exciting, because it links up with many campaigns within and on behalf of the Third World, those countries suffering from the imposition of development processes that originate in the West and which a long history of prophetic warning failed to modify in the so-called 'metropolitan' countries. That process of smothering older, more sustainable practice has been exported all over the globe.

Those traditions do not die; they are merely eclipsed, overshadowed for a time. Philip Conford's painstaking editing has breathed new life into the prescience of John Stewart Collis and his strictures on the effects of deforestation, the lessons on erosion drawn by G.V. Jacks in his book *The Rape of the Earth,* published in 1939, the warnings of Edward Hyams that 'man, over a very great part of the surface of the earth, has become a disease of soil-communities' in the violent assault upon nature. The book is full of vibrant and suggestive prefigurings of the kind of problems that have been 'discovered' in our time. The vitality and immediacy, and above all, the relevance to discussions about 'development' and 'progress', the appeal to proven sustainable practice, will give new heart and courage to those who are fighting the malign spread of these same forms of maldevelopment across the world.

It is worth noting, in this respect, how those people who seek to rescue traditional practice, who speak of conserving what is good and wise in an ancient respect for the earth have been accused, in the late twentieth century, of being romantic or nostalgic. The disgracing of a customary and conserving husbandry is calculated only to clear the way for the rancher and the agri-business entrepreneur, those who see trees only as timber, and land only as investment. This may perhaps lead us to inquire whether it might not be possible to embrace a *radical nostalgia* - a retrieval of sustainable practice allied to a project of our future emancipation. The licensed nostalgias of our time involve interring these ways of life in the gardens of rest of permitted (and highly profitable) regret, or incorporating them into advertisements for adulterated foods to lend them an aura of freshness and naturalness. Nostalgia means epitaphs in our culture; perhaps a radical nostalgia might resuscitate the living lessons. It is not a question of a return to some mythic golden age: it is to confront with the bitter burden they have laid upon the earth and its people those who have jettisoned old wisdom as superstition, and traditional custom as ignorance and sustainable societies as primitive.

Industrial society, both its capitalist begetter and its socialist imitator, those joint and collusive celebrants of progress, have thought only of releasing the productive forces slumbering in the lap of labour: the earth that must bear that progress has paid a price that never entered their calculations. We, who now know that all economic systems depend upon the sustaining capacity of the planet, can no longer permit ourselves such single-minded optimism. Yet even with this knowledge, the same patterns of ruinous and destructive practice are being imposed upon age-old methods of husbandry and farming, destroying forests and lands that have sustained human beings for millennia without loss, until their mass destruction has been required to feed the market economy. A radical nostalgia might take up some of the knowledge and wisdom of sustainable balance with the earth and use it to liberate us from the dynamic of economic systems which are hurtling to extinction. It has nothing to do with going back, the myth of return. It is an intensely practical way of learning to tread more lightly on the fragile and damaged integument of the planet, without taking from it more than we give back. If hope is to be rescued from the workings of blind economic forces that know nothing of human things, let alone of the natural world which they devour in their voracious progression through time, it will be found in ancient sustainable ways of living, the examples set by those farmers and practitioners and visionaries whose words Philip Conford has retrieved from the obscurity with which the prophets of 'modernization' had shrouded their passionate sagacity.

All the development issues that beset and perplex the world in the late twentieth century were foreshadowed within Britain a hundred years ago. It is all so obvious in the simple words of Lady Eve Balfour, who said 'If the nation's health depends on the way its food is grown, then agriculture must be looked upon as one of the health services, in fact the primary health service.' Everything has been known for several decades about the ruin of soil fertility, the effects of chemicals on food, the consequences of deforestation, the degradation caused by monoculture; a wisdom of the ages by-passed by the superior exigencies of profit. We cannot afford the luxury of permitting such precious knowledge to be eclipsed a second time.

Jeremy Seabrook
London
May 1988

INTRODUCTION

In the autumn of 1986 I submitted to Satish Kumar, the editor of *Resurgence*, an article [1] on Edward Hyams and H.J. Massingham, outlining the way in which, despite contrasting political outlooks, they were united by their concern for the health of the soil and by their fear of increasing famine - an anxiety which we know in the 1980s to have been amply justified.

As a result of this article Satish invited me to edit an anthology of writings by British authors, including Hyams and Massingham, who had addressed themselves to the problems of soil fertility, organic husbandry, conservation of natural resources, and the relation between a healthy soil and healthy living creatures, in the years before 'ecology', 'conservation' and 'wholefoods' became increasingly common watchwords. About ten writers should be featured; the extracts should be taken from works published in the first half of this century; and the title Satish suggested was *The Organic Tradition*.

Questions of definition immediately arose, for the word 'organic' can have a variety of meanings, [2] according to whether it is used in the context of the current debates on agriculture, or in the spheres of biology, aesthetics, or social theory - though, as will be seen later, these wider aspects of meaning are also relevant to the philosophy of the organic farming and gardening movement.

At the simplest level the word 'organic' refers to a certain method of growing food, and can be defined negatively: organically-grown produce is that which is grown without the use of chemical fertilizers and pesticides. More positively, the estate-owner Friend Sykes (see chapter 7), one of the most distinguished pioneers of the organic movement, asserted roundly: 'Organic Farming... is another name, as everyone knows, for Humus Farming.' [3] Organic methods are not, therefore, a matter merely of avoiding the use of artificials; they require that the cultivator should encourage the fertility which lies, actually or potentially, in the soil itself, and should regard the soil not as inert matter but as a living organism. Such a definition is circular but the idea of a circle, or cycle, is so crucial to the organic view of the world that this very quality of circularity can be considered appropriate.

The definition is therefore pushed back one stage further: if organic farming is humus farming, what is humus? The easiest answer is that 'humus' is the Latin word for 'earth' or 'soil' and this, as far as it goes, is consistent with the above description of the organic approach. But for the twentieth-century agricultural scientist such a straightforward identification would be over-simplified to the point of hopeless inaccuracy; indeed, this (literally) vital substance, humus, is so complex that definition seems to be almost impossible. The outstanding authority on humus during the first half of this century was the American, Selman A. Waksman, who was Professor of Soil Microbiology at Rutgers University, and Microbiologist at the New Jersey Agricultural Experiment Stations. His research was well known to the leading British exponent of humus farming, the agricultural botanist Sir Albert Howard (see chapter 5).

Waksman's description of humus is as follows:

- a complex aggregate of brown to dark-coloured amorphous substances, which have originated during the decomposition of plant and animal residues by micro-organisms, under aerobic and anaerobic conditions, usually in soils, composts, peat bogs, and water basins. Chemically, humus consists of certain constituents of the original plant material resistant to further decomposition; of substances undergoing decomposition; of complexes resulting from decomposition either by processes of hydrolysis or by oxidation and reduction; and of various compounds synthesized by micro-organisms... Humus is a natural body; it is a composite entity, just as are plant, animal, and microbial substances; it is even much more complex chemically, since all of these materials contribute to its formation. Humus possesses certain specific physical, chemical, and biological properties which make it distinct from other natural organic bodies. Humus, in itself or by interaction with certain inorganic constituents of the soil, forms a complex colloidal system, the different constituents of which are held together by surface forces; this system is adaptable to changing conditions of reaction, moisture, and action of electrolytes. The numerous activities of the soil micro-organisms take place in this system to a large extent. [4]

In addition to offering this lengthy definition, Waksman described eight properties of humus, of which the most important for our purposes here are its dynamic condition and its function both 'as a source of energy for the development of various groups of micro-organisms' [5] and as 'a highly valuable constituent of substrates which support plant and animal life'. [6] Readers who would be happier with a description less precise but more graphic might prefer

Michael Graham's definition of humus as 'a substance resembling soft liquorice that comes from rotting of vegetable matter'. [7]

For advocates of organic farming the major task is to ensure that the soil is enriched by restoring or increasing its humus content. In the view of Sir Albert Howard the example to follow is that of Nature, the supreme farmer, who has never needed to use artificials:

- great pains are taken to preserve the soil and to prevent erosion; the mixed vegetable and animal wastes are converted into humus... ample provision is made to maintain large reserves of fertility; the greatest care is taken to store the rainfall... [8]

Since Nature, if left to itself - or Herself, as Howard would have said - creates its own reserves of fertility, and since the overwhelming majority of human beings throughout the ages have farmed without the use of artificials, by increasing the presence of humus in soils where natural fertility could not be taken advantage of indefinitely, [9] it might be asserted that the idea of an 'organic tradition' is meaningless, since such a tradition in fact stretches right back to prehistoric times. But a conscious advocacy of organic methods can only begin to exist once some alternative approach to cultivation has emerged, and the organic movement has its significance and purpose as a reaction to developments which date from the nineteenth century and have become increasingly powerful in the twentieth.

At the opposite extreme is the frequently-encountered idea that the organic movement is nothing more than an offshoot of the 'hippie' era - a product of the idealistic 1960s - the naive fantasy of the Woodstock generation and their desire to return, in some unspecified fashion, to Nature. The journalist Paul Johnson, for instance, has dismissed concern for the health of the soil as an example of 'fear of science' [10] produced by 'the forces of unreason'. [11] One would not of course look to an ardent defender of Thatcherite capitalism for an accurate picture of the ecology movement but it is disappointing to see a lack of perspective in the writings of one of the most articulate leading figures of the Green movement, Jonathon Porritt, when he refers to Schumacher's *Small is Beautiful* as a 'golden oldie'. [12] Schumacher's book was published in 1973 and the implication of Porritt's description is that eleven years is a very long time in the history of ecology. It is one of the purposes of this anthology to dispel such misconceptions, by showing that concern about the effects of industrialized methods of agriculture already existed at the end of the nineteenth century, and was being systematically expressed in a variety of ways by the 1940s.

The organic tradition, then, can be traced back considerably further than most people are aware, and has to be understood as a response to those developments in nineteenth-century agricultural science and practice without which its existence as a defender of traditional methods would not have been necessary.

If there is one date which is important above all others in the history of modern agricultural changes it must surely be 1840, since it was in that year that Baron Justus von Liebig, Professor at the University of Giessen, published the monograph *Chemistry in its Application to Agriculture and Physiology,* a report to the British Association which was to lay the foundations of agricultural chemistry, and in particular the study of fertilizers and manures. According to Sir A.D. Hall, Liebig 'made little original contribution himself to the theory [[of plant nutrition]], adopting in the main the conclusions that arose from the work of Priestley, Ingenhousz, Sennebier, and de Saussure', [13] but his reputation ensured an enthusiastic response to his views. One major result of his monograph was the inauguration in 1843 of systematic manurial experiments on the estate of J.B. Lawes at Rothamsted in Hertfordshire. Lawes worked with a former assistant to Liebig, J.H. Gilbert - a partnership which lasted until Lawes's death in 1900, and established Rothamsted's importance as a leading institution for research into methods of increasing fertility; or, from the point of view of an advocate for humus farming, as a centre for the new, pernicious orthodoxy of artificials.

The most significant feature of Liebig's thought for our purposes here was his rejection of the view that humus is essential for plant nourishment. Howard attributed this rejection to the fact that Liebig was a chemist, not a biologist, and was therefore unaware that humus is the habitat of fungous and bacterial organisms, though he was correct in appreciating the part played in plant nourishment by the chemical and mineral contents of the soil. In Howard's view Liebig's ideas were dangerous because they omitted consideration of too many other factors, and a more complete understanding of the nature of the soil only became feasible when Charles Darwin published *The Formation of Vegetable Mould Through the Action of Worms* in 1881. [14] Howard seems to have regarded this work as more important even than the theory of evolution, saying that it 'established once for all this principle of interlocked life and, from this point of view, remains a landmark in the investigation of the soil'. [15] But Darwin's essay received far less attention than his earlier, epoch-making works, and in any case the chemical view of the soil was well-established by the time it appeared. According to Prof. J.A. Scott Watson and May Elliot Hobbs:

> Many farmers still believed that muck was the only source of real fertility, and that the new chemicals were no more than whips and spurs wherewith the bad farmer might urge the soil to special efforts and drive it the more rapidly to exhaustion... But Lawes lived to see the fifty-seventh successive crop of wheat, grown without natural manures, flourishing on Broadbalk field, and he could die in the assurance that he had made no very gross mistake. [16]

The Broadbalk field of wheat was a prime source of controversy between supporters of humus farming and defenders of artificials, since it was still producing satisfactory crops after a hundred years. For Sir E.J. Russell, Director of Rothamsted Experimental Station at the time of its centenary, the Broadbalk experiment demonstrated that 'apart from disease, the yield of wheat can be kept up indefinitely by proper artificials'. [17] He further claimed that although farmyard manure was necessary for root crops and potatoes, grain produced by using farmyard manure could not be proved in any way superior to that produced by using artificial fertilizers.

Two years after Russell's article appeared, Howard responded with a bitter counterblast, 'The Unsoundness of Rothamsted', in which he recalled his final visit to Broadbalk:

> I can truthfully say that never in my long experience have I seen arable land in such a hopeless and filthy condition. A more glaring example of bad farming could scarcely be imagined. I took my leave at the earliest possible moment and decided then and there that my last visit to Rothamsted - the Mecca of the orthodox - had been paid. [18]

He considered there to be at least four major flaws in the design of the experiment, the most serious being the fact that the seed sown was obtained each year from a reliable outside source; this meant there was no continuity as regards the wheat itself. Furthermore the plots were not isolated, and could be invaded by burrowing animals - in particular by earthworms. The true effects of artificials, whose use led to the death of such creatures, could not be judged as long as the creatures were still able to colonize the trial plots.

Howard's view of Rothamsted is interesting not only because it illustrates the level of hostility present in the controversy, but for his use of the word 'orthodox'. For thousands of years peasants and farmers had made use of humus, yet within the space of only a century the value of chemical fertilizers had been established as orthodoxy. Why was this?

One possible answer is the fact already mentioned that Liebig was a chemist, not a biologist, and that chemistry, developing in advance of biology - since it has to deal with fewer variables - was able to exert its influence and establish its prominence in the scientific study of agriculture well before the ideas of Darwin, and particularly those of Waksman and his researchers, were published. We have already seen how complex a substance humus was found to be: it is therefore perhaps not surprising that a much simpler view of the process of plant nutrition, supported by the authority of an outstanding figure like Liebig, could rapidly take hold of people's minds in an age when an ideology of progress was helping to discredit traditional values.

This simpler view is generally referred to scathingly by supporters of humus farming as 'the NPK mentality' - the view that nitrogen, phosphorus and potassium, artificially supplied, will provide all the nutrition that a plant requires. Its adoption by so many farmers cannot be explained just by an abstract reference to the nature of scientific advance, though, or by invoking the 'spirit of the age'; there were more pressing, practical reasons why farmers grasped at the apparently obvious benefits of the new fertilizers. Scott Watson and Hobbs, as we have seen above, spoke of the view of traditionally-minded farmers that artificials were being used as 'whips and spurs... [[to]] urge the soil to special efforts...' [19] But if farmers had begun to feel the need to put pressure on their soil, it was because they in turn were being pressurized by economic forces.

Once again the 1840s provide the single most important date: 1846, the year the Corn Laws were repealed and foreign foodstuffs admitted into the country at a nominal fixed duty. It has been said that the Corn Laws were washed away by rain: the disastrous harvest of 1845 and the potato famine in Ireland, combined with the arguments of the Anti-Corn Law League and the gradual erosion of Protectionist policies over a period of some years, led to the acceptance by Sir Robert Peel, the Prime Minister, of the view that cheap food for a rapidly-expanding population was the priority, and that Britain would be able to pay for imported foodstuffs by exporting her manufactured goods. For thirty years or so it appeared that the worst fears of farmers about the possible effects of Free Trade would not be realized - in fact the period from 1853 to the mid-1870s has been regarded as a golden age for British agriculture, with the loss of protection even acting as a stimulus to new developments. There were improvements in drainage, buildings, and the preparation of farmyard manure; a great deal of money was invested in land; enthusiasts like Mechi, at Tiptree Hall in Essex, showed what could be achieved even on poor clay soil; advances were made in the breeding of live-stock; the seasons were favourable, and crops were produced in abundance.

By the second half of the 1870s, though, it was clear that this situation could not last, and successive years of bad weather, combined with the ever-accelerating flow of imports, notably from the United States, culminated in the disastrous summer of 1879, when one of the worst harvests of the nineteenth century devastated British farmers and a flood of American wheat and cheese undercut their prices. The ominous implications of Free Trade could now be more clearly seen, emphasized by the problems occurring in the manufacturing industries. In the words of Lord Ernle:

> English farmers were... confronted with a new problem. How were they to hold their own in a treacherous climate on highly rented land, whose fertility required constant renewal, against produce raised under more genial skies on cheaply rented soils, whose virgin richness needed no fertilizers? [20]

There were various possible responses, but the two which particularly concern our purposes here are specialization - of which more later - and, of course, greater use of artificials. Farming thus grew increasingly industrial in its methods, in the sense that the soil's productive capacity had to be exploited intensively if efficiency - measured in financial terms - was to be achieved. For Howard, the profit motive was at work in this situation in another way, too: the vested interests of those who stood to gain by the sale of artificial fertilizers. (Here we have an example of the anti-capitalist strain which is so prevalent in the organic tradition; though, as will be discussed in more detail, this implies a certain nostalgia for mediaevalism rather than an adoption of socialism.) The nineteenth-century farmers who believed muck to be 'the only source of real fertility', [21] and the twentieth-century advocates of organic husbandry, regarded the use of artificials to increase productivity as a dangerous, short-term expedient. Howard expressed the situation thus:

> Faced with the demand for higher yields, the farmer has grasped at the most desperate of all methods: he has robbed the future. He has provided the huge output demanded of him, but only at the cost of cashing in the future fertility of the land he cultivates. In this he has been the rather unwilling, but also the rather blind, pupil of an authority he has been taught to respect: the pundits of science have urged him to go forward... [22]

The forces set in motion in the nineteenth century have culminated in the agri-business of today, with its monocultural methods and reliance on mechanization, chemicals, and intensive rearing practices. Jonathan Brown's recent book *Agriculture in England: A Survey of Farming, 1870-1947* (Manchester University Press, 1987) gives a clear, concise account of the economic forces at work during the period covered by this anthology, and of the way in which government intervention, necessary though it was, served to increase the dominance of the industrial approach to the soil.

Nevertheless, by the end of the Second World War there also existed a coherent opposition to this orthodoxy, and the spreading influence of the organic movement today is based - whether it is aware of it or not - on the work of those biologists, botanists, farmers, doctors and writers who, during the first half of this century, formulated a countervailing philosophy. Scientific research, which had been used to discredit traditional methods of cultivation, was now used instead to justify and improve them; the work of Howard and his first wife Gabrielle, in India, was of enormous importance in this regard. Howard combined knowledge of Waksman's research on humus with first-hand experience of peasant practice. The peasants of the East were unaware of the scientific basis of their methods yet they had managed for centuries to keep their soil in good heart, whereas modern agricultural techniques appeared to lead rapidly to exhaustion of fertility, as an increasing amount of research on soil erosion, and the evidence of the American Dust-Bowl, persuasively implied. Perhaps chemicals were failing to replace some vital ingredient without which fertility was impossible; perhaps they were contributing to a decline in the quality of any soil to which they were applied, and even, ultimately, to its death.

Two other major figures in the organic tradition were stimulated by their experiences in India during the early part of this century: Sir

Robert McCarrison, and Dr G.T. Wrench (see chapter 8), who were led to consider the relationship between methods of cultivation, diet, and health. Here too, it seemed, was an area where the progressive West could learn from an ancient culture. The science of nutrition might be used to demonstrate the wisdom of a practice which produced such splendidly healthy examples of humanity as the Hunza tribesmen; while evidence from industrial Britain between the two World Wars served to emphasize the poor physical condition of so many of our citizens. Nor was it just a question of *human* health: Howard's work at the Institute of Plant Industry, Indore, suggested that a humus-rich soil would produce disease-resistant plants and that animals fed on the produce of that soil would gain in health. Although Howard was critical of much peasant practice, especially where fruit and tobacco were concerned, he noted that their crops were on the whole free from disease.

In 1928 a Symposium on Soil Organic Matter and Green-Manuring was held in Washington, USA, at which Waksman was the principal speaker. Although his book on humus was not to appear for another eight years, the experiments on which its conclusions were based had been in progress for a considerable time, and it was clear that a scientific justification for a defence of traditional methods and a critique of modern ones were now available. Howard's achievements with the Indore Process (see chapter 5) - scientific knowledge and methods applied to the improvement of peasant practice - and his return to England in 1931 after his first wife's death, gave impetus to the counter-attack. Within ten years the Haughley Research Trust had been founded (see chapter 6), the Indore Process had been successfully used in a variety of countries, the Kinship in Husbandry had been formed around the central figures of Rolf Gardiner and Lord Lymington, and Howard had found disciples such as Friend Sykes (see chapter 7) who were willing to put organic methods to the test on their estates. Furthermore, the supporters of humus farming had by the end of the 1930s found a valuable ally in the literary world, who was to give them an assured outlet for over thirty years - this was Richard de la Mare (son of the poet Walter de la Mare) who edited Faber's agriculture and gardening list from the 1930s until the 1970s. The overwhelming majority of books on the organic movement which appeared in Britain before the 1960s owe their existence to Faber, as the bibliographical details in this anthology demonstrate.

By the Second World War, then, the central importance of this complex substance, humus, was established in the controversy about artificial fertilizers. A clear, non-specialist summary of its origins, nature, and potential value can be found in the first chapter of F.H. Billington's book *Compost: For Garden Plot or Thousand-Acre Farm* (London, Faber, 1942). The main features of the position held by the organic school of thought, and outlined by Billington, can be stated as follows:

- that humus is formed from organic matter which 'includes the residues of plants, animals, worms, insects and myriads of live and dead minute organisms such as fungi... algae and innumerable kinds of bacteria'; [23]
- that earthworms 'excel as humus makers'; [24]
- that good composting, which aims at creating humus, imitates nature's methods;
- that humus provides the medium in which the biological and chemical changes involved in the rotting down of organic matter can occur;
- that humus influences the distribution of plant foods and prevents nutrients being lost because of rain;
- that humus facilitates the process of mycorrhizal association, [25] a kind of symbiosis 'influencing such important qualities as nutritional value, keeping property, disease resistance, reproductive capacity, colour and flavour of plants...'; [26]
- that humus acts as a conditioner, giving soil both cohesion and a crumbly texture;
- that humus enables light-coloured soils to grow darker and therefore warmer;
- that humus has a sponge-like quality which helps soil to absorb rain, thereby preventing run-off and erosion, and prevents the blowing away of top-soil;
- that the chief causes of the depletion of humus are the warmth of the climate; dryness of the soil, resulting from drainage or drought, and excessive or too intensive cultivation;
- that replenishment of humus can be achieved by the use of compost, farmyard manure, or green manures; by crop residues; by temporary leys, and by rotation.

Billington feels it necessary to remind his readers that the supreme value of humus is not universally recognized:

It is necessary to point out that the superior quality of naturally manured produce as compared with that chemically manured and the enhanced fertility of organically-managed soils are not conceded by some authorities. Others are prepared to stake their reputations upon its reality. [27]

A detailed and systematic account of the issues involved in the debate, as it stood at the end of the period covered by this anthology, can be found in *Chemicals, Humus, and the Soil* by Donald P. Hopkins (London, Faber, 1945). In the end Hopkins comes down against the hard-line organic position adopted by Howard and Lady Eve Balfour, but the arguments on both sides are clearly presented. I have concentrated on Howard during this Introduction because he has a right to be regarded as the single most important figure in the organic movement, but it needs to be pointed out that defenders of artificials did not generally deny the value of humus, and that there were supporters of organic methods who were prepared to admit that the use of artificials could sometimes be justified. [28] Another work which gives an account of the debate is Michael Graham's *Soil and Sense* (London, Faber, 1941). Since this book was praised by supporters of the organic movement despite its having a Preface by Sir E.J. Russell of Rothamsted, its fair-mindedness can be assumed.

More than forty years have passed since these books appeared, scientific research on both sides of the argument has moved on, and the effects of chemical methods of cultivation have become increasingly plain - and, to many people, alarming. The success of the centre for organic gardening at the Henry Doubleday Research Association, near Coventry, suggests that the case against artificials may ultimately be proved on the palate of the general public.

If the idea of an organic tradition is to be fully understood, a consideration simply of the arguments about humus and chemicals is insufficient, central though that particular debate may be. The word 'organic', as mentioned at the beginning of this Introduction, has wider reference than just to methods of farming and gardening, though its other possible applications do in fact proceed by analogy from the biological realm.

Towards the end of *Chemicals, Humus, and the Soil* (1945), Donald Hopkins comments that 'the Nature-knows-best philosophy of this [[i.e. the humus]] school tends to appeal to those whose leanings are somewhat artistic...' [29] If this is true - and I believe it to be a perceptive and significant remark - the explanation of the phenomenon can be found in the philosophy of Professor John Macmurray. According to Macmurray, if the processes of life are to be represented symbolically:

> We must represent the unity of what is alive as a unity of differences... the organic whole cannot be represented as the sum of

its parts... It can be represented only in aesthetic terms, as a balance
or harmony... A work of art is always a unity of differences and that
is why we often speak of it as an *organic* unity. [30]

Since what is alive is not static, the different elements in the unity
have to be represented

as themselves in process, and these processes of the different elements
as themselves harmoniously combined to form a unity of processes
which is the life of the organism as a whole... We shall say that each
different element in the living creature has a function to perform in the
whole, for the whole. [31]

Indeed, Hopkins might have gone further, and suggested that the
ideas of the humus school tend to appeal to people of a religious tem-
perament. Among the writers in the period covered by this anthology
one finds Christian belief explicitly expressed by Lady Eve Balfour and
H.J. Massingham, [32] for example; Howard's references to 'Mother
Earth' [33] - a phrase which was also the name of the Soil Association
journal - imply a religious outlook, as does Lord Northbourne's
plea, 'We have tried to conquer nature by force and by intellect. It
now remains for us to try the way of love'; [34] and the approach of the
Bio-Dynamic school of farming drew its inspiration from the ideas of
Rudolf Steiner. [35] More abstractly, it could be argued that the organic
movement is inherently religious in a general sense, since it is based on
reverence for the laws of nature - literally, on humility - rather than on
the arrogant assumption that the earth can be indefinitely persuaded
or forced to do Man's will. In describing mysticism as 'an aesthetic
rather than a religious experience' [36] Macmurray may be making too
absolute a distinction, but when he goes on to say that mysticism
'expresses the point at which the aesthetic attitude seeks to take the
whole real as its object', [37] it is easy to relate what he says to the organic
movement, for at the heart of the organic philosophy is an attitude
which sees the processes of nature in terms of an over-all harmonious
pattern which has been disordered by the techniques of an industrialized mentality.

The pattern takes the form of a universal mandala - the wheel. G.T.
Wrench's book on the relation between soil, diet, and human well-
being uses this image [38] (see chapter 8), and the idea of a 'wheel of life'
is used by Sir Albert Howard in his explanation of the nature of soil
fertility. [39] Very simply, it is a diagrammatical way of expressing the
inter-dependence of soil, plants, and living creatures: the living soil

produces plants; the plants feed animals and humans; the various wastes are returned to the soil, whose health and fertility are thereby maintained or increased. Good husbandry means looking after the soil by observing the Rule of Return, and here the peasant, with his horror of waste, is to be especially admired. Howard believed that not even human urine and excrement need be rejected - indeed, it was far better to use them for making compost than to have water polluted by sewage. The same sort of idea is expressed in imaginative, aesthetic form by Walter de la Mare in his short story 'The Wharf', when Farmer Simmonds tells an urban visitor that his midden-heap may seem 'just filth and waste and nastiness... 〚 but is〛 the very secret of all that is most precious in the living things of the world'. [40] (Since, as we have seen, de la Mare's son Richard edited the Faber agriculture list, it is intriguing to speculate on the extent to which the organic movement in Britain is indebted to a mystical poet.)

When applied to methods of agriculture, the idea of a wheel of life must necessarily mean the practice of mixed farming, whereas the logic of an industrial approach leads to monoculture, in defiance of the variety which is to be found in the natural world. Again, aesthetic judgements are relevant: monoculture, whether in the form of vast fields of wheat, or Forestry Commission evergreens, tends to be unattractive to the eye. For H.J. Massingham, the topographer, the values of the older rural tradition - of peasant farming as opposed to specialization, and the work of the craftsman as opposed to mass production - were reflected in the beauty of the buildings, villages and towns it left behind.

> 〚 The craftsman〛 had sited and built the villages, decorated the roofs and ricks, tilled the fields, tended the sheep, produced the crops, baked the bread, brewed the ale and cider, pleached the hedges, constructed the dry-walls, made the field-gates, conserved the woodlands, named the wild and cottage flowers, carved the churches and celebrated the seasons... 〚 His〛 relation to nature was non-predatory from first to last, from raw material to finished product. He did not conquer nature but married her in husbandry. [41]

Thus we are brought to the political aspects of the organic tradition - the strong element of nostalgia for an 'organic society'. It is not difficult to see how such a longing arises from the outlook described so far, and expresses itself in admiration for the example which once existed, or was believed once to have existed, in the form of pre-industrial Britain. There, it has been felt, was a world in which the profit motive had not yet been enshrined; in which agriculture was the chief occupation; in which husbandry was practised by peasant farmers who cared for their soil out of a long-sighted sense of true economy; in which farming methods respected the value of variety; in which every local area was self-sufficient; in which everyone had a function to perform in the structure of their town or village; in which one dominant view of the world created a sense of unity; and in which humans perceived nature reverently, as God's Creation, rather than rapaciously, as material to exploit for gain. This was the world which had been disappearing ever since the Reformation, and with particular rapidity since the end of the eighteenth century - the world whose passing Cobbett lamented (see Prologue). Small farmers decreased in number; rural poverty, the Enclosures, mechanization, and the pull of the new industrial centres combined to drive or attract people away from the land; land-owners farmed on a large scale in order to make a profit; English society saw the growth of a new, rootless urban population, while the traditional structure of rural society decayed.

The organic movement was therefore concerned not just with advocating the use of humus, or a greater emphasis on mixed farming, but with the restoration of agriculture to its central place in English life. Agriculture, according to this view, was the keystone of society; when it was removed from its position of importance, the effects made their way through one area of national life after another, destroying the beauty of the traditional pattern.

It is possible to see the organic movement as one response to the inter-war crisis, trying to avoid the dilemma of a choice between Fascism (though this requires some qualification in a moment), Communism, and the decrepitude of bourgeois democracy, by opposing the dynamic which underlay all three systems - industrialism. It was argued that a revivified rural life, based on the principles of husbandry, could provide an answer to most of the problems which beset Britain in the 1920s and 1930s. Land-work would reduce unemployment; humus-grown food and open-air tasks would improve standards of health; industry would be smaller-scale and geared to the needs of rural activities, and this would counteract centralization and alienation, thereby contributing to desirable demographic changes; the mass-movements of urban civilizations - particularly Communism - would lose their breeding-ground; rural festivals and rituals connected with the cycle of the seasons would reduce the need for the mechanized entertainments of a jaded proletariat.

The leading figure in the establishment of the Kinship in Husbandry was Rolf Gardiner, and accounts of the movement can be found in the writings of Massingham, Lord Lymington, and Gardiner himself. [42] Massingham edited a book of essays by several of the leading figures in the movement, including Gardiner, Lord Lymington (Earl of Portsmouth), Lord Northbourne, Michael Graham, Edmund Blunden, Philip Mairet and Adrian Bell. [43] Also associated with the Kinship were Sir Albert Howard, Sir George Stapledon, and Sir Robert McCarrison.

For Massingham, as we have seen, the ideal of an organic society lay in the past, beyond the Enclosures, in the England of yeoman farmers and local craftsmen. He therefore hated both Communism and Nazism as exemplars of the worst aspects of the twentieth-century spirit, describing the latter as 'a worse-than-bestial caricature of the drift of all modern civilization'. [44]   But the word 'organic' has been used to describe the totalitarian states of our own age, and Gardiner, Lymington and Blunden showed a sympathy for Nazism which paralleled the admiration many left-wing figures of the 1930s expressed for Stalin. [45] Once again the ideas of John Macmurray provide a possible explanation, when he speaks of

> the facts of plant and animal life... being applied by analogy to the human field on the *a priori* assumption that human life must exhibit the same structure.
>
> The practical consequences are in the end disastrous... The organic conception of the human, as a practical ideal, is what we now call the totalitarian state... If organic theory overlooks human freedom, organic practice must suppress it.
>
> ...We are not organisms, but persons. The nexus of relations which unites us in a human society is not organic but personal. Human behaviour cannot be understood, but only caricatured, if it is represented as an adaptation to environment... [46]

It is a complex question of political theory - or may, perhaps, remain to be seen in practice - whether an organic approach to the soil implies a totalitarian conception of society.

In the 1940s there was a good deal of emphasis among writers in the organic movement on the question of post-war reconstruction, inspired by the same sort of mood which produced the Beveridge Report and the Labour Party's overwhelming victory in 1945   -   the desire to avoid returning to the waste of resources, both agricultural and human, which had characterized the 1920s and 1930s. The war had served to emphasize the importance of home-grown food, and had clearly demonstrated the poor state of health of so many citizens. One major issue was whether land should be nationalized: as is to be expected, this was generally opposed by the supporters of husbandry, though Frances Donaldson and Edward Hyams were in favour of such a policy.[47] The Agriculture Act of 1947 was a major piece of legislation designed to give state support to farmers, but its effect was to increase the tendency towards chemical methods of cultivation. By the end of the period covered in this anthology the forces representing an industrial approach to the soil were poised ready to intensify their hold on farming practice.

But, as I hope this Introduction has demonstrated, all the essential ideas of the organic movement were in existence by 1952   -   the year which saw the death of H.J. Massingham, one of that movement's most humane and expressive advocates. Because, by definition, the organic philosophy attempts to see things as a whole, in relation to each other, the different themes presented in the following chapters can be found referred to in a variety of books from the first half of this century. Thus, for example, the issue of diet is dealt with not only in the writings of Dr Wrench (see chapter 8), but also in those of Sir Albert Howard, Lady Balfour, and Friend Sykes.

My approach has therefore been to present an 'organic' collection of themes, using a different writer to illustrate each of them. Most of the topics vital to an understanding of the organic tradition are here: a historical view of what happens to nations who abuse their soil; the importance of trees and forests in the cycle of nature; soil erosion in the twentieth century; biological methods of maintaining soil fertility; the link between soil and health; objections to monoculture; the avoidance of waste; the importance of craftsmanship; and a sense of religious reverence for the gifts of the earth. All these things are of course ultimately inseparable.

There turned out to be an embarrassment of riches to choose from, and it was with reluctance that I decided against including extracts from, for example, Lord Northbourne's excellent survey of the general issues, *Look to the Land* (London, Dent, 1940), or L.J. Picton's *Thoughts on Feeding* (London, Faber, 1946). The wider question of social organization is not dealt with either; readers wishing to pursue this are referred to Sir George Stapledon's *Human Ecology* (London, Faber, 1964; 2nd edn, London, Charles Knight, 1971); *Alternative to Death* by the Earl of Portsmouth, Viscount Lymington (London, Faber, 1943); and *From the Ground Up* by Jorian Jenks (London, Hollis and Carter, 1950).

Here, then, are some of the people responsible for what Paul Johnson refers to as 'ecological panic'. [48] These 'enemies of society' turn out to be distinguished scientists and doctors, loyal servants of the British Empire, estate-owners, and distinguished horticulturalists and writers, one or two of whose close associates were sufficiently right-wing in their politics to satisfy, one would have thought, even a Paul Johnson.

In the 1960s a popular radio comedy programme starring Kenneth Horne regularly featured Kenneth Williams as 'Arthur Fallowfield', an over-sexed and half-witted peasant stereotype, whose response to every question was 'Well, Oi think the arnswer loies in the soil...' If this anthology serves to show that Fallowfield's claim should never have been a target for metropolitan mockery, it will have performed at least one useful function.

Philip Conford
Chichester
December 1987

References

1   Philip Conford, 'Soil of England', *Resurgence*, no. 120, Jan./Feb. 1987, pp. 8-9.

2   Cf. Raymond Williams, *Culture and Society 1780 - 1950* 〖 1958〗 (Harmondsworth, Pelican Books, 1971), pp. 256-7.

3   Friend Sykes, *Modern Humus Farming* (London, Faber, 1959), p.35.

4   S.A. Waksman, *Humus: Origin, Chemical Composition, and Importance in Nature* 〖 1936〗 (2nd Edn, London, Baillière, Tindall & Cox, 1938), pp. 5-6.

5   Ibid., p.7.

6   Ibid.

7   Michael Graham, *Soil and Sense* (London, Faber, 1941), p.44.

8   Sir Albert Howard, *An Agricultural Testament* (London, Oxford University Press, 1940), p.4

9   Cf. *Farmers of Forty Centuries* by F.H. King (London, Cape, 1927); a book which was a major influence on Howard.

10   Paul Johnson, *Enemies of Society* (London, Weidenfeld & Nicolson, 1977), p.89.

11   Ibid., p.101.

12   Jonathon Porritt, *Seeing Green* (Oxford, Basil Blackwell, 1984), p.244. E.F. Schumacher, *Small is Beautiful: A Study of Economics as if People tered* (London, Blond & Briggs, 1973).

13   Sir A.D. Hall, *Fertilizers and Manures* [[1909]] (4th Revised Edn, London, John Murray, 1947), p.6.

14   This essay was republished under the title *Darwin on Humus and the Earthworm* (London, Faber, 1945), with an Introduction by Sir Albert Howard.

15   Sir Albert Howard, *Farming and Gardening for Health or Disease* (London, Faber, 1945), p.76.

16   J.A. Scott Watson and May Elliot Hobbs, *Great Farmers* (London, Selwyn & Blount, 1937), p.79.

17   Sir John Russell, 'Broadbalk', *The Countryman* (Burford, Oxon), Autumn 1943 edition, p.90.

18   Sir Albert Howard (1945), p. 79.

19   Scott Watson and Hobbs, *Great Farmers*, p.79.

20   Lord Ernle *English Farming Past and Present* [[1912]] (6th edn, London, Heinemann, 1961), p.380.

21   Scott Watson and Hobbs, *Great Farmers*, p. 79.

22   Howard (1945), p. 74.

23   F.H. Billington, *Compost for Garden Plot or Thousand-Acre Farm* [[1942]] (4th revised edn, London, Faber, 1946), p.16.

24   Ibid.

25   Chapter 13 of *Humus and the Farmer* by Friend Sykes (London, Faber, 1946) gives a reasonably non-specialist description of this process.

26   Billington, *Compost*, p. 18.

27   Ibid., p.19.

28   This was true, for example, of Sir George Stapledon and even of Friend Sykes. Cf. Stapledon, *Human Ecology* [[1964]] (2nd edn, London, Charles Knight, 1971), pp. 56-57; Sykes, *Modern Humus Farming* (London, Faber, 1959), p. 39.

29   Donald P. Hopkins, *Chemicals, Humus, and the Soil* (London, Faber, 1945), p. 235.

30   John Macmurray, *Interpreting the Universe* (London, Faber, 1933), p. 110.

31   Ibid., p. 111.

32   Cf. *The Living Soil* by E.B. Balfour (London, Faber, 1943), p. 201; and *Remembrance* by H.J. Massingham (London, Batsford, 1942), p. 125.

33   See, for example, Howard (1945), p. 87.

34   Lord Northbourne, *Look to the Land* (London, Dent, 1940), p. 192.

35   Cf. *Soil Fertility, Renewal and Preservation* by E. Pfeiffer (Revised edn, London, Faber, 1947), p. 182.

36   John Macmurray *Religion, Art and Science* (Liverpool University Press, 1961), p. 44.

37   Ibid.

38   Dr G.T. Wrench, *The Wheel of Health* (London, Daniel, 1938; New York, Schocken Books, 1972).

39   Cf. chapter 2 of *An Agricultural Testament* (London, Oxford University Press, 1940).

40   Walter de la Mare, 'The Wharf', in *Modern Short Stories,* ed. J. Hunter 〚 1964〛 (London, Faber, 1974), p. 214.

41   H.J. Massingham, *Remembrance* (London, Batsford, 1942), pp. 82-3.

42   Cf. H.J. Massingham *Remembrance* (London, Batsford, 1942), pp. 140-6; The Earl of Portsmouth (Viscount Lymington), *A Knot of Roots* (London, Bles, 1965), chapter 5; Rolf Gardiner, *England Herself* (London, Faber, 1943), *passim.*

43   *The Natural Order,* ed. H. J. Massingham (London, Dent, 1945), sub-titled 'Essays in the Return to Husbandry'.

44   H. J. Massingham, *Remembrance* (London, Batsford, 1942), p. vi.

45   Cf. Richard Griffiths, *Fellow Travellers of the Right* 〚 1980〛 (Oxford University Press, 1983), pp. 142-6, 317-29.

46   John Macmurray, *Persons in Relation* (London, Faber, 1961), p. 46.

47   Cf. Frances Donaldson, *Four Years Harvest* (London, Faber, 1945), pp. 113-15; and Mrs Penelope Massingham's Preface to *Prophecy of Famine* by H. J. Massingham and Edward Hyams (London, Thames and Hudson, 1953), p.6.

48   Paul Johnson, *Enemies of Society,* chapter 7.

The Harvest Crown at Springhead, Fontmell Magna, Dorset: Estate of Rolf Gardiner, of the Kinship in Husbandry (see p.57)

PROLOGUE

Lament for a Disappearing Peasantry
William Cobbett
(1763 - 1835)

Although he lived and died before the age of agricultural chemistry, Cobbett's writings on the state of the land anticipate in many respects the concerns of the twentieth-century organic movement. Fundamental to his outlook was a belief that England's rural, agrarian past was greatly preferable to the economic system which was developing so rapidly during his lifetime - the era of the Industrial Revolution, financial speculation, the Enclosures, and much poverty in agricultural areas which led to the 'Captain Swing' riots of 1830. The emphasis on 'efficiency' in farming meant in practice that more of the land was owned by wealthy men, that cottagers lost common rights, and that smallholders either became landless labourers, or had to join the increasing populations in the expanding manufacturing towns. The independent freeholder was in decline, and the majority of farmers were tenants. In Cobbett's view the new landowners were men who had made money through trade and finance and wanted to run their estates for profit (in which aim the Napoleonic Wars had greatly assisted them) while having no real commitment to the land they farmed. Mechanization was the application to agriculture of industrial techniques. It was destroying a tradition of craftsmanship and a social system which had been rooted in the soil.

As is often so with radicals, there was a deep strain of conservatism in Cobbett, in his case easily attributable to his origins in the way of life which was under attack. The changes he considered necessary consisted in a return to the world of the yeoman, where well-being was measured in terms of one's ability to support oneself from carefully-tended land, by mixed farming.

THE 'SYSTEM' AND ITS FALSE PROSPERITY

The truth is, that the system which has been pursued in England from the time of the Revolution ⟦ of 1680⟧, the system of government debt, is a system which begins by totally debasing the labouring classes, and that ends by producing its own overthrow, and generally, that of the state along with it. It draws property into great masses; it gives to cunning the superiority over industry; it makes agriculture a subject of adventure; it puts down all small cultivators; it encloses every inch of that land which God himself seems to have intended for the poor.

(*The Autobiography of William Cobbett,* ed. William Reitzel; London, Faber, 1967, p.16); ⟦ first published by Faber in 1933 under the title *The Progress of a Plough-Boy to a Seat in Parliament* ⟧

Could you have seen and heard what I saw and heard during ⟦ my⟧ Rural ⟦ Rides⟧, you would ⟦ not have said⟧ that the House 'worked well'. ⟦ There⟧ were two hundred thousand men, who by the Acts of this same House, saw wives and children doomed to beggary, and to beggary too never thought of, never regarded as more likely than a blowing up of the earth or a falling of the sun. It was reserved for this 'working well' House to make the fire-sides of the farmers scenes of gloom.

(*Autobiography:* 181)

The coaches and chariots and landaus that rattled through the squares and streets of London; the forests of masts that rose in the seaports; the loads of pearls and diamonds that shone at the court; even the beautiful mansions and pleasure grounds that were seen all around the metropolis; these: no one, no, nor all of these put together, were proof of the prosperity of a nation: all these could exist, and the nation ⟦ yet⟧ be plunged into the deepest of misery and degradation.

⟦ By the enclosing of land⟧ numerous families of the children of labourers were crammed into the stinking suburbs of towns, amidst filth of all sorts, and congregated together in the practice of every species of idleness and vice. In the stinking houses of towns, the labourer's children could not have health. If they had not health they were miserable in themselves and a burden to the parish.

(*Autobiography:* 140 - 1)

I have never been able clearly to comprehend what the beastly Scotch *feelosofers* meant by their 'national wealth'; but, as far as I could understand them, this was their meaning: that national wealth meant, that which was left of the products of the country over and above what was consumed, or used, by those whose labour had caused the products to be. This being the notion, it followed, of course, that the fewer poor devils you could screw the products out of, the richer the nation was. What, then, was to be done with this over-produce? Was it to go to pensioners, placemen, gendarmerie, and, in short, to whole millions, who did no work at all? By national prosperity, ⟦ such ⟧ writers meant something very different indeed from that which I, who had no desire to live upon taxes, should have called national prosperity. They looked upon it as being demonstrated in the increase of the number of chariots and fine-dressed people in and about the purlieus of the court. This was a demonstration of the increase of the taxes, and nothing more. National prosperity shows itself in very different ways: in the plentiful meal, the comfortable dwelling, the decent furniture and dress, the healthy and happy countenances, and the good morals of the labouring classes of the people. National wealth means, the Commonwealth, or Commonweal; and these mean, the general good, or happiness of the people, and the safety and honour of the state; and, these were not to be secured by robbing those who laboured, in order to support a large part of the community in idleness.

⟦ One had only ⟧ to look at the face of the country, including ⟦ the ⟧ Wen ⟦ of London ⟧, to behold the effects of taking property from one man and giving it to another. The monstrous streets and squares, and circuits, and crescents; the pulling down of streets and building up new ones; the making of bridges and tunnels, till the Thames itself trembled at the danger of being marched and undermined: the everlasting ripping-up of pavements and the tumblings up of the earth to form drains and sewers, till all beneath us was like a honeycomb... ⟦ One had only ⟧ to look at the thousands employed in cracking the stones upon the highways, while the docks and thistles and couch-grass were choking the land on the other side of the hedges; to see England, land of plenty and never-ending stores, without an old wheat rick, and with not more than a stock of two-thirds the former cattle upon the farms: to see the troops of half-starved creatures flocking from the fields, and, in their smock-frocks and nailed shoes, begging their way up to ⟦ the cities ⟧, in order to get a chance snap at the crumbs and the orts rejected by idleness and luxury - of all the destructive things that could fall upon a nation; of all the horrid curses that could afflict it, none was equal to that of robbing productive labour of its reward, of taking from the industrious and giving to the idle.

To have plenty of everything that made life easy and pleasant was formerly one of the great characteristics of the English people. Good eating, good drinking, good clothing, good lodging; without these, people do not really live: it is staying upon the earth. Good government is known from bad government by this infallible test: that, under the former the labouring people are well fed and well clothed, and under the latter, they are badly fed and badly clothed.

(*Autobiography:* 183-6)

THE STATE OF THE PEASANTRY

⟦ On the same journey I ⟧ crossed the River Wey. Here I found a parcel of labourers at parish-work. Amongst them was an old playmate of mine. The account they gave me of their situation was very dismal. The harvest was over early. The hop-picking was over; and they were employed by the parish; that was to say, not absolutely digging holes one day and filling them up the next, but at the expense of half-ruined farmers and tradesmen and landlords, to break stones into very small pieces to make nice smooth roads lest the jolting, in going along them, should create bile in the stomachs of tax-eaters. ⟦ This ⟧ was a state of things where all was out of order; where self-preservation, that great law of nature, seemed to be set at defiance; for here were farmers unable to pay men to work for them, and yet compelled to pay them for working in doing that which was really of no use to any human being. There lay the hop-poles unstripped. You saw a hundred things in the neighbouring fields that wanted doing. The fences were not nearly what they ought to have been. The very meadows, to my right and left in crossing ⟦ the ⟧ little valley, would have occupied these men advantageously until the setting in of the frost; and here were they, not, as I said before, actually digging holes one day and filling them up the next; but, to all intents and purposes, as uselessly employed.

I am sure I saw produce enough in ⟦ some ⟧ farmyards, to feed the whole of the population of ⟦ some ⟧ parishes. But the infernal system caused it all to be carried away. Not a bit of good beef, or mutton, or veal, and scarcely a bit of bacon was left for those who raised all this food. The labourers looked as if they were half-starved. Good God! what a life to live! What a life to see people live; to see this sight in our own country, and to have had the base vanity to boast of that country, and to talk of our 'constitution' and our 'liberties'. The fact was, that, where honest and laborious men could be compelled to starve quietly, with old wheat ricks and fat cattle under their eyes, it was a mockery to talk of their 'liberty' of any sort; for, the sum total of their state was this, they had 'liberty' to choose between death by starvation (quick or slow) and death by the halter! I really was ashamed to ride a fat horse, to have a fully [[*sic*]] belly, and to have a clean shirt on my back, while I looked at these wretched countrymen of mine.

(Autobiography: 181-3)

Having done my business at Hartswood today about eleven o'clock, I went to a *sale* at a farm, which the farmer is quitting. Here I had a view of what has long been going on all over the country. The farm, which belongs to *Christ's Hospital,* has been held by a man of the name of *CHARINGTON,* in whose family the lease has been, I hear, a great number of years. The house is hidden by trees. It stands in the Weald of Surrey, close by the *River Mole,* which is here a mere rivulet, though just below this house the rivulet supplies the very prettiest flour-mill I ever saw in my life.

Everything about this farm-house was formerly the scene of *plain manners* and *plentiful living.* Oak clothes-chests, oak bedsteads, oak chests of drawers, and oak tables to eat on, long, strong, and well supplied with joint stools. Some of the things were many hundreds of years old. But all appeared to be in a state of decay and nearly of *disuse.* There appeared to have been hardly any *family* in that house, where formerly there were, in all probability, from ten to fifteen men, boys, and maids: and, which was the worst of all, there was a *parlour!* Aye, and a *carpet* and *bell-pull* too! One end of the front of this once plain and substantial house had been moulded into a *'parlour';* and there was the mahogany table, and the fine chairs, and the fine glass, and all as bare-faced upstart as any stock-jobber in the kingdom can boast of. And, there were the decanters, the glasses, the 'dinner-set' of crockery ware, and all just in the true stock-jobber style. And I dare say it has been *'Squire* Charington and the *Miss* Charingtons; and not plain Master Charington, and his son Hodge, and his daughter Betty

Charington, all of whom this accursed system has, in all likelihood, transmuted into a species of mock gentlefolks, while it has ground the labourers down into real slaves. Why do not farmers now *feed* and *lodge* their work-people, as they did formerly? Because they cannot keep them *upon so little* as they give them in wages. This is the real cause of the change. There needs no more to prove that the lot of the working classes has become worse than it formerly was. This fact alone is quite sufficient to settle this point. All the world knows, that a number of people, boarded in the same house, and at the same table, can, with as good food, be boarded much cheaper than those persons divided into twos, threes, or fours, can be boarded. This is a well-known truth: therefore, if the farmer now shuts his pantry against his labourers, and pays them wholly in money, is it not clear, that he does it because he thereby gives them a living *cheaper* to him; that is to say, a *worse* living than formerly? Mind he has a *house* for them; a kitchen for them to sit in, bed rooms for them to sleep in, tables, and stools, and benches, of everlasting duration. All these he has; all these *cost him nothing;* and yet so much does he gain by pinching them in wages that he lets all these things remain as of no use, rather than feed labourers in the house. Judge, then, of the *change* that has taken place in the condition of these labourers! And, be astonished, if you can, at the *pauperism* and the *crimes* that now disgrace this once happy and moral England.

The land produces, on an average, what it always produced; but, there is a new distribution of the produce. This 'Squire Charington's father used, I dare say, to sit at the head of the oak-table along with his men, say grace to them, and cut up the meat and the pudding. He might take a cup of *strong beer* to himself, when they had none; but, that was pretty nearly all the difference in their manner of living. So that *all* lived well. But, the 'Squire had many *wine-decanters* and *wine-glasses* and 'a *dinner set*', and a '*breakfast set*', and '*dessert knives*'; and these evidently imply carryings on and a consumption that must of necessity have greatly robbed the long oak table if it had remained fully tenanted. That long table could not share in the work of the decanters and the dinner set. Therefore, it became almost untenanted; the labourers retreated to hovels, called cottages; and, instead of board and lodging, they got money; so little of it as to enable the employer to drink wine; but, then, that he might not reduce them to *quite starvation,* they were enabled to come to him, in the *king's name,* and demand food *as paupers.* And, now, mind, that which a man receives in the *king's name,* he knows well he has *by force*; and it is not in nature that he should *thank* any body for it, and least of all the party *from whom it is forced.* Then, if this sort of force be insufficient to obtain him *enough* to eat and keep him warm, is it surprising, if he thinks it *no great offence against God* (who created no man to starve) to use *another sort of force* more within his own controul ⟦ sic ⟧? Is it, in short, surprising, if he resort to *theft* and *robbery?*

This is not only the *natural* progress, but it *has been* the progress in England. The blame is not justly imputed to *'SQUIRE CHAR-INGTON* and his like; the blame belongs to the infernal stock-jobbing system. There was no reason to expect, that farmers would not endeavour to keep pace, in point of show and luxury, with fund-holders, and with all the tribes that *war* and *taxes* created.

(William Cobbett, *Rural Rides* ⟦ 1830 ⟧ , ed. George Woodcock, Penguin, Harmondsworth, 1973, pp. 226-8)

THE IMPORTANCE OF TREES

That melancholy, mean fellow, Doctor Johnson, observes, that when a man plants a tree, he begins to think of dying. If this were the fact, is that to prevent the planting of trees? I have been planting of trees in every spot that I have ever occupied, all my lifetime; and ⟦ in America ⟧ , I collected seeds of trees to carry home, and to sow in England. I expected to sit under the shade of the trees which ⟦ those ⟧ seeds would produce; and, if I only saw them six inches high, had I not the enjoyment of so much of them?

(*Autobiography:* 165)

I derived the greatest of pleasures from the reflection, that I caused millions of trees and shrubs to be planted in England, that would never have been planted in England, for ages to come, had it not been for me. ⟦ Years later, when in Scotland, I saw in an orchard ⟧ some American ⟦ apple ⟧ trees, sent by me, which were beginning to bear. 'Cast your bread upon the waters', says the precept, 'and have patience to wait to see it return.' I had sent from England to Long Island ⟦ for ⟧ some cuttings of apple trees; they had come to me at Kensington; Mr. M'Gavin, at Hamilton (four hundred miles from

Kensington), had got some of the cuttings after they came from Long Island; he had put some of them upon some of the branches of his trees: and he showed me a bough which had proceeded from this cutting, from which he had gathered forty pounds weight of fine apples!

(Autobiography: 204)

This is a tract of Crown-lands, or properly speaking, *public-lands,* on some parts of which our *Land Steward,* Mr. HUSKISSON... is making some *plantations of trees,* partly *fir,* and partly other trees. What he can plant the *fir* for, God only knows, seeing that the country is already over-stocked with that rubbish...

If I were a Member of Parliament, I *would* know what timber had been cut down, and what it has been sold for...

(Rural Rides: 86)

TERRACE CULTIVATION

I saw, on my way through the down-countries, hundreds of acres of ploughed land in *shelves.* What I mean is, the side of a steep hill, made into the shape of *a stairs,* only the *rising parts* more sloping than those of a stairs, and deeper in proportion. The side of the hill, in its original form, was *too steep to be ploughed,* or, even to be worked with a spade. The earth, as soon as moved, would have rolled down the hill; and, besides, the rains would have soon washed down all the surface earth, and have left nothing for plants of any sort to grow in. Therefore the sides of hills, where the land was sufficiently good, and where it was wanted for the growing of corn, were thus made into a sort of *steps* or *shelves,* and the horizontal parts (representing the parts of the stairs that we put our feet upon), *were ploughed and sowed,* as they generally are, indeed, to this day.

(Rural Rides: 349)

GOOD PEASANTRY AND GOOD LIVING

The land here, and all round CRICKLADE, is very fine. Here are some of the very finest pastures in all England, and some of the finest dairies of cows, from 40 to 60 in a dairy, grazing in them. Was not this *always* so?... Aye, it was always so; and there were formerly *two churches* here, where there is now only one, and five, six or ten times as many people. I saw in *one single farm-yard here* more food than enough for four times the inhabitants of the parish; and this yard did not contain a tenth, perhaps, of the produce of the parish; but, while the poor creatures that raise the wheat and the barley and cheese and the mutton and the beef are living upon potatoes, an accursed *Canal* comes kindly through the parish to convey away the wheat and all the *good food* to the tax-eaters and their attendants in the WEN!

(Rural Rides: 362-3)

I [used to go] around a little common, called Horton Heath on a Sunday. I found the husbands at home. The Common contained about 150 acres; and I found round the skirts of it, and near to the skirts, about thirty cottages and gardens, the latter chiefly encroachments on the common, which was waste (as it was called) in a manor of which the Bishop was the lord. I took down the names of all the cottagers, the number and ages of their children, and number of their cows, heifers, calves, ewes, pigs, geese, ducks, fowls, and stalls of bees; the extent of their little bits of ground, the worth of what was growing, the number of apple trees, of the black-cherry trees, called by them 'merries', which was a great article in that part of Hampshire. I have lost my paper, and, therefore, I cannot speak positively as to any one point; but, I remember one hundred and twenty-five, or thirty-five stalls of bees, worth at that time ten shillings a stall, at least. Cows there were about fifteen, besides heifers and calves; about sixty pigs great and small; and not less than five hundred head of poultry! The cattle and sheep of the neighbouring farmers grazed the common all the while besides. The bees alone were worth more annually than the common, if it had been enclosed, would have let for deducting the expense of fences. The farmers used the Common for their purposes; and my calculation was, that the cottagers produced from their little bits, in food, for themselves, and in things to be sold at market, more than any neighbouring farm of 200 acres! The cottagers consisted, fathers, mothers, and children, grandfathers, grandmothers, and grandchildren, of more than two hundred persons!

[I learnt to hate] a system that could lead English gentlemen to disregard matters like these! That could induce them to tear up 'wastes' and sweep away occupiers like those I have described! Wastes indeed! Give a dog an ill name. Was Horton Heath a waste? Was it a 'waste' when a hundred, perhaps, of healthy boys and girls were playing there of a Sunday, instead of creeping about covered with filth in the alleys of a town?

(*Autobiography:* 107-8)

My ride yesterday, from *MILTON* to this city of *SALISBURY,* was, without any exception, the most pleasant; it brought before me the greatest number of, to me, interesting objects, and it gave rise to more interesting reflections, than I remember ever to have had brought before my eyes, or into my mind, in any one day of my life; and therefore, this ride was, without any exception, the *most pleasant* that I ever had in my life, as far as my recollection serves me. I got a little *wet* in the middle of the day; but, I got dry again, and I arrived here in very good time...

Let us now, then, look back over this part of Wiltshire, and see whether the inhabitants ought to be '*transported*' by order of the '*Emigration Committee*' of which we shall see and say more by-and-by... The farms are all large, and, generally speaking, they were always large, I dare say; because *sheep* is one of the great things here; and sheep, in a country like this, must be kept in *flocks,* to be of any profit. The sheep principally manure the land. This is to be done only by *folding;* and, to fold, you must have *a flock.* Every farm has its portion of *down, arable,* and *meadow;* and, in many places, the latter are *watered meadows,* which is a great resource where sheep are kept in flocks; because these meadows furnish grass for the suckling ewes, early in the spring; and, indeed, because they have always food in them for sheep and cattle of all sorts. These meadows have had no part of the suffering from the drought, this year. They fed the ewes and lambs in the spring, and they are now yielding a heavy crop of hay; for, I saw men mowing in them, in several places... though it was raining at the time.

The turnips look pretty well all the way down the valley; but, I see very few, except *Swedish turnips.* The early common turnips very nearly all failed, I believe. But, the stubbles are beautifully bright; and the *rick-yards* tell us, that the crops are good, especially of *wheat.* This is not a country of *pease* and *beans,* nor of *oats,* except for home consumption. The crops are *wheat, barley, wool* and *lambs,* and these latter not to be sold to butchers, but to be sold, at the great fairs, to those who are going to keep them for some time, whether to breed from, or, finally to fat for the butcher. It is the *pulse* and the *oats* that appear to have failed most this year; and, therefore, this Valley has not suffered. I do not perceive that they have many *potatoes;* but, what they have of this base root seem to look well enough...

The stack-yards down this Valley are beautiful to behold. They contain from *five* to *fifteen* banging wheat-ricks, besides *barley-ricks,* and *hay-ricks,* and also besides the *contents of the barns,* many of which exceed *a hundred,* some *two hundred,* and I saw one at PEWSEY ... and another at FITTLETON... each of which exceeded *two hundred and fifty* feet in length. At a farm, which, in the old maps, is called *Chissenbury Priory*... I think I counted twenty-seven ricks of one sort and another, and sixteen or eighteen of them *wheat-ricks.* I could not conveniently get to the yard, without much longer delay than I wished tomake; but, I could not be much out in my counting. A very fine sight this was, and it could not meet the eye without making one look round (and in vain) *to see the people who were to eat all this food;* and without making one reflect on the horrible, the unnatural, the base and infamous state, in which we must be, when projects are on foot, and are openly avowed, for *transporting* those who raise this food, *because they want to eat enough of it to keep them alive;* and when no project is on foot for *transporting* the idlers who live in luxury upon this same food; when no project is on foot for transporting pensioners, parsons, or dead-weight people!

A little while before I came to this farm-yard, I saw, *in one piece,* about *four hundred acres* of wheat-stubble, and I saw a sheep-fold, which, I thought, contained *an acre of ground,* and had in it about *four thousand sheep and lambs.* The fold was divided into three separate flocks; but the piece of ground was one and the same; and I thought it contained about an acre. At one farm, between PEWSEY and UPAVON, I counted more than 300 hogs in one stubble. This is certainly the most delightful farming in the world. No *ditches,* no *water-furrows,* no *drains,* hardly any *hedges,* no *dirt* and *mire,* even in the wettest seasons of the year; and though the *downs* are *naked* and *cold,* the valleys are snugness itself... The *shelter,* in these valleys, and particularly where the downs are *steep* and *lofty* on the sides, is very complete. Then, the trees are every where *lofty.* They are generally *elms,* with some *ashes,* which delight in the soil that they find here... By the water's edge there are *willows;* and to almost every farm, there is a fine *orchard,* the trees being, in general, very fine, and, this year, they are, in general, well loaded with fruit. So that, all taken together, it seems impossible to find a more beautiful and pleasant country than this, or to imagine any life more easy and happy than men might here lead, if they were untormented by an accursed system that takes the food from those that raise it, and gives it to those that do nothing that is useful to man.

Here the farmer has always an *abundance of straw.* His farmyard is never without it. Cattle and horses are bedded up to their eyes. The yards are put close under the shelter of a hill, or are protected by lofty and thick-set trees. Every animal seems comfortably situated; and, in the dreariest days of winter, these are, perhaps, the happiest scenes in the world; or, rather, they would be such, if those, whose labour makes it all, trees, corn, sheep and every thing, had but *their fair share* of the produce of that labour. What share they really have of it one cannot exactly say; but, I should suppose, that every labouring *man* in this valley raises as much food as would suffice for *fifty,* or *a hundred persons,* fed like himself!

(*Rural Rides:* 302-5)

...where manufacturing is *mixed with agriculture,* where the wife and daughters are at the needle, or the wheel, while the men and the boys are at plough, and where the manufacturing, of which one or two towns are the centres, is spread over the whole country round about, and particularly where it is, in very great part, performed by females at their *own homes,* and where the earnings come *in aid of the man's* wages; in such case the misery cannot be so great; and, accordingly, while there is an absolute destruction of life going on in the hell-holes, there is no *visible* misery at, or near, Worcester; and I cannot take my leave of this county without observing, that I do not recollect to have seen one miserable object in it. The working people all seem to have good large gardens, and *pigs* in their styes; and this last, say the *feelosofers* what they will... is the *only* security for happiness in a labourer's family.

(*Rural Rides:* 394-5)

For many years there existed a fashion of looking upon the working people, and particularly the labourers in husbandry, as an inferior race of human beings, and of treating them as such. ⟦ It still goes on.]] They are the contrary of this; they are the superior race, and they have always been so; they are content as to their station in life; they are unpresuming; they are honest; they are sincere; and he who says the contrary is a base and infamous slanderer. It has been amongst the greatest delights of my life to see them happy, and amongst my most ardent desires to contribute to that happiness. I have admired their character and their conduct ever since I was able to estimate them; and I would willingly strike dead at my feet the insolent brutes who speak contemptuously of them.

I was born and bred a farmer, or a sort of labourer; and I have never desired to have any rank, station, or name, or calling, more and other than that of a farmer. [[Everyone had known]] that I wanted nothing for myself, but they knew that I wanted to take [[away]] the power of oppressing and pillaging the order to which I belonged; admire my industry, my perseverance, my wonderful exertions; but there was at bottom, to balance against all these, my strong and implacable hatred of oppression of all sorts; and particularly the partiality of taxation; the stripping of the working people of their earnings, and the heaping of these earnings upon idlers. This has been the constant ground of hostility to me; and I must say, that I trust in God that I shall so conduct myself as to cause the hostility to continue until the last hour of my life.

(Autobiography: 225-6)

Cobbett's Cottage Economy [[*1822*]] *both looks back to the pre-industrial world of peasant farming and can be seen as a fore-runner of the self-sufficiency movement, with its advice on home brewing, straw plaiting, making bread, keeping animals and poultry, and so on: again we encounter the paradox that in order to look to the future it is necessary to study the methods of the past.*

There are many books about Cobbett, but two can be mentioned in particular: G.D.H. Cole's Life of William Cobbett *(London, Collins, 1924) is a biography written from a socialist perspective, emphasizing Cobbett's radical politics;* Great Cobbett - The Noblest Agitator, *by Daniel Green (London, Hodder & Stoughton, 1983) is a detailed study of Cobbett's life, with a good bibliography, written by a Tory.*

H.J. Massingham's The Wisdom of the Fields *(London, Collins, 1945) begins with a chapter on Cobbett, 'Rider of the Shires', and his historical survey,* The English Countryman *(London, Batsford, 1942), gives an idea of the yeoman tradition whose destruction Cobbett so bitterly regretted. According to Raymond Williams in* The Country and the City *(London, Chatto and Windus, 1973; St Alban's, Paladin, 1975) Massingham's book is 'one part record, two parts ideology';* [1] *Williams's own book, which includes detailed reference to Cobbett, can be read as an ideological counter-balance.*

Reference

1   Williams (Paladin, 1975), p.313.

Dust Over Dakota: The Results of Exploited Soil

1

A Historical Perspective

Edward Hyams

(1910-1975)

Edward Hyams was a writer who produced several novels, a history of the New Statesman, *and studies in viticulture. A passionately keen gardener, he was sufficiently well-respected to be appointed consultant to the government of Iran during the construction of its national botanic garden and herborium.*

His concern for the problems of soil conservation stemmed not only from his interest in gardening, but from his study of history. He learnt in particular from the works of Toynbee and Spengler, and their analysis of the factors which lead to a civilization's decline. Another major influence was the survey of twentieth-century soil erosion in The Rape of the Earth *by Jacks and Whyte (London, Faber, 1939; see chapter 3).*

Hyams' study of mankind's relation to the soil resulted in his book Soil and Civilization *(London, Thames and Hudson, 1952), which looked at the rise and fall of human societies from an ecological perspective. All the following extracts are taken from the 1976 edition of the book, published by John Murray (London).*

THE CONCEPT OF A SOIL COMMUNITY

Man in nature prospers when he is working in such a way as to move with life's pattern, collaborating with the other members of the *Soil Community* to which he belongs. Far too much weight seems to have

been given to fear of the environment as a formative influence in the
story of mankind, far too little to the sense of belonging, of being in
place.

(Soil:12)

What happens when men are introduced into a soil community?

If the men are hunters and food collectors there is no reason why
they should not fit into the community, be members whose activities
are held in balance with those of all the others. Like all the other
members, these men will be checked from growing so numerous or
predatory as to upset the balance of the community, by the limitations
of their own powers, and that measure of hostility between species and
species which is an important factor in maintaining equilibrium. The
men will be eaten by other beasts, preyed upon by micro-organic
members of the soil community, poisoned by some of their
fellow-members who are plants or reptiles, and will also, perhaps,
check their own numbers and powers by internecine war. Life exists by
virtue of cannibalism and of nothing else, so that there can be no
practice so irrational as that of vegetarianism 'on principle': who eats
grass, eats flesh.

But when men pass the stage of food collecting and hunting; or
when men who have passed this stage enter upon a hitherto
undisturbed soil community, their powers are such that they are able
to disturb the balance of the community to the detriment of other
species and the advantage of themselves. If the men be few and the
community large, this disturbance need not be disastrous. But if or
when the men become numerous relative to the size of the
community, the result may be very terrible: it may be the destruction
first of the soil balance; then, as a consequence, of fundamental soil
fertility; and this being the basis of life of the soil in question, all living
members of it perish, including, in the end, the community of men
which has brought this death about by turning from a contributing,
co-operating member of a delicately adjusted organism, into a
parasite upon it, and a parasite which it is not constructed to endure.

(Soil:26-7)

...the earliest men of whom any record survives were hunters and
food-gatherers. They were not, however, without creative powers; on

the contrary, they included notable artists, and perhaps, by analogue with the recently extinct African bush-folk, whose painting is reminiscent of some prehistoric work, had a genuine literature of spoken tales and poems.

Men hunting and gathering food are full soil-community members and on a par, in relation to the soil, with all the other animal members. Most sophisticated literatures express traditions of a remote Golden Age, when men were simple and virtuous. This tradition must refer, as in the Jewish example of Adam and Eve in the Garden of Eden, to the primal hunting and food-gathering phase of our history as a species, when, speaking ecologically, men, although rather unenterprising, were virtuous indeed.

As soil-community members enjoying no special privileges, men would have been held in balance with soil fertility; they would have been subject to the checks which keep all soil members in equilibrium, the hazards which keep all member species from becoming excessive in relation to the other member species, and to soil-fertility increment.

In such conditions men, however talented, cannot make a civilization: competing, on more or less equal terms, with other and equally predatory genera; under the law of return, entailing specific sacrifice for communal advantage, men cannot become so numerous and so prosperous as to stockpile the surplus out of which civilization is made. *For the first step towards civilization is soil exploitation.*

Before a stable hunting and food-gathering community of men can begin to exploit soil as parasites, instead of living with it as members, a new economic tool is required. Such men may already possess language, aesthetic sensibility, artistic talent, weapons, tools, and the control of fire, yet still they are objects of natural history... and cannot become makers of history.

Two economic instruments of emancipation were devised. Some men tamed and battened upon animals; they learnt to use the stomachs of fellow-species for the digestion of grass in their own interest, and became herdsmen, shepherds, and horsemen. Others tamed and battened upon esculent plants, particularly cereal grasses, and thus became farmers... In both cases the men were parasitic upon soil fertility by means of animal and plant instruments, with which, in time, they learnt to live symbiotically. The ancient balance of natural soil communities had at last been upset by opportunist intelligence. Man stepped outside the scheme of nature, and started the process we call history.

(Soil:31-2)

MAN AS A DISEASE-ORGANISM

Here... is a simplified demonstration of the dominance of a soil community by a single species, which thus becomes distinguishable as a disease organism...

(Soil:77)

There is a wood of sweet-chestnut trees in which also grow honeysuckles. No satisfactory balance could have been produced between these two species, since the honeysuckles are so vigorous that, growing unchecked, they would choke the sweet-chestnuts, enjoy a brief dominance, and perish for want of support and leaf-mould and shade. However, in the wood lives a family, a man and his wife and six children. Their only food is chestnuts, but they are not so primitive as to be mere food-gatherers; for recognizing that unless they take action the honeysuckles will choke their food-trees to death, they undertake the labour of keeping the honeysuckles in check.

It does not, however, occur to them to destroy the honeysuckles entirely. Perhaps the plant is a sacred one in the man's religion; and indeed he only prunes it with fear and propitiatory rites. As for his wife, she is not a religious woman, but she likes to have a few flowers in the house, and to do what pleases her husband.

The balance once established is stable while the children grow up, and even when they are adult it is not, at first, disturbed. The daughters, in this austere but not unpleasing soil community, like the flowers of honeysuckle with which to decorate their persons; one of the sons, a practical man, finds the bines useful as rope; another, the youngest, has an attitude towards the honeysuckles resembling that of his father, and yet not quite the same: his pleasure comes from beholding the way the plants grow, the colour of the flowers, the shape of the leaves, and he likes to make drawings of them on bits of chestnut wood.

The third son, however, is different. He is not conservative, and he does not hesitate to call his father's religion superstitious, his brother's art a waste of time, his sisters' vanity disgraceful. He proposes that instead of spending months every year in pruning the honeysuckles, they would do well to grub them all up and be done with it; that, he says, is the scientific, the rational way. And since everyone is rather ashamed of being irrational, and because the third brother is a forceful and determined man, his opinion prevails, and out come the honeysuckles. And in no time at all the bees, which lived in the wood for the honeysuckle, and incidentally fertilized the flowers of the chestnuts, abandon the wood and leave the human members of the community without food.

By what means do species rise to dominate, unbalance and destroy a soil community? In natural conditions this almost certainly happens much more rarely than in artificial soil communities. Just as savage cultures are ponderously stable, whereas civilized cultures are precarious, so natural soil communities are difficult, artificial ones easy to upset.

Consider, for a minute, a market garden as an artifical soil community in isolation. One of its common members is the cabbage white butterfly. The cabbage white butterfly in a natural soil community has to seek wild cabbages on which to lay its eggs, and wild cabbages are not particularly common - indeed I have only seen them growing once and in one place, in anything like profusion. But the market gardener having planted perhaps an acre of cabbages, the cabbage white suddenly finds its commodity with unnatural ease, and in unnatural quantity. These temporarily favourable conditions might enable it to rise to unexampled heights of prosperity as a race, to multiply very rapidly in conditions where the predators which keep it in check are not, until attracted later, present in their ordinary numbers. As a result, and supposing the market gardener to abandon brassica culture for some other crop, an exceptionally large number of cabbage whites would be forced to seek their living in natural conditions, and the wild cabbages would succumb to a plague of caterpillars, with a whole chain of related consequences which we need not follow here.

In the first half of the nineteenth century the rising class of machine-owning capitalists in Britain required hands to man their rapidly growing factories. Men and women were attracted away from work on the land, or in cottage industries, where the food they ate was only what they could produce by their own actions applied immediately, or at only one remove, to the soil. They were brought together in great and crowded numbers and food was brought to them in exchange for machine minding. Conditions were, in fact, created, in which they could propagate their kind, for a time and very uncomfortably, *without reference to "natural" supplies of food*, to weather, to the season. The consequence was a temporary and fantastic specific (not, of course, individual) prosperity of mechanical man. Mechanical or machine-minding man became numerous out of all proportion to the supply of food within the range of action of individual machine-minding men. Among the consequences of this destruction of balance were the American dustbowl and the British Empire.

...man, over a very great part of the surface of the earth, has become a disease of soil communities, and...this catastrophe derives quite as much from his past relations with the soil, as it does from his present ones: either he has reacted from past practices, or he has failed to learn from them, or he has transferred practices which succeed in one environment, to soils where they are pernicious.

Fleas are parasitic upon men: if they are few they cause him minor discomfort, but no serious harm, so that his vitality and power to continue functioning are not impaired. If the fleas become excessively numerous, they may so weaken their host by their depredations as finally to destroy him and, in the absence of any other host, themselves. A few men can live parasitically upon a soil, without destroying it, but should they become too many they inevitably and invariably destroy it unless they find means to enhance its annual increment of fertility. For, as fleas suck men's blood, so men suck the fertility of soils...

When a people grows up as a member of a soil community, its agricultural or pastoral practices grow out of the conditions of the country, and are consequently adapted to it, just as the life-maintaining practices of other native species arise out of, and are adapted to, the ruling conditions.

When peoples intrude into a virgin soil community, at an early and primitive stage of their own technical development, the soil community will impose upon them, by its superior strength, modifications of their agricultural practices which suit its own well-being. The intruders are allowed in, but by no means on their own terms. The terms are laid down by the stable community into which they are trying to thrust themselves.

People whose farming (and sometimes even industrial) practices derive from either of these beginnings have a past - that is they possess a continuum of traditions which joins them to their origins as members of their particular soil. Such a past is of enormous practical value: it may mean, for example, being able to take 30 cwt. of wheat from an acre of land which has already yielded crops in two or three thousand seasons, instead of a wretched 8 cwt. from an acre almost barren and dead after only a century of cultivation. The farmer who works land similarly worked by his spiritual, if not physical, ancestors during a score of generations, need not be stupidly conservative: he may employ new methods, grow new crops, and use new tools. But he will, by a sort of intuition which rises out of his organic relationship with his land, test each novelty before he adopts it, by reference to a code of morality in his relations with soil, a code which he has inherited. He will respect the land as a life, never exploit it as a mineral.

But when a people at a very high technical level intrude upon a virgin soil community, or upon an old artificial soil community, they possess the means to impose their will: they will offer no terms, make no adjustments in their native practices, concede little or nothing to the invaded soil. They will probably introduce their own native practices at that level of efficiency which they have reached at home, and which, perhaps, their own soil has been adapted to during hundreds, even thousands of years. Or they may, by their scientists, devise, intellectually, new practices, with an insufficient understanding of the conditions in which these practices are to be applied.

Both these catastrophic things happened when white men took control of Africa; and, what is worse, the methods evolved by the native inhabitants, out of the conditions of their environment, were made impossible to practise.

(Soil:79-83)

The vast herds maintained by ancient peoples, herds of horses in the case of the Tartars and Mongols, the peoples of Jenghiz, of Timur, of the Golden Horde; of Attila, and of their remote ancestors, were only relatively vast. The horses and other cattle were grazed over very great regions, for ever shifting across hundreds of miles, indeed right across central Asia and eastern Europe, the herdsmen adapting their culture to their moving economy. By this means the grasses, the grass soil communities, were never overtaxed. It does not in the least matter whether the herdsmen knew, intelligently, why they acted as they did. But in the absence of knowledge, rational knowledge, of the real nature of their environment, an intruding people who have not grown up out of their adopted countryside, have no tradition of conservation, no respect for the life of the soils off which they propose to live. The

South American cattle men had no tradition from which to derive wisdom. They had only the ethos and the example of the great Republic to their north, and this they adopted. Industry and application are certainly virtues which the American peoples possess almost to excess. The South American ranchers saw that the thing to do was to work hard and make money. They stocked the *steppe* of their countries without regard to the consumption of a soil fertility which they did not even know was consumable. They bartered the future of their soils for Packards, mistresses, electric light, palaces in their capitals and apartments in Paris. They did not begin to make a culture out of their soil: they bought an alien one with their soil's fertility.

Not only do modern cattle men destroy the fertility of their *steppe* soils and thereby put the life of the grass soil communities in danger. They sell it oversea.

Between 1920 and 1950, that is in thirty years, the Argentine alone exported to Britain 11,683,000 tons of beef, not to mention other meats. This represents approximately 50,000,000 head of cattle. The average age of these beasts would be 3 years. In 3 years a steer consumes 10 tons of grass. A ton of grass represents, in terms of plant nutrients taken from the soil, perhaps 1 cwt. Such nutrients can, of course, be replaced as artificial fertilizers; whether they are so replaced is another matter. In any case, the texture of the soil is none the less not restored. An immense quantity of organic material has been removed. A small proportion of it can be restored by manuring with steers' dung, but there is a steady and continuous loss. What then, has happened as a result of this export of meat? A quantity of top-soil equal to about a million fertile acres has been sent away from the soil community to which it belonged, eaten by the English, assimilated into their flesh, or, by way of their sewers, thrown into the sea.

If it were literally true that every atom of energy borrowed from soil by animals living on and off it, must be returned whence it came, then man, as a semi-parasite, could not live at all. The factor left out of account is the usufruct, the annual increment of fertility won by plant-populated soils. It would be perfectly sound to kill and eat so many cattle as could feed off the Argentine *steppe* without breaking into soil-fertility capital. But no more; or not until the cattle men had done what the farmers of Europe have done, made an artificial soil capable of yielding far more than a natural soil.

(Soil:89-90)

THE EXAMPLE OF ROME

The fact is that, for its salvation, a human community must, like a community of any other creatures, be founded in a soil. When Carthage fought Rome there was no clash of two valid nations: there was a struggle between a nation and a vast and powerful cartel of joint-stock trading concerns which happened, among other properties, to own and work some agricultural land. When, at the head of any army of mercenaries and impressed colonials, supported by trained fighting elephants, and by a gorgeous and devoted bodyguard of young Carthaginians of good family, Hannibal went out of Spain into Gaul, over the Alps and down into Italy, he there performed the most incredible *tour de force* in military history: in the teeth of his own government, almost without supplies or reinforcements from home, he stayed in the enemy's country for sixteen years. He made half Italy Hannibalic, thus assuring that when he did withdraw the Romans themselves would, by furious punitive measures, wreak havoc even where he himself had not done so. He consistently defeated Consular army after Consular army, for there was no man living anything like capable of matching his military talent. The armies of Rome were citizen armies, they were Goldsmith's proud peasantry, under arms. With the slow, obstinate, unspectacular heroism of their class and nation, they got themselves massacred by thousands. They were irreplaceable; the land which they worked could not spare them if the Roman character was to be spared. Half the farmlands lay derelict, during nearly two decades.

At a certain moment in the course of this war, Hannibal could have taken Rome. There can be no question of that: he did not do so, and that refusal to do what every soldier aims to do, capture the enemy's capital, is one of the major mysteries of military history. To the question which this strange behaviour on the part of Hannibal propounds, Captain Liddell Hart once gave a very suggestive answer. In a brilliant essay on the subject of Hannibal's career, he wrote that Hannibal did not take Rome because to have done so would have been to end the war too soon: before his god he had sworn to destroy Rome and, like Shylock, he might have said:

> An oath, an oath, I have an oath in Heaven:
> Shall I lay perjury upon my soul?
> No, not for (Rome).

Hannibal, Captain Liddell Hart suggested, had devoted his life to revenge, and that revenge must be satisfied by making sure that Rome died in agony and by inches, not still half intact.

It is a very possible answer: Hannibal's people and his father had been shockingly wronged by Rome. The Carthaginians were notoriously vindictive and ruthless, and their religion one of the most frightful, in its rites, of which we have knowledge. Had Hannibal taken Rome when the city lay open to him, he must have ended the war, and thereafter have been the instrument of making a rational peace, dictated by the commercially-minded Carthaginian Senate. He preferred to make sure of the destruction of Rome.

In a way, he succeeded.

It is true that he had, although undefeated in the field, to withdraw at last from Italy; that he was beaten in battle, in Africa, by Scipio; that he witnessed the humiliation of his city; that he had to fly for his life from Roman vengeance; that that vengeance caught up with him; that he was sold by the king with whom he had taken refuge; and that he died by his own hand rather than fall into Roman ones. Meanwhile he had made sure that the subsequent career of Rome, instead of being a great and splendid triumph of civilization and culture, was a slow agony of decline and degradation into the worst manifestation of slave-supported imperialism.

The foundation of the Roman character was the Roman soil community. Hannibal destroyed it, and with it Rome's power to act with generosity and charity. She was no longer capable of making what, in her beginning as a great power she seemed to be making, a Commonwealth. She could only make a spiritually barren, aesthetically contemptible, socially decadent monstrosity.

*

...The spirit of the old Rome had been made by men who believed, with Alexander Pope... that:

> Happy the man, whose wish and care
> A few paternal acres bound,
> Content to breathe his native air
>   In his own ground.
> Whose herds with milk, whose fields with bread
> Whose flocks supply him with attire
> Whose trees in summer yield him shade,
>   In winter fire.

Whether the remaining Romans still had these sentiments is uncertain: that they could no longer live in the manner described is only too certain.

In Cato, in Varro and in Columella we have three monographists from whose writings the new, evil and inevitable soil policy of Rome can be examined... Despite the persistence in some places, of the old, sound system of soil-man relationship, of the small-holding subsistence farmer, Roman soil had become primarily a vast Slave-manned Plantation, the slaves, of course, being provided by Carthaginian prisoners-of-war.

Thus, the whole nature of the Roman *polis* had been shockingly and mortally changed, in such a sense as to bring upon Rome, inevitably, the Gracchan revolution, the Social War, the Civil Wars, the failure of Republicanism, the transformation of Democracy into the totalitarian monster-state of Augustus and his successors, and the economic decline of the Roman Empire into the vicious and ridiculous system desperately imposed by Diocletian.

(Soil:133-7)

OKLAHOMA: DIFFERENT ATTITUDES TO THE SOIL

During several decades the pressure applied to the United States government by the farmer-citizens and by commercial and industrial interests, to open up the Indian Territory, was unremitting. And it is eternally to the credit of several United States governments that they so respected the objections of the Indians to this course, although what was proposed seemed very fair and just, that they resisted pressure to the point of risking insurrection and civil war. They did not hesitate, time and again, to use military force against their own people in order to keep their pledges to the Indians, and that in the teeth of the angry violence of their constituents. Nevertheless, they were, in the long run, forced to break every promise they had ever made to the Tribes.

The real difficulty in this situation inhered in the fundamentally different attitudes towards soil, and particularly towards land-tenure, of the two conflicting peoples.

The white people were the heirs of an ancient high civilization which had passed its cultural and spiritual zenith some time before. They were, even in their simplest and humblest members, sophisticated, in fact corrupt, in their attitude to land. A symptom of this intellectual corruption was, and is, the degradation of women and soil to the status of personal chattels. It seemed to the European colonists of America right and proper that each head of a family should own a piece of land, and should exercise upon it a patriarchal right. In short, these people had sunk into the same condition of spiritual blindness, in the matter of man's place in the living world, as affected the Romans towards the end of the Punic wars.

The Indians, on the other hand, had no conception of soil as property. Such an idea must have seemed to them immoral and irreligious; land tenure among them was not several but tribal, not personal but communal. There is no clearer nor more final answer to those who still believe that there is something "natural" about the idea of each man as a freehold smallholder, than the persistent, obstinate and despairing resistance offered by the Indians to the apparently reasonable suggestion, often reiterated, that land should be distributed among them in severalty, that every adult Indian should receive 160 acres of good land together with enfranchisement as a citizen of the United States. The Indians were implacably hostile to the idea that land could be held as private property, could be bought, sold, given away or bequeathed.

This ecologically invaluable instinct was, of course, debauched. It was probably among the half-breeds that the idea of soil as property first gained admittance; then the more sophisticated Indians consented to it; and lastly the mass. But it is significant that the earliest tribes to accept land-holding in severalty were the smaller ones, whose tribal organization had long been breaking down under the pressure of the white invasion. The Indian Territory was at last deprived of the protection which native human customs, grown up within its influence, had extended to its health and integrity. It lay open to disease.

(Soil:142-3)

WESTERN EUROPE: THE CREATION OF PERFECT ARTIFICIAL SOIL

A soil consultant of international reputation told a branch meeting of the British National Farmers' Union: "Whenever I get back to Britain it is a relief to handle English soil." He was making a very favourable comparison between the texture, and therefore the fertility and stability of English soils, and those of other parts of the world. He

added that there were one or two other places in Europe similarly
endowed. These fertile and stable soils are, with rare exceptions,
confined to Atlantic Europe. Their nature is a product of their past,
and they have been slowly transformed from forest soil communities
into artificial soil communities: transformed and maintained.

It is probable that an observer from another planet who understood
human values would judge the achievements of Western Christian
man, in religion, philosophy, science and the arts to be of a higher
order than those of any other men in the world. It is true that these
achievements have resulted in the building-up, in the soul of Western
Christian men, of an overweening, blind pride which now becomes his
hubris. It is, ironically, in an alien, classical tradition that out of
hubris rises the *atê*, whereby the sinner against the earth shall be
chastised: Western Christian man appears to be about to destroy himself by means of his powers over nature, and if he is spared after all it
will perhaps be because there is one great sin against earth which he
has *not*, at least on his native heath, committed. As a peasant, a
farmer, he has shown a remarkable and almost singular sense of responsibility, a respect for valuable traditions, and a sure and subtle
tact in making use of new devices and techniques with intelligent
moderation. Atlantic European soils are not only *not* exhausted by
seven or eight thousand years' association with man; they are probably more fertile and stable today than they have ever been. The crop
per acre taken annually from North-west European soils is much in
excess of the world's average, and equal or superior to that taken, in
classical times, from the richest soils available to Hellenic man, for
example, the volcanic soils of Sicily.

This greatest of the many great achievements of European man has,
moreover, been accomplished not, as in South America, by a unified
culture under a theocratic communist dictatorship; nor with the
enormous advantage of a soil-worshipping religion enduring from
primitive to highly civilized times. European man has kept himself
tolerably free, and as for his religion, though anciently the Europeans
worshipped their soil, during the last three thousand years of their
history they have adored gods and goddesses with less and less interest
in or association with agriculture; and during two thousand years they
have worshipped a group of Mediterranean deities whose own creative
background was singularly inappropriate to Atlantic European
conditions. These handicaps are very real, very grave; God and soil are
so immediately connected that unless an alien God can be
acclimatized, modified in his nature to flourish in the soil he is

colonizing, the people who worship him or her on that soil will suffer serious psychic and psychological wounds. Recall the sound religious instinct of Naaman, who, in order to worship Jehovah for cleansing him of the leprosy, carried Palestinian soil back with him to Syria.

(Soil: 230-1)

There was no property in land among the Celts. As among all peoples in an Heroic stage of society private property in personal goods was like gentry and aristocracy, class pride and distinction, important: in spirit the Celts were not egalitarian, but in the important particular of land-holding, the holder was the clan. Pastures belonging to a clan were the exclusive right of that clan (though even this does not imply the idea of ownership as we know it), and the limits of the pastures were marked, maintained and defended at need. But not even the greatest man of a clan could properly say "this is *my* land"; at most he could say, "this is *our* land"...

It is comparatively simple for a community to own and work pasture in common - in fact it is difficult to do otherwise with any regard for equity, but arable is another matter, for the governing factor in successful tillage is quality of labour, and goodwill. The tilled land of the Celtic septs was held in common but worked in severalty, each head of a household being allotted land from the common holding, in strips, so that there should be a fair distribution of good, bad and indifferent soils. These strips were redistributed at intervals, and no man ever "owned" one, but simply had a right to it for the subsistence of his family and the maintenance of his social position as a free and equal member of the clan. His sons inherited, but what they inherited was not property, but rights - the same rights as their father's. If population declined, each man's share increased proportionately, until population rose; then the shares declined again, and continued to decline until the level of subsistence was endangered by want of land, when either a colony was thrown off, or the metropolitan holding was increased by "assartage" - that is by clearing the waste land...

All this applies to Celtic free tribesmen in good standing. The aboriginal inhabitants, descendants of the earlier farmers, had no such status. In some cases... they were enslaved, at least enserfed. But on the whole they existed in their own communities, holding their own land, and paying tribute to the Celts but not otherwise troubled by them. There was no question of these natives being made working slaves of the Celtic freemen, to labour on the freeman's land. Whatever the natives may have suffered as men, by becoming a tributary state within the dominant Celtic state, the soil was spared the ill effects of slave exploitation, and the Celtic overmen were not tempted to forget their responsibility to the soil, nor spared the constant lessons deriving from close manual contact with it.

Celtic good sense in soil management saved the soil from another ill effect which might have been expected to arise from their system of dividing the land equally among the heirs of the tribesmen, at the latter's death... Such an arrangement tends, as we have seen elsewhere, to a progressive reduction of the size of the holdings, to pulverization as it is called, until the smallness of the holding which must support a household is such that the abuse of the soil becomes a condition of survival. The Celts got over this by making their attributions of allotments ideal, not real; a piece of land continued to be worked as an integer, if its nature demanded it, and although rights in its working might be held by several and even by numerous tribesmen, no attempt was made to divide it physically. Moreover, the tendency, as population increased, was not to resort to intensive farming, as in Italy, but to clear virgin soil. It was realized that share-holding in the right of a strip might not suit all temperaments, and such share-holding was therefore voluntary; no man was forced to accept such an arrangement, to "hold in joint tenancy", if he did not want to. That, in practice, such joint tenancy was common argues a fine sense of unity in the clan, and of responsibility towards the community and the soil.

The Celtic agrarian communities, then, were villages of joint and equal tenant farmers, the "landlord" being the community itself, and with a gentry distinguished by birth, and also by wealth in anything but land, until the system began to degenerate and land-owning was introduced. Meanwhile, during the course of many centuries, the Celts kept the soils of Atlantic Europe in growing heart.

(Soil: 242-4)

TOOLS AND PHILOSOPHIES

When men do work upon matter they employ tools which are of two kinds: physical tools of wood, bone, stone, metal; and psychological tools which are expressed in methods, and which become formalized as techniques. Philosophically, there is no difference between these two classes of tools: the plan a man makes concerning the way in which he will move a boulder, is just as much a tool as the lever he uses to carry out his plan. The psychological tools can be divided into two sub-classes, the intellectual and the spiritual; the intellectual tools are concerned with method and collected in sets as sciences; the spiritual tools are concerned with relationships with the rest of the universe, and are collected together in mythologies and religions. A man using all three kinds of tool to turn a piece of waste land into a farm, uses the spiritual tool to invoke the help of the God whose writ runs in that parish, and thereby puts himself into an effectively wilful and purposeful state of mind; he uses the intellectual tools to decide how to set about the work; and the physical tools to cut down trees and plough the virgin soil.

(Soil: 274)

In the beginnings of rationalism the various sciences and arts are felt to be manifestations of a single superior state of mind and spirit, and poets are philosophers, painters, mechanics, sculptors, chemists or physicists. In the early days of the Royal Society, scientists and artists were allies, almost indistinguishable, and serving one discipline. With specialization , necessary consequence of the rapidly growing bodies of the sciences, this unity was lost. The specialist is by himself, he has no body of philosophy, no grand general idea to which his work subscribes. When ordinary men are led by a creative minority in a state of spiritual and intellectual anarchy, then they no longer sense or know the world as a unity of which they are a part, the principal motive for action becomes a brutal self-interest; and even in his dealings with his fellow-men, man's "nature", his feeling tends to vanish away, and heacts at best intelligently, at worst "bestially", and almost never feelingly. If the prospect before us were one of the continued fragmentation of art and science into special techniques, then our industrialism, our divorce from the soil community, could have no issue but the most frightful disaster.

There is, however, an alternative, and it has been suggested by the need, in America, to rehabilitate soils: for this purpose, various sciences become the servants of a kind of aesthetic insight, and in that service they are reunited. The process is likely to be assisted by the fact that, in any case, the actual advance of certain sciences is bringing about the overlapping of one special field by another which gives rise to such bastard sciences as bio-chemistry, and even bio-physics. The chemist, the biologist, the botanist, the crystallographer, the electrician are finding that their work is converging; when the poet and the musician and the painter and the sculptor begin to be drawn in by the same unifying force, then a new integrity for man will have been made, a relationship with the universe as valid as that expressed in the ancient myths will become possible.

The ecologists of America, and the practical men working to their plans, have found that they can restore dead soils to life by recreating upon them a "natural" and balanced soil community. They begin by introducing some undemanding weed which will colonise the most exhausted soils, they gradually introduce nobler vegetables species; they have to work with great care and great insight, balancing species against species, making sure that the trees they plant, when that becomes possible, will find themselves able to establish a mode of life with the ground plants. In the course of time species intrude of their own accord, and the ecologist has to decide whether these intruders shall or shall not be allowed to stay. Some of the artifically introduced species may grow too prosperous at the expense of others, and must be checked; others, too meek, encouraged. In time animal species are introduced, some living off the vegetation, and others, predatory on the former, to hold them in balance. The work must be like building a house of cards, excepting that when every single feat of delicate balance has been successfully accomplished, then the equilibrium of the finished artifact will be massive, not precarious. Now this creative ecology, if that will do as a name for it, is unquestionably an art: aesthetic insight, right feeling for the grain of life is what must animate it. Yet its servants are the sciences. And its end product is a fertile soil which, in time to come, can be safely cleared and ploughed and sown, and will yield harvests..

If man can also think of himself as one of the materials of this new art, as well as the artist, he may yet learn from his ancient contact with soil how to live nobly and at peace.

(Soil: 290-2)

Hyams is rare among writers on ecology in that he approached the subject from a socialist point of view. His article 'Soil and Socialism', published in the New Statesman *(8 December 1951), is therefore of special interest, and has a further significance in that it led to his collaboration with H.J. Massingham (see chapter 10) on* Prophecy of Famine, *(London, Thames and Hudson, 1953). In chapter 7 of that book Hyams suggests what a flourishing modern peasantry might be like, and attempts to dispel the widely-accepted travesty of peasant life which has been created by urban prejudice.*

A Rain Forest in Kenya

2

Trees in Nature's Economy

John Stewart Collis
(1900 - 1984)

John Stewart Collis produced a number of books on literary topics before the Second World War, but is now best known for his writings about Nature. During the war he worked first as an agricultural labourer, then as a forester on the estate of Rolf Gardiner - where the Kinship in Husbandry was based - near Shaftesbury in Dorset, describing his experiences in While Following the Plough [[1946]] *and* Down to Earth [[1947]] . *These books were republished jointly in the 1970s under the title* The Worm Forgives the Plough *(London, Charles Knight,1973; Harmondsworth, Penguin, 1975). He also wrote books of what might be described as 'poetic natural science', and it is from one of these,* The Triumph of the Tree *(London, Cape. 1950) that the following extracts are taken.*

THE HYDROLOGIC CYCLE

Loam soil is said to be composed of one-quarter water, one-quarter air, and one-tenth organic matter - 'it thus swims, breathes and is alive.' So say the authorities. Whatever the exact proportion of water in soils may be, we know that it is very great, and that in fact nothing in all nature is more important than water... If John Ruskin had handled this theme, he would undoubtedly at this point have done a volume on Water. But I am all for sticking to one thing at a time. This is difficult of course, since *inter-relatedness* is the very definition of nature. The full theme of Water is a great subject and can lead us into many places and unveil some surprising spectacles; and perhaps if I get back to trees the reader will not refuse to join me at some future time in a consideration of water. But something must be said here and now about the hydrologic cycle since trees play an important part in the smooth working of its flow.

(The Triumph of the Tree: 138)

...there is a complication which makes a neat statement of the cycle, or the circle, impossible. In fact it makes the words cycle or circle a little dubious. I am thinking of the evaporation from vegetation. There is the evaporation from the ocean, and of rain sent up again from bare land under heat. That is one kind. There is another kind. There is the water sent up, invisibly sprayed into the sky by vegetation itself. A full-grown willow can transpire up to five thousand gallons in a single summer day. How much then a forest? Clouds can be made that way over the land, without benefit of seas. These are tree-clouds, not ocean-clouds. There is a cycle all right, and a constant amount of water in perpetual circulation. But we must not forget this cloud-feeding by plants.

(The Triumph of the Tree: 140)

TREES AND TEMPERATURE

We have seen how vulnerable the soil is. It could so easily be tossed about by the elements, if unprotected. Happily it is protected, in the natural state, either by a carpet of grass whose network of deeply diving roots holds it down firmly, or by trees that on a tremendous scale stake it down, the tree-roots ramifying in all directions, so that only a hundred trees occupying an area of five miles will be actually supplying, in sum, three or four miles-worth of cordage for holding the soil together. Thus when trees were regarded by the uninstructed minds of superstitious men as the guardians of fertility there was some sense in it. When they become simply 'timber' in the eyes of unsuperstitious and instructed men who cut them down indiscriminately the consequences are so bad that modern science is busy restoring the idea that after all trees do guard the fertility of the soil.

Let us now plunge into the centre of our subject. On closer examination we find that trees perform many more offices in relation to the soil than that of merely pegging it down. By virtue of cooling the air and spraying the sky and multiplying the clouds they exert considerable influence upon the fall and distribution of rain; by virtue of sponging the earth around their feet they enormously influence the behaviour of floods, the discipline of rivers, the supply of springs, the health of fish, and (when man arrives), the welfare of navigation; and by virtue of their power to suck up moisture by the ton they dry the swamps and control the malarian mosquitoes. Forests are so much more than meets the eye. They are fountains. They are oceans. They are pipes. They are dams. Their work ramifies through the whole economy of nature.

The rays of the sun beat down upon a barren place. The naked earth becomes very hot and the temperature of the air very high. But if vegetation covers that ground the temperature will be altered. It will be considerably cooled. For the vegetation will evaporate water. It has been proved that, in terms of corn, for every pound of dry substance produced there is an evaporation of two hundred and thirty-five pounds of water; and in terms of turnips, for every pound of substance nine hundred and ten pounds of water are sent up. Under good cultivation an acre can produce seven tons of dry substance. On these terms we can calculate that a given acre will easily evaporate, during the vegetative period, about three thousand five hundred tons of water which will mount upwards to moisten and cool the regions of the sky.

If this is true of crops, how much more does it apply to forests. And further, we must remember that leaves do not become heated nearly as easily as rock or open soil, while the ground under the shade of trees can never be greatly warmed. The result is that forests exert a moderating influence on temperature. That great mountain, the Brahmaputra, has not many trees; but its middle part is covered by forest - and there the temperature is less than at the bare parts by twenty degrees! The largest forest area in the world is at the upper Amazon, six hundred and twenty miles from the Atlantic on one side, and cut off from the Pacific by high mountains. So far from seas, so near the Equator - will not the temperature be very high and very dry? Yet no, it is not greater than at the coast, and not as high as some temperatures in the middle latitudes. This remarkably moderate temperature is attributed to the enormous transpiration of water from plants in the tropics. The rainfall-down is about sixty inches a year. The rainfall-up (or evaporation) amounts to forty inches a year. Between the two lots the air is considerably cooled.

(The Triumph of the Tree: 140-2)

TREES AND RAINFALL

This capacity of trees to moderate the temperature, besides being so
agreeable, is also a factor bearing upon the quantity and distribution
of rainfall. Water comes down from the sky in the form of rain or
snow or hail, and is further found as dew, hoar-frost, and other
condensations of moisture which form on the surface of foliage,
branches, and trunks. And before it comes down, as everyone knows,
it is tanked in clouds, or as clouds. What induces the exchange? Cold
obstruction. That is why mountains promote precipitation. But
wooded mountains are still more effective in deflating the fleeting
vapours. Denuded hills do not always induce rainfall, while
tree-clothed hills do. Dr. Paul Schrieber, a noted meteorologist, after
giving elaborate data for Saxony, reached the conclusion that in a
district completely covered by forests the influence of the forest in
increasing rainfall would be equal to elevating the region six hundred
and fifty feet. We cannot easily raise mountains when we wish to
increase the rainfall. It is therefore worth realizing that by judiciously
planting trees we can lever-up a mountain about six hundred feet.

This cold obstruction induces greater condensation in the
air-currents - and hence precipitation. But also, forests, whether on
mountains or not, add to the weight of clouds by the evaporation we
have been speaking of. And since they add to their weight they induce
their downfall. The amount of water evaporated, that is, thrown off
by forests into the air, is so enormous that they have been given the
name of 'the oceans of the continent'.

(The Triumph of the Tree: 143-4)

Supposing that tomorrow there were no vegetation over the face of the
earth - then much less rain would fall over the continents; the clouds
would frequently pass over without unloading. If on the next day trees
covered the same space, then the rainfall would be enormous in
comparison. Therefore if continentals (we are not thinking of
islanders such as the British, at the moment) wish to be sure of their
rainfall, they should be careful about their forests. They have not
always been thus careful. The result is that in some places after
reckless lumbering, men have looked up to see the clouds steadily
passing them by day after day without discharging their moisture, like
ships refusing to put into port. The primitives were nearer the truth

when they paid special honour and made peculiar sacrifices to certain trees as the producers of rain...

...it is clear from the foregoing that if we are entitled to say - Put up some trees and you can pull down some clouds (always supposing the actuality were anything like as simple as that!) we are certainly not entitled to think that this will always add to the moisture of the soil on which they stand. On the contrary, they suck up moisture, as we have just seen...

And from this it also follows that trees could be used to suck up swamps and bogs. Swamps are agriculturally useless and often the breeding-places of malaria and swamp-fevers. In fact trees have already been planted for the purpose of draining swamps. It has been done with great success in Landes and Sologne. It would be delightful to see the half-useless peat-bogs of Ireland's Calary Common in County Wicklow transformed in this way.

The above considerations, then, entitle us to say that trees have a decided influence upon temperature; that by offering obstruction to clouds on high places they increase rainfall and in effect raise the height of mountains; that though forests promote a greater fall of rain than do open spaces, they themselves give back almost as much water as they receive, raising invisible oceans which moisten the pastures of the sky and favour a far-flung distribution of rain; and that this very fact enables them to soak up swamps and cleanse their malarian pollutions.

(The Triumph of the Tree: 147-8)

TREES, MOUNTAINS AND RIVERS

Imagine if you can - it is not something we could ever see in the state of nature - a long mountain slope consisting of soil without grass or trees on top. When the rain-storm beats down upon it, what happens? Some of the water sinks in and is sponged up; and a great deal more runs down into the valley below to form a torrent making for the lowlands and the sea. The rain-storm continues: and now the water is hardly absorbed at all and ninety per cent of it runs down, *taking with it* a proportion of the top of the soil. The process continues. This very unnatural erosion continues and the rivers increase, while their freightage of soil and silt piles up in the regions far away. The process goes on until all the top of that soil has been carried down. Then the bottom of it follows, the stones, the rubble follow and pile up on the soil which went first, so that matters are now upside down in the valley beyond. The storm subsides. The rivers decrease. The beds dry up. There is a period of drought. Then once again the storm breaks out. This time the water rushes down so unhindered and so swiftly, that what with inadequate river banks and gross siltage, floods sweep over the land.

This never happens, of course, in the Natural Order. It could happen if someone came and rolled up the carpet of grass and pulled out the cover of trees.

Now let us imagine the same area of mountain slope covered with forest. Again the storm breaks out and the rain pours down. This time it does not reach the ground all at once. It must first fall upon the leaves and the branches of the trees, and thence trickle to the bottom where it is easily absorbed. There is no running straight down the hill into the valley. For not only is there so much less force in the rainfall by virtue of the living-leaf obstruction which cushions the blow, but the dead-leaf and twig obstruction, the litter, serves in the nature of a colossal sponge, a single acre of which can sometimes harbour forty-six tons of water. This absorption on the floor is the chief thing and a very great thing: but the check first received at the roof is also important. This is particularly evident in the case of snow, the rapid melting of which is so often a cause of sudden flood where there are no trees. In a dense forest only half the snow-fall reaches the ground. A white roof is formed on top of the trees, so that airmen passing across forest lands have sometimes confused the foliage with the floor. When the false upper floor melts it must first trickle down the barks or fall in lumps to the ground. This capacity of litter to detain moisture is called seepage, which in many places on the steepest slopes has been found so marvellously absorbative that it 'creates conditions with regard to surface run-off such *as obtain in a level country'.*[1] It can turn almost a perpendicular into a flat in terms of gravitation.

It is this seepage which promotes the discipline of rivers, the always wonderful sight of water running on and on all the year round, neither flowing over its banks nor drying up nor becoming clogged with silt. It is seepage which makes severe floods extremely rare in the natural state. It is seepage which preserves the water clean and wholesome for the fishes. It is seepage which keeps the rivers dependable for navigation when men arrive on the scene. Indeed it is already a well-known truth that if we strike at our trees and thus at seepage, we strike at our inland ships: thus (to anticipate the Argument for a minute), at the period of Roman rule in France the river Durance was perfectly navigable, while now, the watersheds being cleared of forests, you can hardly float a skiff on it; and the Loire, once a navigable river of the highest order affording communication between Nantes and the Central Provinces, so that in 1551 the Marquis of Northumberland, Ambassador from England, could sail from Orleans to Nantes panoplied in a magnificent suite 'in five large many-coloured boats', is now unnavigable above Saumer, owing to the detritus brought down from the mountains with every flood.

Moreover, this seepage provides such a system of sieving, such a network of small tributaries, such a check on too swift surface evaporation, that it not only regularizes the rivers but creates and maintains the springs. There is a world we know little about, we dwellers on the upper earth; a world open only to the eye of the spelaeologists, those daring travellers into the nether regions in which are discovered underground rivers and lakes and wells in the silent majesty of mighty halls and the total darkness of long winding corridors and caves. Here is the beginning of rivers. Here is the fountain-head of the flow, the primal source of the glittering glory we behold far away in the valleys and the plains. And it is *maintained*. It is fed slowly and continuously from the great sponges that cling to the mountains. This is the protection against drought no less than the only true damming against flood.

(The Triumph of the Tree: 150-3)

TREES AND WIND

The consolidation of mountains and the just administration of water do not exhaust the offices of trees in relation to the earth. There is an invisible agent we have to reckon with; necessary and beneficial in the motions of the sphere, but at times a most blasting bane, an unseen foe that needs no cloak of darkness. We must consider the wind on the plain. It is not so drastic an element as water, but it can be a fearful one. Its invisible whips can be the scourge of man and beast and plant. The only thing to do is to break it. An impossible task, we might think. It is easy to break hard things, by simply tapping them or by elaborately blasting them to bits. It is very difficult to break a really soft thing; and when that thing is the unseen element of wind whose arm is yet strong enough to raise up liquid mountains on the sea or cast down houses on the land, the only thing we can do is to wall ourselves away from it. We cannot wall up the open country, so we must try and break that fury. Again we call trees to our rescue, and speak of Wind-breaks. And it is astonishing to how great an extent they do break it. I have stood on a field protected by a line of poplars when almost a hurricane was blowing across the country, and I have felt hardly enough wind to blow my hat off; while the difference in the temperature between my side and the far side of the trees was remarkable - no wonder, since it is found that even a hedge of only six feet high can raise the average soil temperature three or four degrees to a distance of four hundred and fifty feet.

We take this sort of thing for granted in the British Isles where agriculture is not yet so much the enemy of silviculture that hedges at least are still in abundance. One writes 'not yet' because hedging is a big job in itself, as I can vouch for from personal experience of it, and does not lend itself to any mechanical instrument. But since so many hands have recently been turned into steel, so many men exchanged for machines of one sort or another, the man who looks after hedges may soon be no longer found on a farm; and thus the farmer is increasingly showing a tendency to do without hedges and to put up one long piece of wire instead, charged with electricity for the benefit of the amazed and affrighted cows. I suppose there will have to be a decade of bovine electrical education before these monstrosities are exchanged again in favour of hedges. But elsewhere in the world, on great stretches of plain, neither trees nor hedges are naturally abundant and 'the wind which sweeps over the plain unhindered, increasing in fury and breadth, is its greatest enemy. In drying out the plain, it creates a hard soil crust. By increasing evaporation, it draws off the soil moisture and cools the soil. Then it tatters and dries the finer soil parts. A plain constantly exposed to wind pressure will be driven back to the most primitive conditions of life and growth'. [2]   And should there ever come a time when large areas of level forest are cut and the land ploughed and the soil loosened, then, the hitherto harmless wind in that region will be no longer harmless, and ruined farmers will face that cloud of dust which is their day of judgment.

(The Triumph of the Tree: 153-5)

AMERICAN SETTLERS AND THE DESTRUCTION OF THE FORESTS

Having conquered the Indians, they turned to nature. They found themselves confronted with a mighty host. It stood before them, erect and menacing, battalion behind battalion. But it was unarmed. It could not defend itself. It could not even retreat, for it was rooted to the ground. Being pious folk, the invaders saw that God was clearly not on the side of these green battalions. The forest was an enemy that could be destroyed. And they set to work to destroy it.

Two immediate objectives were to be gained: first, room in which to grow crops, and second, the supply of timber with which to build the new civilization and to maintain it with fuel. It was a big job, this subduing of the wilderness. It took toughness and time before the first 100 million acres of trees had been brought down. They went at it with a will. They launched a campaign against the forest with a virulence that seemed akin to hatred - (an attitude towards trees which seems to have remained with Americans to the present time, for in 1917, according to Dr. Pfeiffer, when some French peasants asked American soldiers to thin out a few trees, they were appalled by the recklessness and violence with which they set to work). They went out against the forests with the thoroughness of an invading army, attacking first one stronghold then another. For a hundred years the white pine trees of New England held out. Then one day it was found that all had fallen on that field. After the white then the yellow. The movement of destruction advanced relentlessly onwards from the forests of Maine to New York. In ten years those battalions were defeated and the lumber-troops entered Ohio and Indiana and Pennsylvania, from whence they moved in turn to Michigan, to Wisconsin, to Minnesota and thence again to the Gulf and Pacific coasts. That was the Northern campaign against the trees. There was a similar offensive in the South, through the Rocky Mountain region, through Arizona, Colorado, and Idaho, and from the Carolinas to Texas.

Such is the briefest possible outline of the onslaught. Today it is reported that seven-eighths of the continent's virgin forests has gone, and that only the douglas fir is making a last stand along a fifty-mile front between the top of the Cascade Mountains and the Pacific.

The method throughout this tree-war was that of clean cutting, complete clearing without any policy of further yields. It was applied to areas which had no farming possibilities with as much zest as on the fertile loams. Whole mountain ranges were burned off, though quite useless for farming. The attackers advanced upon the enemy with steel and fire - with quite as much fire as steel. Burning down forests by deliberate intent was one of the quickest means of advance, for in a wind fires sometimes spread at sixty miles an hour. Speaking of the Southerners, Paul Sears says: 'To the settler, here as in the North, the forest was a hostile thing, occupying the ground which he needed for corn and beans, even though it furnished him with game, fuel and building material. All was fair in the struggle against this handicap, and no weapon, not even his sharp ax, was more powerful than fire. So the use of fire against the forest became a ritual of the poor white. He has literally burned his way west, from the pine-lands of the Carolinas to the blackjack cross-timbers of Oklahoma and Texas.'

There seems to have been no sense of waste in those days. Often enough they did not stack the logs for later use - it was easier to get them out of the way by burning them at once. Thus it is told how, in the neighbourhood of Michigan, huge slabs of white pine were dumped into the open fields in great pyres and burned day and night - with such a blaze that there was no darkness in the town. Such pyres were sometimes kept burning for two or three years! Furthermore, accidental fires were extremely common, and still are in America to the extent of one hundred and fifty thousand a year. When at last this became recognized as a menace and men were engaged at high wages to fight forest fires, it only made matters worse - the number of fires increased because out-of-work men started some more in order to be paid for putting them out.

It will be seen from the above that at first the lumber trade was of less account than the actual business of clearing the ground for cropping. But the steady growth of mill-power at length made the lumber merchant very rich and powerful. When we realize that the first water-power mill in 1631 could only cut 1000 board feet a day; that in 1767 the gang-saw cut 5000 a day; that in 1820 the circular saw cut 40,000 a day; that in 1830 the steam saw cut 125,000 a day; and that the figure is now 1,000,000, we can appreciate what the lumber industry began to mean, and with what ruthlessness the Lumber Kings would ravage their way through the trees with an even greater recklessness than the farmers. Forests once covered six-sevenths of the State of Wisconsin with hemlock and pine, and by 1899 the lumbermen, employing 1033 saws, were cutting 34 billion feet a year, until in 1932 there was nothing left. We may fairly call these lumber merchants tree-butchers since wood bore no relation in their minds to the living object than slabs of meat are related to an animal in the eyes of the butcher. The trees were not trees but dollars in terms of 'timber' to be translated by the marvellous ingenuity of man into all the things, the endless things, required by civilization.

One of these things is paper. Perhaps it is when we turn from the saw mills to the paper mills of the factories in the towns that we get the clearest picture of such transformation. Let me bring the story up to date. At the time of writing this book - 1948 - the remarkable metamorphosis of trees into print is still in full swing and the facts concerning it are forthcoming from reliable sources of information. An average issue of the *New York Times* of ninety-two pages, plus book supplement and magazine pages, requires *one hundred acres* of forest for its production. Some American Sunday papers run to one hundred and twenty-eight pages and have a circulation of one million. This requires the pulp-wood production of *one hundred and forty* acres for each issue. Since this means the consumption, for each issue, of one thousand one hundred and twenty cords of pulp-wood, the operation demands the use of fifteen thousand, six hundred and eighty trees.

In my mind's eye, as I write these words, I can very clearly see what fourteen acres of trees mean. For it was once my job, as a woodman, to thin a wood of about that size. [3] It seemed quite a large area to me. That a space of one hundred and forty acres should be needed for a newspaper edition, is difficult to believe; and I did not believe it until I received an authoritative and very detailed communication on the subject from the Director of the Canadian Forestry Association - and the facts are as given above. So I must accept it as a fact that every Sunday when an American family open their weekly newspaper, they are entitled to say - Here goes another fifteen thousand trees.

We have come a long way from the conception of trees as gods.

(The Triumph of the Tree; 203-7)

MODERN ATTITUDES TOWARDS NATURE

... A very long way indeed. It is not a happy contrast. Could we draw back and regard these operations of our forefathers in America, with the eye, not of a human being but of an animal involved in the invasion, they would offer a fearful spectacle. Since we cannot do this we can at least try and see it as from a high place. For many centuries the land had remained under the equilibrium of the Natural Order. Suddenly it was broken in upon by a race of men from across the sea. And with what violence, with what hatred against all living things! There had never been anything like this before in the history of man and nature. There had been many civilizations. Men had grown up with nature in this place and that place. They had seldom been wise or good in their relations with earth. They had made many mistakes, huge blunders in tree-killing, soil-injury, and water-wastage for which they had been repaid with dust and sand. But there had never been anything like this that occurred, and occurs, in modern days under the sign of mechanism. When we think of the ripping up of the grass in every direction, of the crashing down of huge trees under the axe and the deliberately lit forest fires rushing forward at the rate of an express train while thousands of animals shriekingly fled in terror from the crackling flames till exhausted they were burnt alive, our minds and our hearts turn back to the primal days of religion and reverence. For what had those beauty-blind mechanical destroyers, those reality-scared lumberjacks, to do with any sort of religion? Do they not seem only as large insects, or as a plague of locusts eating everything before them without the excuse of being driven blindfold in the coils of necessity?

(The Triumph of the Tree: 216-17)

THE TREATMENT OF TREES IN WESTERN EUROPE

The whole world has heard of the Tennessee Valley Authority. What they did there, what they are doing elsewhere in the replanting of their forests and the conservation of their soil, may save them from total disaster and eclipse.

The story of man and trees in Western Europe has not been so calamitous in result as the American. Nevertheless nearly a thousand years war was declared against trees in Western Europe. It is not the fault of the deforesters that the land is not now in worse shape than it is - the fact is of course that the invaders of the American continent had the conditions for a real rape of the earth, not hitherto available. The European situation with regard to deforestation is too complicated to be subject to a general statement. But it is only too obvious that today, the Scandinavians, who have largely kept their trees, are in a very much better position with regard to fertility than Southern Europe, especially Spain whose once tree-covered country is now a scene of almost Eastern poverty. Again, the Germans are world famous for their forests and their foresters. Today the trees are falling fast under the axe of the occupying powers. But let us remember that it was the Nazis who first set about exploiting German and Austrian forests without any regenerative policy whatever. They wished to use their trees as weapons of war, and did so with such thoroughness that by 1942 it could be written: 'Clad in fabrics produced from wood, living on wood sugar, wood proteins, and meat and cheese from wood-fed cattle, with a schnapps ration made from "grain" alcohol obtained from sawdust, German soldiers move to the Russian battle lines in wood-gas-driven trucks, which are greased with tree-stump lubricants and run on Buna tyres made from wood alcohol. Spreading misery and destruction with explosives manufactured from the waste liquors of woodpulp mills, they are assisted in their nefarious work by squadrons of plywood planes, while the German propaganda division takes a motion-picture record of selected items of the action on a film made of wood cellulose acetate.'   [4]

The trees have had their revenge all right. And, one way or another, it will return on us, we may be sure, if we further deface the German forests.

In England forests once covered nearly the whole land. Envoys returned to Caesar saying that they could not penetrate to the end of them. In due course they also were cut down. There has been much re-growth since, and reckless cutting of the re-growths, but still many woods remain to the tree-loving British, while of course a supply of rainfall has never been a problem for the islanders.

For my part, I think that the danger to England caused by the primary destruction of her forests, goes very deep. The nemesis is very real and very terrible. It goes underground. Already by the fifteenth century so many forests had been cut down that wood as fuel was beginning to become scarce. When Aeneas Sylvius, later Pope Pius II, paid a visit to England in 1458 he noted in his diary how pleased the poor people were when they were given stones for alms... 'Now we have seen begging at the temples, poor people almost naked: who, when they had been given stones for alms, went away happy. That kind of rock, which may contain sulphur or some other rich material, is burned instead of firewood when the district is bare.' That is to say already coal had been discovered, and that branch of forestry which we call coal-mining, had begun. First we cut down the forests standing above ground. When they were exhausted there remained the woods underground - the carboniferous forests. Coal mining is a branch of forestry and agriculture: but we dig deeper, we cut without planting, we reap where we have not sown.

Thus that great day came when the carboniferous forests were located and the properties of coal were realized. Perhaps this was the most exciting discovery of all. We are weary of such things now. Our hearts are cold and cowed. But we shall be lacking in imagination if we cannot realize what it must have seemed like in those days, the excitement which the words of George Stephenson must have held for all who heard them: 'We are living in an age when the pent-up rays of that sun which shone upon the great Carboniferous Forests of past ages, are being liberated to set in motion our mills and factories, to carry us with great rapidity over the earth's surface, and to propel our fleets, regardless of wind and tide with unerring regularity over the ocean.'

We must allow a certain epic grandeur in their theme. The power was divined. The wealth was realized. The possibilities seemed boundless. Naturally there was a coal rush. Claims were staked out by the enterprising and adventurous, and messengers were sent down into the primitive forests. A strange journey indeed! Strange wanderings in those sunken lands! Pioneering down into the darkness, the travellers explored that green old world of long ago. They made perpendicular roads and descended as far as three miles into the buried woods. They carved out galleries within them. They ran trucks through tunnels chiselled from the petrified leavings of the rotten reeds. And as they passed along those corridors encased by the corrupted ferns, and penetrated ever further into the lost regions of the sunlit lands, the danger from gases obliged them to go in darkness with nothing to lighten their way save the phosphorescent gleam from dried fish...

They encountered more perils than explosive gases. In making their way through the subterranean forests they sometimes came upon tree-trunks standing erect, the interior being sandstone and the bark converted into coal, so that as soon as the stance of such trees was weakened they often suddenly fell, killing the men below. 'It is strange to reflect', says Sir Charles Lyell, 'how many thousands of these trees fell originally in their native forests, in obedience to the law of gravity, and how the few which continued to stand erect, obeying, after myriads of ages, the same force, are cast down to immolate their human victims.' But nothing daunts the spirit of man. In heaving out these precious rocks, this bottled energy, for expansion in the upper world, no effort was too much, no sacrifice in flesh and tears too great, and hundreds, even thousands of these visitors to the ancient woods gave up their lives and lay down eternally entombed amidst the sepulchres of the trees.

This enterprise was pursued with such zeal and concentrated industry that during the nineteenth century England cut out more of these forests, this coal, than was cut out elsewhere over the *whole world*. This changed England utterly. Her history was altered. She was forced to enter on a road all unforeseen. It caused the colossal industrialism of the country. That is by far the most important effect which trees have had upon England. They had been sleeping below. They were disturbed. When they were carried to the surface they were in the form of great potential activity. Once they had got to work they changed everything, including characters and faces. As for their effect upon population, a twenty million increase is an underestimation. Thus England became one of the most powerful countries in the world. Then the most vulnerable. And now?

Everyone knows her dilemma now. No country in the world, or in history, has ever been less ecologically sound than the England of today with its population of fifty million, ninety per cent of whom work at non-agricultural activities caused by the carboniferous forests. That is the fact. When food fails presently to come in from other countries how will the fifty millions get on? The question is enough to make a tree laugh. This ever hanging threat is the cause of the gloom which has fallen upon the English of late - they feel they have no *footing* on earth.

(The Triumph of the Tree: 238-42)

THE NEED FOR AN ECOLOGICAL OUTLOOK

It seems to me that the time has come for Advanced Guards - philosophic, educational, poetic, scientific - to cohere for once and make their countrymen conscious of the ecological situation. It is a comprehensive theme. 'We have learned to see in mythology', says Dr. Pfeiffer, 'a good deal of physiology and natural scientific wisdom.' In this book I have tried to bring together the intuitions of the past with the factual knowledge of the present. We have reached a time when we can get our bearings. We can discard superstition without replacing it with irreverence. We can sense the invisibilities on a higher plane of apprehension. Edward Carpenter said that he once managed to glimpse at any rate a partial vision of a tree. 'It was a beech, standing somewhat isolated, and still leafless in quite early Spring. Suddenly I was aware of its skyward-reaching arms and upturned finger-tips, as if some vivid life (or electricity) was streaming through them into the spaces of heaven, and of its roots plunged in the earth and drawing the same energies from below. The day was quite still and there was no movement in the branches, but in that moment the tree was no longer a separate or separable organism, but a vast being ramifying far into space, sharing and uniting the life of Earth and Sky, and full of a most amazing activity.' [5]

We cannot all reach these visionary heights, nor can any man remain there. But we can all be ecologists. There are in England today agriculturalists with astonishing practical genius combined with comprehensive ecological insight. Trust England to produce such men! If they are supported and allowed to lead the way and show the means towards the greatest compromise England has ever been called upon to make, the compromise between industry and agriculture, then England could regain her balance. But she must make up her mind about it. The English can do anything if they make up their minds upon a course of action - but they do not like doing so, they would rather drift. Can we afford to drift any longer? If the present unecological life is continued and other countries are relied upon to support us - why, then that cutting down of the forests which led to the cutting out of the squashed and hoarded wealth of wood below, will have meant disaster. For trees always have the last word.

(The Triumph of the Tree: 245-6)

The majority of The Triumph of the Tree *has been reprinted in* The Vision of Glory *(London, Charles Knight, 1972; Harmondsworth, Penguin, 1975). Richard Ingrams's biography* John Stewart Collis - A Memoir *(London, Chatto, 1986), gives an account of the long period of neglect which Collis suffered until the growth of interest in ecology led to the success of* The Worm Forgives the Plough, *though it does not deal in any great detail with Collis's ideas on the environment.*

Rolf Gardiner (1902-1971), for whom Collis worked, was a leading figure in the organic husbandry movement, and particularly concerned with forestry, publishing England Herself *(London, Faber) in 1943, a book about his 'ventures in rural restoration' on the Springhead estate.* Water Springing From the Ground, *edited by Andrew Best (Springhead, Fontmell Magna, Shaftesbury, Dorset; 1972) is an anthology of Gardiner's writings. He contributed an essay on rural reconstruction to* England and the Farmer, *edited by H.J. Massingham (London, Batsford, 1941), and one on forestry to* The Natural Order, *also edited by Massingham (London, Dent, 1945).*

Alternative to Death, *by Gardiner's friend Lord Lymington, Earl of Portsmouth (London, Faber, 1943) contains a chapter on forestry and its place in farming.*

References

1   Paul Sears, *Deserts on the March.*
2   Ehrenfried Pfeiffer, *The Earth's Face.*
3   *See Down to Earth* Part II.
4   'The Rediscovery of Wood', *American Forests,* September 1942.
5   *Pagan and Christian Creeds.*

Basin-Listing, Nebraska, U.S.A.: a method of collecting and storing moisture, to prevent soil drift

3

Water, Wind, and Soil Erosion

G.V. Jacks and R.O. Whyte
(1901 - 1977)　　(1903 - 1986)

The Rape of the Earth: A World Survey of Soil Erosion *(London, Faber, 1939), published in the same year as Steinbeck's* The Grapes of Wrath, *has as its frontispiece the photograph entitled 'Dust Over Dakota' (see page 36) which shows a solitary figure in a featureless landscape, bent against the wind which is blowing away the exhausted top-soil.*

At the time of the book's publication, G.V. Jacks was Deputy Director of the Imperial Bureau of Soil Science, which was based at Rothamsted Experimental Station, Harpenden, under the direction of Sir E.J. Russell, while R.O. Whyte was Deputy Director of the Imperial Bureau of Pastures and Forage Crops, which was based at Aberystwyth under the direction of R.G. Stapledon (see chapter 9). Jacks was later editor of the Journal of Soil Science, *and a member of the Nature Conservancy Council, while Whyte went to work for the Food and Agriculture Organization of the United Nations.*

The authors drew their evidence not merely from the USA, but from Australia, New Zealand, India, China, Japan, Palestine, Turkey, Russia, and Africa, considering Africa's plight to be the most serious of all. Little information could be gathered from South America, though the problem of de-forestation in Brazil was already manifest.

The Rape of the Earth is a classic, to which many works of the 1940s refer, and which clearly foresaw the probability of the scenes of famine now so familiar. The sections on Africa are of particular relevance to the 1980s, but I have chosen to deal chiefly with the relation between a healthy soil and the management of water, and the effects of wind on soil which is deteriorating. These issues follow on logically from those referred to in the previous chapter.

NATURE AND MAN-MADE SOIL EROSION

Erodibility is not an inherent property of any mature and fertile soil; it is a property induced, most commonly, by human interference. No undisturbed mature soil (with the possible exception of certain sparsely clad soils in dry regions) exhibits any appreciable erodibility, otherwise it would have disappeared long ago. Natural vegetation and soils form non-eroding systems under the climatic conditions prevailing where they occur.

(The Rape of the Earth: 93-4)

Erosion in Nature is a beneficent process without which the world would have died long ago. The same process, accelerated by human mismanagement, has become one of the most vicious and destructive forces that have ever been released by man. What is usually known as 'geological erosion' or 'denudation' is a universal phenomenon which through thousands of years has carved the earth into its present shape. Denudation is an early and important process in soil formation, whereby the original rock material is continuously broken down and sorted out by wind and water until it becomes suitable for colonization by plants. Plants, by the binding effects of their roots, by the protection they afford against rain and wind and by the fertility they impart to the soil, bring denudation almost to a standstill. Everybody must have compared the rugged and irregular shape of bare mountain peaks where denudation is still active with the smooth and harmonious curves of slopes that have long been protected by a mantle of vegetation. Nevertheless, some slight denudation is always occurring. As each superficial film of plant-covered soil becomes exhausted it is removed by rain or wind, to be deposited mainly in the rivers and sea, and a corresponding thin layer of new soil forms by slow weathering of the underlying rock. The earth is continuously discarding its old, worn-out skin and renewing its living sheath of soil from the dead rock beneath. In this way an equilibrium is reached between denudation and soil formation so that, unless the equilibrium is disturbed, a mature soil preserves a more or less constant depth and character indefinitely. The depth is sometimes only a few inches, occasionally several feet, but within it lies the whole capacity of the earth to produce life. Below that thin layer comprising the delicate organism known as soil is a planet as lifeless as the moon.

The equilibrium between denudation and soil formation is easily disturbed by the activities of man. Cultivation, deforestation or the destruction of the natural vegetation by grazing or other means, unless carried out according to certain immutable conditions imposed by each region, may so accelerate denudation that soil, which would normally be washed or blown away in a century, disappears within a year or even within a day. But no human ingenuity can accelerate the soil-renewing process from lifeless rock to an extent at all comparable to the acceleration of denudation. This man-accelerated denudation is what is now known as soil erosion. It is the almost inevitable result of reducing below a certain limit the natural fertility of the soil - of man betraying his most sacred trust when he assumes dominion over the land.

Man-induced soil erosion is taking place to-day in almost every country inhabited by civilized man, except north-western Europe. It is a disease to which any civilization founded on the European model seems liable when it attempts to grow outside Europe. Scarcely any climate or environment is immune from erosion, but it is most virulent in the semi-arid continental grasslands - the steppes, prairies and velds of North and South America, Australia, South Africa and Russia which offer the greatest promise as future homes of civilization. It is also the gravest danger threatening the security of the white man and the well-being of the coloured man in the tropical and sub-tropical lands of Africa and India. Until quite recently erosion was regarded as a matter of merely local concern, ruining a few fields and farmsteads here and there, and compelling the occupiers to abandon their homes and move on to new land, but it is now recognized as a contagious disease spreading destruction far and wide irrespective of private, county, state or national boundaries. Like other contagious diseases, erosion is most easily checked in its early stages; when it has advanced to the stage when it threatens the entire social structure, its control is extremely difficult. In the main, unimportant individuals have started erosion and been crushed by it, until the cumulative losses in property and widespread suffering and want have brought governments and nations, with their immense powers for good or evil, into the fray.

(The Rape of the Earth: 19-20)

GULLY FORMATION AND SHEET EROSION

The most significant physical deterioration resulting from cultivation is a reduction in the porosity and cohesion of the soil. Rainwater, that was formerly absorbed by the soil, then runs off the surface, carrying soil with it, and 'sheet erosion' begins. This is usually unnoticed, as only a fraction of an inch of soil is removed in a season, but the trouble is already well advanced, for the next layer of soil exposed at the surface is less absorbent than was the eroded layer, the amount of run-off water increases further, and the rate of erosion is steadily accelerated. In a very short time, the run-off collects in rivulets where its erosive and transporting powers are enormously increased. The rivulets become gullies and the gullies coalesce to become chasms, penetrating through the soil into the barren subsoil. Stuart Chase in *Rich Land, Poor Land* describes how a chasm, 3,000 acres in extent and 200 feet deep, in Georgia, USA, started to grow forty years ago from water dripping unheeded off a barn roof and forming a little rill that became a rivulet that became a torrent that tore away the soil and subsoil over an ever-widening area and flung whole farmsteads into the gaping wound. Other chasms and gullies, tributaries of this greatest, cover 40,000 acres in the neighbourhood. Chase likened the scenery to the Yellowstone canyon which Nature fashioned in millions of years. Men have worked quicker; only half a century has been needed to fashion the new canyon of Georgia.

Gullies are among the more spectacular results of erosion; without them the far more insidious and widely destructive processes of sheet erosion might pass unnoticed for much longer. Sheet erosion is like a wasting disease that affects the whole body but exhibits no serious outward symptoms until it is so far advanced that only a complicated treatment can effect an uncertain cure. The ugly scars on the landscape produced by gully erosion are often the first warning taken that something serious has been happening for several years over a much greater area of still unscarred land. For gully erosion which, if unchecked, can cause incalculable havoc, is the direct consequence of, and can only be controlled by preventing, sheet erosion.

When gully formation has begun, the land has already lost, apart from soil material, much of the most important element in soil fertility and stability - the water-holding capacity of the soil. The capacity to absorb and retain water is a very characteristic property of a mature, fertile soil. It is scarcely, if at all, developed in bare weathered rock formations (except heavy clays) that have never carried vegetation and contain no humus. Normally the water-holding capacity of soil is confined mainly to a few inches on the surface where fresh humus, formed from decaying plant and animal remains, accumulates. Sheet erosion, by removing the most absorbent layers, not only greatly increases the amount of run-off water which is the principal eroding agent, but equally decreases the value and usefulness of the rainfall. In semi-arid countries, where every drop of rain is needed to maintain some life, this consequence of erosion is far more serious than the actual loss of soil. The recent spells of drought years in North America, South Africa and Australia would not have been so devastating fifty years ago, as much more of the rain would have been held by the absorbent soil and utilized by the crops. To-day an abnormally high rainfall is required to produce the same results as an average rainfall would have produced then; but to-day a high rainfall also tends to wash away more of the remaining soil than a low one. Where erosion has occurred, rain is no longer an unmixed blessing. In many parts of these countries drought has come to stay, regardless of the weather.

What happens, and does not happen, when as a consequence of a little sheet erosion, a part of the annual rainfall runs off the surface? In countries with a strictly limited water supply, the total natural productivity of the land is immediately and permanently reduced, since the maximum productivity is fixed by the amount of rain retained by the soil rather than by the total rainfall. As run-off is accompanied by erosion, the water-holding capacity of the soil is further reduced, the proportion of run-off to total rainfall increases, and productivity decreases, progressively. At the same time the underground water supply, normally fed by water filtering slowly through the soil, diminishes. Wells and springs dry up or only flow intermittently, town water supplies are endangered and a progressive desiccation of the whole country is observed.

(The Rape of the Earth: 29-31)

FLOODING AND SILTATION

The run-off water is, however, water, and it would not appear to be beyond the capacity of man to store or utilize it for productive purposes before it is lost in the sea. In actual fact, run-off water is ordinarily worse than useless, and human ingenuity is fully occupied in preventing it from completing the chaos started by sheet erosion rather than in utilizing it. The drainage system of a river basin (which forms a natural unit of country in questions of erosion control), has been shown to be so related to the topography, soils, vegetation and climate of the basin that it is perfectly adapted to deal with the normal discharge of water into the main river. Widespread floods are unusual in regions undisturbed by man. Even the immense volumes of water released by the spring thawing of snow on mountains are sufficiently retained by the porous litter and soils of undisturbed forests to prevent an excessive discharge into the rivers. But when man cuts down the mountain forests and destroys the sponge-like properties of the forest floor, flood, after a thaw or heavy rain, is almost inevitable, as the forest was an essential part of the natural drainage system. Deforestation, with or without perceptible soil erosion, of mountain watersheds is, indeed, the commonest cause of recurrent floods the world over. The most costly works of mountain flood control are hopelessly inefficient in comparison with actual forest.

Similarly when natural grassland, on even the gentlest slope, is mismanaged by injudicious cultivation, say, or by overgrazing, soil fertility is reduced, erosion commences, and soon the amount of run-off water begins to rise. It is not unusual for the run-off from a cultivated prairie to increase in a few years from a normal 1-2 per cent to 10-20 per cent of the annual rainfall - i.e. ten times. When the whole or the greater part of a natural drainage basin is thus mismanaged, the result is that enormously excessive quantities of water are discharged into the rivers during the wet, and abnormally small quantities during the dry seasons. Hence rivers associated with eroded regions are characterized by marked irregularity of flow, periods of flood being followed by periods of very low water, which (apart from flood damage) greatly reduces their utility for navigation, town water supplies, hydro-electric power, irrigation, etc. It is obvious that the loss and damage caused in this way by erosion are not confined to the eroded regions but may extend over the whole length and breadth of a great river basin like that of the Mississippi - which in many places is now more a menace than a blessing to the country through which it passes. There can be no doubt that the increasing frequency and catastrophic nature of the Mississippi floods are largely due to soil erosion in both neighbouring and distant regions.

(The Rape of the Earth: 31-2)

The task of restricting the damage done by, and of utilizing productively, the excessive and often priceless run-off water is of the utmost difficulty, owing to the fact that the water carries a load of soil. When soil is washed from a field, with its irreplaceable content of vitality and fertility, it might be thought that the damage, as far as the soil was concerned, was completed, but it has only begun. The water breaks down the transported soil crumbs into their constituent particles of sand, silt and clay thereby destroying most of the characteristic soil properties and fertility, so that even when the eroded particles are re-deposited on cultivable land, they have lost much of their former productive capacity. The transported particles themselves have a powerful erosive effect, tearing away more soil as they pass over the land, and widening and deepening gullies until the run-off water is loaded to full capacity. The capacity of running water to hold soil in suspension depends upon the velocity of flow and the size of the suspended particles; doubling the velocity increases the carrying capacity no less than 64 times, and the size of particle transportable 128 times. Thus gullies, by continually eating into the land and thereby increasing the angle of slope and the velocity of run-off water, enormously accelerate erosion. They grow with amazing rapidity and form rushing, muddy torrents after every rain. The torrents find their way into the tributary rivers and natural drainage channels where the inclination is usually less and, as the velocity of flow decreases, the coarser suspended particles are deposited on the river beds. The river beds rise, and continue to rise with each deposition of sand, the excess of water pours over the country in uncontrolled flood. In time, the normal drainage channels become clogged and new channels form but *without regard to the natural drainage requirements of the region.* The result may be heavy flooding and waterlogging in some parts, overdrainage in others, further extensive erosion and landslides - in short the dislocation of the productive mechanism, whether natural or man-controlled, of the entire region.

Besides a tendency to flood and irregularity of flow, a further characteristic of rivers associated with eroding regions is muddiness. The waters are saturated with fine silt and clay that fall out of suspension only very slowly and at low river velocities, and give rise to conditions inimical to fish life. Fish are disappearing, or have disappeared, from many rivers which once ran clear but now are turbid with soil that perhaps has been transported from hundreds of miles away.

When the waters reach a main river, the danger of flood is multiplied by the confluence of many overladen tributary streams, and the damage inflicted by flood is also likely to be greater, since dense human settlements tend to concentrate near the banks of main rivers. A main river generally flows more slowly than its tributaries, causing the deposition of some of the fine mud that remained in suspension in the more rapidly flowing streams. The river bed rises and the flood menace increases in magnitude and frequency. Cities threatened with inundation have to be protected by building high banks, sometimes towering above the roofs of the houses, to confine the river, agricultural land is intentionally flooded to relieve the pressure on more densely populated districts and huge dams are constructed in an attempt to regulate the flow of turbulent water. But experience has shown that the engineer alone cannot permanently control a great muddy river continually being supplied with millions of tons of eroded soil. The artificial banks must be raised, ultimately to breaking point, as the river bed rises, the dams built to trap the water trap also silt and clay which choke the reservoirs behind the dams, and the last state of the river is far worse than the first. There is nothing on land more beneficent to organised life than an orderly river, or more perpetually menacing than a river run amok.

It would, indeed, make things much easier for mankind if all the soil of which men rob their fields were lost for ever in the depths of the ocean. Siltation - the deposition of eroded soil on river beds - is among the worst and most intractable consequences of erosion. It may take several centuries for siltation to put a river out of control, but other troubles, beside the incessant danger of flood, arise long before the uncontrollable stage is reached. River navigation, which often constitutes an essential link in a country's chain of commerce, is seriously impaired or destroyed by siltation; storage reservoirs, whether constructed for flood control, irrigation, hydro-electric purposes or public water supplies, become silted up and useless with incredible rapidity, for the dam that blocks the reservoir stops the water flowing, and down comes all the suspended soil. In fact, almost every useful function that running water is expected to perform in an organized community is impaired by erosion and siltation, and every danger that it may threaten is brought nearer to realization.

The consequences of erosion by water may be summed up as the localized reduction of productive capacity due to direct losses of soil and (often still more serious) of soil moisture, and the general disorganization of whole regions resulting from the cumulative dislocation of the natural water régime. The various destructive processes react upon each other and gather accelerating momentum as they proceed. It is this fact which makes the present world-wide erosion a matter of the greatest import to humanity at large. There is danger in complacency continuing because the earth is still rich enough in capital resources, expressed as soil fertility, to support its human population for a long time to come. One day we may realize that the capital is exhausted and no more dividends will be paid. It is not so much the damage already done that matters as the final and inevitable disaster to civilisation that will occur if the contagion is allowed to spread until it is uncontrollable. A war-scarred country can be restored to prosperity in a few years; a field stripped of its soil is finished, at least as far as providing for the living generation is concerned, but can continue to spread destruction over other land.

(*The Rape of the Earth: 32-5*)

SOIL CONSERVATION

There is nothing new in the idea of soil conservation. Soil conservation is as old as, and in former times was almost synonymous with, agriculture although nobody used the synonym, which is a recent American invention. Good husbandry consists not only in producing but in continuing to produce good crops. If we wished to distinguish between agriculture and soil conservation, we might define agriculture as cultivation for present and soil conservation as cultivation for future production. Good husbandry combines agriculture and soil conservation.

In humid regions, before the advent of machines and artificial fertilizers, good crops could in general only be obtained by adopting measures like organic manuring, mixed farming and crop rotations which at the same time tended permanently to improve the soil. One type of 'vertical' erosion was very liable to occur, namely, the removal by leaching from the soil of soluble salts and plant nutrients, and many common agricultural operations were designed to prevent this. 'Lateral' erosion did not occur to any serious extent, largely on account of the absence of strong winds, protracted droughts and torrential storms. Nowadays the prevention of 'vertical' erosion seems a very simple matter, but it took several centuries for mankind to learn how to counteract the drain on plant foods to which humid soils under cultivation are subjected.

Another way of distinguishing between what we have called 'vertical' and 'lateral' erosion respectively would be to say that the former involves the washing-out of the soluble parts of the soil and the latter mainly the washing (or blowing) away of the insoluble parts. 'Vertical' erosion is always liable to occur in humid regions where the movement of water in the soil is predominantly downwards, but not in arid regions where water is drawn upwards by evaporation. 'Lateral' erosion is very liable to occur on unprotected soils in arid regions because the soil pulverizes and loses its water-absorbing power when it dries out. Both 'vertical' and 'lateral' erosion occurs in the humid tropics owing to the effects of extreme heat and torrential rain.

The natural vegetation counteracts 'vertical' erosion by keeping the soluble plant nutrients in circulation through the plants and back to the surface of the soil when the plants die, and 'lateral' erosion by the soil-binding effect of the plant roots, by the physico-chemical effect of decaying humus on the soil structure, and by mitigating the impact of rain and wind on the soil.

The technical problem of preventing 'vertical' erosion in soils under cultivation has been solved by manuring and by ploughing, harrowing, rolling and so on, with the object of keeping soil moisture near the surface. These cultural practices were adopted because they were found to produce good crops and keep the soil in good heart; the idea that by tilling the soil he was recompensing it for the loss of protection against leaching afforded by the natural vegetation did not enter the farmer's head. He probably recognized the importance of keeping the plough layer moist, but soil chemistry was a closed book to him. Nevertheless he managed to avoid the main dangers of the washing-out of plant nutrients as successfully as if he had possessed the half-knowledge of soil chemistry now available. 'Agriculture' and 'soil conservation' were inseparable and indistinguishable. Technical advances in agriculture may render them less inseparable in the future. Agriculture, however, had its beginnings in arid lands where precautions against 'vertical' erosion were unnecessary. Indeed, in the very arid plains irrigation was used to induce some 'vertical' erosion and remove the excess of soluble salts as well as to supply water for the crops. On less arid, sloping land the principal cultural operations were evolved to prevent 'lateral' erosion and the run-off of water from the slopes. Early agriculture (in North China, the Philippine Islands and

Peru, for example) was particularly notable for the remarkable systems of terraces that it produced. As soon as the land was cultivated it was found necessary to throw up small earth barriers to catch the soil washed down from above, and each year, as more soil came down, the barriers had to be raised and lengthened until in the course of centuries a complete terrace system came into existence. Terracing performed a similar function in early, semi-arid agriculture to that of ploughing and harrowing in later, humid agriculture - it conserved the soil. In one form or another it is the traditional form of cultivation through the semi-arid East.

In South and Central China the primary function of the innumerable terraces on hill slopes has been to hold back water for the rice fields, but at the same time the terraces have accomplished quite effective erosion control. That it was the need for irrigation water rather than a desire to save the soil that impelled the Southern and Central Chinese to undertake these tremendous engineering feats is shown by the traditional way they cultivated - and still cultivate - unirrigated rice by planting in rows running up and down slopes, causing rapid erosion and abandonment of the fields after a few years. These people do not appear to have been really 'erosion-conscious'. Their object in terracing was to save the scanty water supply and keep it in the top layer of the soil. Where they could attain their object without terracing, they gave little attention to protecting the actual soil against erosion.

Soil conservation, in the sense of counteracting the destructive effect of rain on cultivated soil, has been an essential, albeit sometimes incidental, feature of all successful agricultural systems. It was none the less essential for being incidental. As long as men, guided by intuition and with crude implements helping the work of their hands, treated the soil to their best advantage, soil conservation looked after itself. Only since science has shown the way to multiply the natural output from the land has soil conservation come to be regarded as something almost distinct from normal agriculture. Unfortunately for the soil, it was found that the agricultural systems that prevented 'vertical' erosion on humid land could be adopted to produce large profits on semi-arid land where 'vertical' erosion was practically non-existent. Thus the soil-conservation side of agriculture was gradually eliminated as redundant, and fat profits continued to be made from the soil by pure exploitation until there were no more profits left.

The principles of soil conservation that will have to be reintroduced into modern semi-arid agriculture are fundamentally the same as those which evolved naturally as part of the agriculture of the ancient East, but profoundly modified in detail to suit the changed conditions of the age. The first object of soil-conservation measures on semi-arid land is to make the best use of rain. When this has been achieved, the problem of preventing 'lateral' erosion by either water or wind is already half solved. In the humid tropics the matter is complicated by the fact that both 'vertical' and 'lateral' erosion is threatened, and the experience gained in soil conservation in both humid-temperate and arid-temperate regions needs to be taken into account. But wherever the soil-conservation side of agriculture has been neglected for the sake of economic opportunity, its re-introduction will mean that somebody must suffer a reduction in immediate profit or incur a greater loss than would otherwise have been necessary. That is the rub. The fundamentals of soil conservation on semi-arid land were worked out by the ancients; they are simplicity itself on paper, but cause revolutions now that circumstances are compelling their re-introduction after a highly profitable period of neglect.

(*The Rape of the Earth: 106-9*)

VEGETATION AND WATERSHEDS

Probably in few cases where floods now occur will it be possible to dispense with downstream engineering works, at least for some considerable time to come, but the value of these works in their present state can be greatly increased by the adoption of all possible conservation practices in the headwaters. The water which accumulates in streams and rivers may arrive in two ways, either as surface run-off or from the ground water-table in the form of seepage water or springs. It is obvious from the frequent references which have been made in the foregoing chapters to the measures which can be adopted to control excessive run-off that, in spite of the complexity of the hydrologic cycle, something can be done under most cirucmstances to influence the amount of run-off water which passes direct into the rivers, frequently causing them to flood. Other references have already been made to the action of forest or grass covers in guiding rainwater safely to the underground storage, from which it reappears over a considerable period from springs and seepage, maintaining a steady supply to the river in place of the sudden rush of run-off water which follows an excessive downpour on a non-retentive watershed. The adoption of cultural and other practices to reduce run-off and soil wash and the maintenance of a good vegetative protective cover are the bases of effective upstream engineering in any part of the world. The reduction of run-off will mean that more water is passing into the soil and to the water-table, that streams will have a steadier supply; the vegetation which facilitates this transit generally itself benefits from the higher water-table, at least in semi-arid climates, and thus the vicious cycle of denudation, erosion and flood changes to the beneficent cycle of revegetation, water storage, soil retention and reduction in the number and height of floods.

The processes of degeneration in a watershed or catchment area, resulting from excessive clearing, burning or overgrazing, may result in flood damage in a very short time, whereas the processes of regeneration are slow, the rate of revegetation decreasing with an increase of the period since the denudation began. Thus again we must conclude, as we have already stated in the chapter on the advance of the desert, that the urgency of the commencement of reclamation work in affected watersheds and catchment areas cannot be over-stressed. It is not necessary to quote examples, as the problem arises in all countries suffering from erosion, whether temperate or tropical, arid or semi-arid.

(The Rape of the Earth: 190-1)

WATER CONSERVATION

Grandiose schemes of irrigation of fertile valley lands are frequently put forward as a cure for the agricultural troubles of a country, but, as already noted, the source of the water, its silt-load, its permanency and the conservation requirements of the upper watershed must also be considered carefully. Whether the irrigation is to be carried on with floodwaters from permanently flowing silt-laden rivers, or with the almost silt-free water supplied from reservoirs which store the wet-weather spates of intermittent streams, any scheme must be part of a complete and well-balanced plan for a drainage basin as an entity. In arid and semi-arid conditions, water collected in contour furrows on pastures and range grassland, in contour trenches in degraded scrub and forest land, or in terraces in arable land, may be stored in small or large reservoirs, for use in irrigation of cultivated lands in the dry season; this may, however, not be feasible in a country with a high evaporation, as for example in semi-arid parts of East Africa, where the rate is of the nature of 1 to 2 cm. (½ to ¾ inch) or more per day during five, six or seven months of the year.

Where the rain which falls on a particular area of semi-arid grassland is not required for storage for irrigation or stock, and where it might do damage in eroding gullies, it may be collected behind a special system of dikes and spread over a large area of level grassland. This method is adopted in the Navajo Reservation in New Mexico, where it is intended to accelerate the regeneration of the overgrazed grassland. This object may be achieved if the silt deposited by the flood water does not choke the grass vegetation.

The whole question of water conservation and use is one of the most complex and involved of the practical problems discussed in this book, and little justice can be done to the subject in one brief chapter. There is so much yet to be learnt. For example, in Africa, practical conclusions   cannot be drawn as to the measures which will be of lasting benefit both to the soil and to the people until more is known of the hydrologic cycle, the precipitation, and its more efficacious utilization, and the relation between evaporation, run-off, absorption and transpiration, in different climatic zones, in different soils, and vegetation types; there are vast regions where the actual climate would permit the production of subsistence or even of export crops, but where the unreliable domestic water supply permits the land to maintain only a very small population. The rapid deterioration of rainfall efficiency now proceeding in East Africa is due to deforestation and soil erosion, and any soil and vegetation conservation measures adopted would automatically improve the water balance. Mr. C. Gillman, Water Consultant to the Tanganyika Government, states that there can be no doubt 'that our ⟦ East African⟧ ground-water resources are among our most valuable, if not *the* most valuable asset, that their extent should be accurately mapped, the possibilities of their improvement be carefully studied with the help of the geologist and plant ecologist and every possible precaution be taken, by reforestation and anti-soil-erosion measures, against further deterioration of rainfall efficiency. The destruction of a country's arable soils is bad enough; infinitely worse is the concurrent destruction of its ground-water regime because it is a process faster even than that of soil deterioration and, therefore, liable to put areas that still possess soil out of action because there is no more water for the tillers of the soil.' When the water balance has been restored and a suitable and economic method of storing water for human requirements has been evolved, the situation will be regarded with more equanimity, but that day is far distant, and is rapidly receding with every delay in tackling the problem as a whole.

(The Rape of the Earth: 195-7)

PROSPECTS FOR WESTERN EUROPE

Finally, let us contemplate the prospects for Western Europe, which can still claim to be the centre of modern civilization, but has hardly suffered at all from the destruction of its soils - that otherwise almost universal disease of civilization. The area that has escaped erosion represents a distinct ecological region of humid deciduous forest whose soils were, originally, not naturally suited to growing the grain crops upon which civilization depends. The conversion of the humid forest environment to a less humid agricultural environment in which wheat could compete successfully with the indigenous flora was a tremendous achievement. Except in the more arid Mediterranean with its dry summers, deforestation was not accompanied by severe, accelerated erosion, partly because of the well-distributed, gentle rainfall, partly because the process was so gradual that soil changes could keep pace with vegetation changes. Localized erosion has occurred on mountain slopes, in France and Switzerland for example, where extensive deforestation has been done for lumbering rather than for agriculture, and definite evidence of former erosion can be seen on the now grass-clad hills of Wales.

The conversion of the European forest lands to their present condition of immense agricultural productivity has taken at least a thousand years to complete. Little technical progress in agriculture took place in the early stages of the conversion while the soil would have been particularly liable to deteriorate under flagrant exploitation. During the Dark and Middle Ages, the soils were not subjected to any abnormal strain and evolved into an agricultural type almost as naturally as though agricultural crops had somehow supplanted the trees without human intervention. When, after centuries of adolescence, European civilisation blossomed out in the nineteenth century, the countries of the New World were called upon to feed the flower. The enormous increase in Europe's population was accomplished without disturbing the established equilibrium between humanity and the soil although, as we have seen, it has very clearly prevented equilibria from being established elsewhere. Europe did not need to strain the productive capacity of her soils until the World War; new fertilizers enabled the soils to produce without difficulty enough to make good any year-to-year deficiencies from overseas.

The War displayed the full potentialities of European soils. Within four years the overcrowded warring nations became almost self-sufficient in food. It was not a comfortable nor a lasting self-sufficiency but then the main energies of the nations were not directed towards food production. Since the War economic circumstances have compelled them, one after another, to perpetuate policies of self-sufficiency and thereby to give a great impetus to the growing movement of soil conservation in the rest of the world. For diverse reasons the surpluses producible in the thinly populated countries will not again be freely available to Europe. Whether for her ultimate good or not, Europe will have to rely to a far greater extent than hitherto on her own soils to feed her teeming populations. For the first time since they came under cultivation the soils will be subjected to a serious strain.

We cannot even guess whether or for how long the soils will be able to stand the strain. A comparable situation has never arisen before. Our knowledge of how certain soils react to certain external circumstances is derived from a few years' observation only, and is totally inadequate to help us here. It may, however, be regarded as highly improbable that the soils of Western Europe, if they should become exhausted by prolonged, intensive cultivation, will ever suffer the catastrophic erosion that has overtaken the exploited prairies or the cut-over forest soils of Eastern America. They will inevitably grow old, but they will not die. A gradual deterioration of soil structure, imperceptible perhaps within a single generation, will be the most probable manifestation of the strain on the soils. Something - but not enough - is being done in most countries to counteract the cumulative ill effects on soil structure of a falling humus supply, increasing acidity, and the single-minded enthusiasm of all people for the outward insignia of a healthy countryside - high yields. More could be done if the principal aim of agricultural policy were to preserve soil structure for the next century even at the cost of curtailing production and weakening the first line of 'national defence.' Were another war to come, ploughs would tear up the structure-forming meadows and pastures, humus-providing animals would be slaughtered, soil improvement would be neglected, the vital reserve of soil fertility would be mercilessly broached. Unlike America, Europe cannot adopt a long-term soil-conservation policy in which the eventuality of war is a secondary consideration. Europe must build for the immediate future which has little significance in the eternal process of soil evolution.

A deterioration of the soil structure slowly built up during the past centuries would produce conditions favouring a less exacting flora than agricultural crops. Such conditions would not necessarily terminate Man's dominance over the soil. A highly industrialized civilization does not live by bread alone. To an ever-increasing extent it needs wood - for newspapers and books, for clothing, for fuel, for explosives, for paints and varnishes and for a hundred other things. A time may come when self-sufficiency in wood is more urgent than in wheat, when civilized Europe will welcome and encourage the irresistible return of the forest on to agricultural land. The mild, maritime climate of Western Europe is a guarantee that the soils will not erode away as a result of any conceivable mismanagement. Our civilization will be spared the fate that overtook its predecessors but in the end the forests will claim back their dominions as the deserts of the East have claimed back theirs.

(The Rape of the Earth: 298-301)

The year before The Rape of the Earth *appeared Jacks and Whyte produced* Erosion and Soil Conservation *(Harpenden, Imperial Bureau of Soil Science, Technical Communication no. 36, 1938) which dealt in detail, country by country, with the state of the soil throughout the world.*

G.V. Jacks later wrote a book simply entitled Soil *(London, Nelson, 1954), and R.O. Whyte wrote* Crop Production and Environment *(London, Faber, 1946).*

Another major work on desertification is one by the American ecologist Paul Sears: Deserts on the March *(Norman, USA, University of Oklahoma Press, 1935).*

A chapter on soil erosion can be found in Famine in England *by Viscount Lymington (London, Witherby, 1938); and there is a chapter on the same topic, referring particularly to the work of Jacks and Whyte, in* The Discipline of Peace, *by K.E. Barlow (London, Faber, 1942).*

R.H. Elliot of Clifton Park

4

Maintaining Fertility (I):
The Clifton Park Method

R.H. Elliot
(1837 - 1914)

R.H. Elliot, who owned land in Southern India, Ireland, and Scotland, published his book Agricultural Changes *in 1898. The fourth edition of it, which came out ten years later, was re-titled* The Clifton Park System of Farming, *after his estate in Roxburghshire. A new edition was published in 1943 (London, Faber), with an Introduction by Sir George Stapledon (see chapter 9), who had been much influenced as a young man by Elliot's ideas on ley farming and the improvement of grassland.*

The Clifton Park System was a response to the depression which had affected British agriculture since the 1870s. Elliot was concerned at Britain's dependence on imported foodstuffs, but was also anxious about the possible effects of artificial fertilizers, and developed his system to show that fertility could be improved by other means.

THE IMPORTANCE OF GOOD TURF

... it may be said that the solution of all our agricultural difficulties, so far as they can be solved by the wit of man, resolves itself into one expression - the cheap production of a good turf. That is the principle, which, as I shall show, dominates the whole subject, and that it does so is evident if we consider carefully the following points:

(1)   The success of our agriculture depends on the cheapening of production.
(2)   The cheapest food for stock is grass.

(3) The cheapest manure for soil is a turf composed largely of deep-rooting plants.

(4) The cheapest, deepest, and best tillers, drainers, and warmers of the soil are roots.

But before proceeding to prove that a cheaply created turf is the only solution for our agricultural difficulties, it may be well to notice the solutions that are thought by some to present certain prospects of cure for the unfortunate conditions of our times; for, by first of all disposing of these, we shall be able to fix our attention more exclusively on those factors which alone can set our agriculture on a footing with the requirements of the age.

(R.H. Elliot, *The Clifton Park System of Farming*,
5th ed. London, Faber, 1943, 41-2)

... if corn growing should never again become profitable, there can be no doubt of the good that will arise from the adoption of the farming system recommended in these pages; and should corn growing for sale again become profitable, then the land laid down to temporary pasture, on a system of not less than four years in grass, may have the system shortened to three years, or even to two, and both such lands, and those laid down to permanent pasture, again brought under the plough will be the more fitted for profitable corn growing than ever they were before.

I have said that the production of stock at the lowest possible cost is what the farmer has solely to rely upon, and this, of course, involves the production of their food at the lowest possible cost. Both these facts must obviously govern the farming policy of the future. How, then, can the farmer most cheaply provide food for stock? This, again, depends, of course, as to the way manure can be most cheaply supplied. Now, as every gardener and cultivator well knows, the cheapest and best form of manure is a good turf, for the decaying sod not only supplies the plants with food, but, what is nearly as important, and some might say of even greater importance, provides a good nest, or, in other words, good physical conditions in the soil. And it was on this turf that for so long a large proportion of our agriculture in Scotland depended, when vast quantities of land, enclosed within the last fifty or sixty years, were ploughed up. But in the process of time this resource has become exhausted. It must be again supplied, and this can only be effectively done within a moderate period of time by growing a mixture of large-rooting and deep-rooting plants, managing them well after they have grown, and giving them four to six years' time to form into a turf.

(*The Clifton Park System:* 43)

THE VALUE OF THE CLIFTON PARK SYSTEM

... I quote the following from a Roxburghshire tenant farmer, as it illustrates so conclusively the national importance of the work that has been carried to most successful results at Clifton-on-Bowmont. The passage, I may mention, has already appeared in my letter in *The Times*, under the heading of 'Agricultural Depression', on 12th October 1904. The tenant farmer alluded to writes as follows:

'From the short experience I have had on my farm of practising a modification of your system, I am now thoroughly convinced that most of the poor land in this country could be profitably farmed and give more employment to labour than it possibly can do at present. Clifton-on-Bowmont proves beyond question how much can be done to cheapen production and maintain the fertility of the land through natural and scientific methods. Your example should prove a guide and a warning to many who would run to extremes in laying too much land, thought worthless for growing crops, to grass of inferior quality. Such land can never be profitably held in that way. Clifton-on-Bowmont teaches a different lesson, and conclusively proves that much poor land going out of cultivation, and carrying a poor short stock in consequence, can be successfully cropped by a proper rotation; and that, instead of driving more people off the land to make room for a few sheep, it can be made to give employment to more people, and produce much more and better sheep. This is the first year I have adopted your system as regards cropping, and I am highly pleased with the results so far, as I never had turnips do so well, and the system saves certainly 30 per cent in labour ... and manure. By another year I hope to work much more of my land on your system.'

But the system, which is now widely known as the Clifton Park system, will do much more than produce the effects so forcibly pointed out by my correspondent. It will arrest the steady decadence of all British arable soils. For the last thirty years I have had them through my hands on a large scale, from alluvial flats up to thin soil 800 feet above the level of the sea, and find an only too ample confirmation of the general complaint of practical farmers. At the first great meeting of 400 Aberdeenshire farmers, held more than twenty years ago, exhaustion of the soil was declared to be one of the greatest causes of their difficulties. In the course of discussion with ten leading farmers at Clifton-on-Bowmont last year all seemed to agree in thinking that the soil had declined owing to the exhaustion of organic, or vegetable, matter. With the aid of liming, and a freer and freer use of artificial manures, the decadence thus caused is steadily continuing. And the farmer expects that foreign competition may be met by ever augmenting bills for purchased fertilizers, which will cause the soil still further to decline in fertility, while the agricultural chemist, aided by the manure merchant, is emptying his pockets, and at the same time enabling the farmer to run out the remaining fertility of the soil. When, some months ago, I told a very old and experienced practical farming friend that I proposed to grow a fine crop of turnips without the aid of any manure he laughed in my face, and evidently thought the assertion the best joke he had heard for some time; yet this has been done, and on land that never has had any farmyard manure, and the previous turnips of which had only received some artificials.

(*The Clifton Park System:*28-9)

... the system I have to advocate - one depending entirely upon stock - will be much safer than our old arable culture. For with that we had the maximum of risk, combined with the maximum amount of destruction to the fertility of the soil. And as to that point we have the testimony of the first great meeting of 400 Aberdeenshire farmers, held upwards of twenty years ago, who declared that one of the three great causes of their difficulties was the exhaustion of the soil. But the system which I have to urge in these pages will continually enrich the soil, and, what is often of greater importance, improve its physical condition. And it may be well to notice in this connection that the system to be proposed will not only suit the times, but also the interests of both the landlords and tenants. Formerly, their interests were in a great measure opposed, the object of the tenant being to take all he could out of the land, and the object of the landlord to retain all the strength he could in it; and, with the aid of artificial manures, the tenants have been only too successful in depleting the soil, and, in a large number of instances, after having sucked the orange, have thrown the empty peel in the landlord's face. But with the system I advocate it will be as much to the tenant's as to the landlord's interest that all the strength possible should be retained in the land, for, in the future, on no other principle can farming in these islands be profitably carried on. And here it may not be uninteresting to notice that similar principles were laid down by M. Porcius Cato (born 234 B.C.) in his agricultural treatise, *De Re Rustica*. He was asked what was the most certain profit rising out of land. 'To feed stock well,' he replied. Being asked what was the next point of importance, he said, 'To feed with moderation.' Evidently meaning to the extent that paid best, or, in other words, that the farmer should aim at a low cost of production. He also, I may add, laid down that ' a good husbandman should be a seller rather than a buyer', which, of course, means that he should breed his own stock, and produce for himself everything that he profitably can. And it seems hardly necessary to add that the Act which now requires that all imported animals should be slaughtered at the port of debarkation still further enforces the necessity for adhering, as far as possible, to these old Roman agricultural maxims. It is interesting to note that Cato estimates the value of manuring as below ploughing, and thus recognized as Sir John Lawes did that the physical condition of the soil is of more importance than its strictly speaking chemical composition. 'If I am asked,' says Cato - 'what is the first point in good husbandry, I answer good ploughing; the second ploughing of any kind, and the third manuring.' 'In a very important sense tillage is manure' (Bailey's *Principles of Agriculture*, p. 65, Macmillan, New York). Tillage by the agency of roots is the best and by far the cheapest form of tillage, and that it is the best anyone can see for himself by digging up the soil in forest-clad land, and that it is the cheapest as well as the best in arable land is evidenced by the great depth to which chicory and burnet roots penetrate.

(*The Clifton Park System*: 36 -7)

VEGETABLE-MATTER AND DEEP-ROOTING PLANTS

The preceding remarks I have quoted all indicate the really great difficulty connected with laying down land to grass - the want of good physical conditions in the soil, which can only be supplied by permeating it with vegetable matter. The manurial conditions, from a strictly speaking chemical point of view, may be good, but they cannot make up for the want of good physical conditions; and the more I have studied the whole subject by the light of theory confirmed by practice, the more certain do I feel that the importance of keeping up a good physical condition of soil, though generally recognized, has never been sufficiently acted up to. [1] My first practical experience regarding this point dates a great many years back, and has ever since been the means of my continually observing and studying the effects of the presence or absence of good physical conditions of soil. I think it would be difficult to find a more thoroughly practical experience than that which I will now proceed to describe.

In conjunction with a planter friend in India I once endeavoured to ascertain the consumption by coffee trees of potash, with the view of seeing how far it was advisable to add it to our manures, and there were accordingly taken with great care two samples of soil - one from the virgin forest land, and the other from land immediately adjacent to it, from which twelve crops of coffee had been taken without any manure being applied to the soil. The samples were sent to Professor Anderson, of Glasgow University, and he was asked to spare neither pains nor expense in carefully examining the soils, with the view of seeing how far the cropped soil had been exhausted of potash. The result seemed at first sight to be remarkable; for the soil from which the twelve crops had been taken was found, from a chemical point of view, to be very little deteriorated except as regards lime, which was rather less than in the virgin soil. But the explanation evidently was that the leaves shed from the shade trees and stones decaying in the soil had supplied the small quantity of potash and other ingredients removed by the crops. 'Why, then,' asked my friend, who had called on the Professor to hear the result of the inquiry, 'can young coffee plants easily be grown on the virgin soil while we have the greatest difficulty in growing them on the cropped soil?' 'Simply,' was the answer, 'because the virgin soil is in a fine granular state, and in perfect physical condition, while the soil in the plantation, after having been rained upon, and walked upon, and exposed to the elements, has lost its original fine physical condition.' In other words it had become more or less consolidated, and therefore was a bad nest in which to grow young coffee plants. Here, then, we have an important practical illustration of what, I feel sure, must frequently be the case - namely, that what is often attributed to manurial deficiency, or, in other words, poverty of soil, is largely owing to physical defects. And if these tell largely on a, comparatively speaking, strong shrub like coffee, how much more must they tell on tender-rooted grasses, and how much, further, must such deficiencies tell in a climate like ours, which is so much subject to changes which tend to run the soil together, and so injure its physical condition. And if, again, a planted out plant of coffee is, as we have seen, liable to fail from being put down in a defective nest, how often, too, must grass seeds fail from a similar want of a proper home to germinate in, and how frequently must the tender, newly grown grass plant fail from the want of suitable conditions for establishing itself in the soil. I think, then, that a little consideration of these points will show that I may safely declare, as I have in the beginning of this chapter, that one of the most important points connected with the whole subject of laying down land to grass, either to lie for a period of years or permanently, is the disintegration of the soil, and the intermingling with it of a sufficient portion of vegetable matter, so that, after being disintegrated, it may not readily again run together. The question which naturally occurs is this: How can such conditions be most economically provided? And, first of all, let us take the case of laying down land to permanent pasture.

When laying down land to grass, the usual practice has hitherto been to do so after a crop of turnips, and when the land has, in the course of its previous cultivation, been regularly supplied with farm-yard manure, and thus with applications of vegetable matter, and is of a quality that does not readily run together, and so becomes tough and hardened, there is nothing to be said against so doing. But where the land has not been well supplied with vegetable matter, or is of a quality which soon loses whatever physical condition has been imparted by tillage, I have now reason to think, from my own practical experience, that it is decidedly best to lay down permanently after first of all growing a turf mainly composed of deep-rooting plants, and plants which leave much vegetable matter in the soil. For I have found in the case of alluvial flats containing rather heavy land that, after having laid down the land and left it in grass for about eight or ten years, we have, on again ploughing up and laying down, after a course of crops, had by far the most successful takes of grass that I have ever seen. There were two evident reasons for this favourable result. The first was that the soil was well permeated with vegetable matter, and the second that, being so, a thoroughly satisfactory and well aerated bed was provided for the springing of the seed, and the subsequent growth of the young plants. And in the cases previously alluded to, I am satisfied that a still better result would have been obtained had I, when first laying down the land in question, been acquainted with the deep-rooting chicory, burnet, and kidney vetch, and the advantage of using, from a vegetable-matter-creating point of view, a large amount of cocksfoot and yarrow. It may be urged that the process would be a costly and tedious one, and with the old system of laying down with a large proportion of ryegrass, which entailed a falling off of the pasture in the fourth year, this would have undoubtedly been the case; but, with our recent experience here, I have found that land of tough quality, and deficient in vegetable matter, may be loosened, ameliorated with vegetable matter, and deeply cultivated with the agency of roots in about three or four years; and then, after our usual four-course rotation of cereal and root crops, laid down to permanent pasture with satisfactory results. Having thus dwelt upon the importance of disintegrating the soil, and permeating it thoroughly with vegetable matter, before laying it down to permanent pasture, I now propose to allude to the equal, or even greater, advantage of doing so in the case of land to be left in grass for five or more years, and which is to be again broken up for the winter support of the stock on the farm.

I have been told by a very intelligent gardener, who is practically acquainted with the great importance of soil disintegration through the agency of roots, that if he trenches land a foot deep, and takes from it a crop of parsnips, he finds, on taking up the crop, that the land immediately below the part dug is in finer physical condition than the cultivated land above. And this, of course, arises from the fact of the parsnip roots penetrating, and minutely sub-dividing, the soil, which, from its depth, has the advantage of being largely removed from the action of the weather. And, to give another illustration, we find the same thing in India when the forest is allowed to gradually extend itself into the adjacent grass land, and when the roots of the trees gradually permeate the land below the reach of the roots of the grass plants, and so turn the whole soil to a considerable depth into a beautifully cultivated subject. Or to take yet another illustration, it may be mentioned that agriculturists in France, to improve certain arable lands, sow on them a mixture of gorse and grass (to be cut for hay) with a view of improving the depth and texture of the soil, which, after the lapse of a certain number of years, is again brought under the plough. Of all cultivating agencies, then, roots stand by far at the head, and it is by applying this principle to our arable lands that we shall at once manure, aerate, and cultivate them in the cheapest manner. All agriculturists recognize this in a general way; but, as regards the cultivation of our lands with the agency of deep-rooting forage plants, it can hardly be said to have been, practically speaking, recognized at all in this country. And I may go as far as to say that, till it is so, our agriculture will never be placed in the position of safety it ought to occupy.

(The Clifton Park System: 52 - 5)

… I have found, from using chicory, burnet, kidney vetch, and a liberal supply of yarrow, that there are other attendant advantages besides that of disintegrating the soil and supplying it with vegetable matter, for all light land is, of course, very liable to suffer from drought, and all these plants resist drought to a wonderful degree. Of this fact I had a remarkable confirmation in 1895, in the case of a large flat field on the margin of a stream (called haugh in Scotland) - a field interspersed at intervals with gravel beds, the grasses in which, of course, are quickly burned up in periods of drought. In that year there was a very severe drought, and, therefore, an excellent opportunity for testing the value of these plants in dry weather. When the drought was at its height, I, on 17th June 1895, carefully examined the field, and especially the shingly beds on it. On these the grasses and clovers were withered down to the ground, and the clover leaves crumbled in the hand as if they had been scorched by fire; but the drought-resisting plants were green and sappy, though in various degrees. Chicory and burnet clearly stood the drought best, then came kidney vetch, and then yarrow. Of the lucerne plant I cannot speak so positively. Some were dried up and yellowish, while others looked fairly well. I was particularly struck with a plant of burnet. It was touching one of cocksfoot (which stands drought well as compared with other grasses) which was withered yellowish-white down to the ground, but the burnet was as green and fresh-looking as a thriving strawberry leaf.

(The Clifton Park System: 59)

ARTIFICIAL MANURES

… the chemist must become more of a farmer, and the farmer more of a chemist, before either can work effectively in arresting the downward course of our British soils. And is it not obvious that if, when the blind lead the blind, the result is liable to be unsatisfactory, the leading of the semi-blind by the semi-blind is certain to end in much more serious disaster? In the former case both are proverbially liable to be abruptly aroused to the inadvisability of their proceedings, and that, too, before they have gone very far; but when a chemist who is agriculturally semi-blind leads a farmer who is chemically semi-blind, still more unsatisfactory results are, as we shall see, certain to ensue, for they are sure to be the means of doing much harm by the propagation of that most dangerous form of knowledge known by the name of half-truths. In order to prove this it is only necessary to look into the seventh annual report on experiments with crops and stock at the Northumberland County Demonstration, Cockle Farm Park, Morpeth. It is there evidently assumed that the British farmer has done all he can for himself by fully employing the natural resources within his reach, and that all that remains is for the chemist to step in and assist the farmer either to increase his crops or improve the condition of his animals by the aid of commercial fertilizers. But the chemist (though adding the name agricultural would lead people to suppose that he is an agriculturist as well as a chemist) really knows nothing of agriculture, and indeed it is obvious that he does not, for otherwise he would first of all inquire whether the farmer does make a full use of all the natural resources at his disposal before advising that various kinds of chemical manures should be used. But the chemist makes no such inquiries. He takes British soil in hand as he finds it exhausted more or less by long courses of limings and artificial manures, and tells the farmer that all he has to do is to replace what he has taken out of the soil, and that if he wants more produce from it he must at once apply an increased supply of the chemical ingredients that have been carried off the land. By this process the chemist manures the plant and not the soil, while the farmer puts down as little as he thinks will serve to grow the plant, which he could not otherwise effectually do, and the plant, grown through this aid, searches through the soil to absorb the remains of its natural fertility. Thus the decline of our soils proceeds till the humus of the soil becomes so thoroughly exhausted that the diseases of plants increase, and they are more and more at the mercy of the vicissitudes of unfavourable seasons. Then as the fertility of the soil declines, and natural sources of plant food diminish, and are not replaced, or only in most inadequate degrees, by natural agencies, the artifical manure bill must be increased, and it has been so increased that farmers now complain that it amounts to another rent. But such manures, even if they could be had for nothing, would not enable the plants of the farmer to contend successfully with climatic shortcomings which so frequently occur in these islands - excessive drought, or excessive wet, or excessive cold. If the season is perfect the artificial manure will act fairly well. If it is too dry there may be too little water present to convey the plant food into the plant, and if very wet much of the manure may be washed away, and other parts of it, if not used at once, are liable to enter into insoluble compounds in the soil; while if the season is cold the artificial manure cannot raise the temperature of the soil as humus does. It is evident then that what the farmer requires is at once a chemical and a physical agent provided at the lowest cost, which will act with the greatest certainty, no matter what the season may be, and which will continuously increase the humus of the soil, and add to its depth. This he can provide, as I have abundantly shown, by growing a turf of deeply rooted, and powerfully rooted plants. The chemist with his artificial manures can only provide, of course, a costly chemical agent which must always be, as I have shown, at the mercy of the season, and not only cannot permanently ameliorate the fertility of the soil, even in the most favourable seasons, but, unless supported by dung or turf, must deplete the soil. To the agriculturist who has what Locke terms 'Large, sound, roundabout sense', the preceding statements are, of course, mere truisms; but as there are many of my readers who, to use Locke's words again, 'have not a full view of all that relates to the question, and may be of moment to decide it', it is advisable to refer them to the statements I have made as regards the crops grown without manure, and also to allude to some facts with reference to the experiments made at Cockle Park County Demonstration Farm. These, as we have seen, are made on the assumption that the British farmer has done, and continues to do, all he can for himself, and that it only remains for the chemist to show him how, by the application of artificial manures, he may derive increased crops from exhausted soil. If the assumption is correct then the results of the experiments are valuable to the farmer, but the assumption, as I have abundantly shown at Clifton-on-Bowmont, is not correct, and the experiments are really only of value to show the farmer how, with the present low price for agricultural produce, he may lose his money if, after having adopted my system and manured his land with turf, he chooses to add artificial manures.

(*The Clifton Park System*: 125 - 7)

THE IMPORTANCE OF AGRICULTURE

... there never was a time in our history when the landed interests in our country should be more carefully guarded, and every incentive provided for full justice being done to the land by the landowners, for the conditions throughout the world are such that, taking into consideration the immense foreign competition, and the heavy burdens imposed on land, it is certain that no tenant will embark on those landed improvements which are so necessary for the welfare of the country. And even if the capitalist tenants were inclined to lay out money in landed improvements, the possibility of having their farms wholly or partially seized for the creation of small holdings, would be a sufficient check to any tendency they might otherwise have to lay out money on the land. I have said that there never was a time when more attention was required to be bestowed on what is still the biggest industry in the kingdom, and if we look forward to the progress of manufactures and mining in Asia, we shall find that the development of our agricultural resources is a subject which must be one of ever-increasing importance to our national welfare. People generally, and Englishmen in especial, have seldom any inclination to look ahead (as Cobden did when he said, 'I have often thought what ugly ruins our mills will make'), more especially when doing so is at all likely to disclose a rather disagreeable prospect, but if it is desired to attract attention to the necessity for following American lines as regards State aid to agriculture, we should take into careful consideration our manufacturing and mining prospects. To look forward here with accuracy, it is both advisable and interesting to look back to the beginning of our manufacturing progress - to the time when machinery was introduced, and when, with the aid of protection (which levied import duties so high that we find the weavers of Bengal petitioning the English Government to be allowed to compete on equal terms with English manufacturers) the skill and capital of the West overcame the cheap hand labour of the East. Having established our manufactures with the aid of Protection we then called out loudly for free trade all round. But the skill and capital of the West have now gone out to ally themselves with the cheap labour of the East, and the numerous mills in India testify to the initial steps of the vast changes that are slowly but steadily advancing. But this is far from being all. The Japanese, the Chinese, and the native capitalists of India are rapidly learning all that Europe can teach, and, ultimately, will carry manufacturing and mining industries to the utmost limit attainable. Then will be seen the greatest labour struggle the world has ever beheld - the competition between the cheap dark and the dear white workman. When that period arrives, and it cannot be far distant, calico may once more come to us from Calicut (a town on the west coast of India), which gave its name to the cotton productions we once imported from the East, and if we wish to manufacture even for our own people it is plain that we should only be able to do so with the at present despised agency of Protection. That resource alone will be left to us as far as cloth manufactures are concerned. The same remark will also apply to every other product which we now export. For the rest we must rely upon the development of our biggest industry - agriculture. What is agriculture? As the Indian proverb goes, 'the ploughers are the linchpin of the world'. Pull it out and the whole machinery of life tumbles to pieces. Amidst the din of hammers, the whirl of machinery, and the tall smoking chimneys, we seem to have quite forgotten this fact. We shall once more have occasion to remember it, and perhaps sooner than we anticipate. It is of obvious importance then to set our house in order betimes, and prepare to furbish up our agricultural armour to the utmost. We have tried to do so by calling in the aid of costly artificial manures, and costly mechanism in the shape of subsoil ploughs, and other earth-stirring implements; we must now call in the appliances of nature in the shape of deep-rooting plants, which will at once till, manure, aerate and drain our soils with the utmost degree of efficiency and economy. When an eminent agriculturist was one day looking at a field on my property laid down with the mixture of grasses used in my system of farming, and carrying a large stock of sheep at least double what can be kept on the old system under rye-grass and a little clover - he said 'we have no idea of the stock this country could carry were this subject attended to', and if that is so, and in my opinion it undoubtedly is so, then the possible increase of the fertility of our soils through the agency of the vastly increased stock that may be maintained, far exceeds anything that could be conceived as possible under our present system of agriculture. What is its greatest defect? That it has no true rotation of crops and no self-acting manurial, drainage, and tillage system. What is a true rotation of crops, or, to put it in another way, what is that principle which ought to guide the farmer when he grows a rotation of crops? It is important to remember that crops of various kinds may be found on a farm, and that you may have a different crop

every year for a series of years and yet be far removed from carrying out
a scientific rotation of crops, i.e. a system which will yield the best
results to the farmer at the smallest cost, and the only effective way of
carrying out the most profitable form of rotation lies in the cultivation
of crops which take nitrogen - equal in the end to ammonia - from the
air with those which can only derive it from the soil. In Scotland at
least there is no such rotation excepting in those occasional cases where
a crop of beans is grown. The only nitrogen collecting crop grown, or
rather attempted to be grown, consists of the clover sown along with
the grass seeds, and this clover is not only insignificant in amount, but
is commonly a partial and often a complete failure. From a nitrogen
collecting point of view then there is practically no rotation of crops at
all, and never will be till, as is the case under my system, large crops of
red clover and other nitrogen collecting plants are grown. When such
crops can be generally grown, and as I have proved under my system,
can be grown with certainty, then, and not till then, will our
agriculture be placed on a sound footing, and it will be on a sound
footing because the greatest possible amount of manure will be
derived free of cost from the atmosphere. With the aid of these
agencies will be kept the greatest possible amount of stock on the land.
This, of course, will enrich it with manure cheaply supplied, and
evenly distributed free of all cost for placing it in the soil. With this
agency, also, will be grown the greatest amount of vegetable matter in
the turf, which will be ploughed down when the grass period of my
eight course rotation comes to a close - turf enriched with four years'
manure from the stock kept on the land. When this ample plant food,
and what is of even more importance, these ample physical conditions
are supplied, the four succeeding crops of the rotation may be grown
without any artificial manure excepting the small supply necessary to
stimulate the growth of the turnips, and so to remedy the too often
defective growing power of our climate. By this system we have an
extreme economy of production, and it is only by this economy that
our agriculture can be profitably continued in the face of the
enormous competition coming on in ever-increasing severity from
almost all quarters of the globe. But turn where one may, a universal
agreement will be found as regards the essential point of all others in
any soundly economical agriculture which will maintain and augment
the fertility of the soil, and, for one instance, I may quote the very
decided opinion expressed in America, which tells us that: 'In general
agriculture in Illinois, whether it is grain farming or ordinary live

stock farming, the growing of legumes is absolutely essential in any economic system which shall maintain the fertility of the soil.'[2] When this principle is recognized and acted on there can be no more running out of land, chemically and physically, as there is at present, and fertility will continuously increase to the benefit of both landlord and tenant, and I need hardly add, to the general augmentation of the national welfare, and especially the increase of employment in the rural districts, for it is perfectly obvious to all experienced observers, that while we cannot look for any increase of the rural population from turning the present labourers out of their cottages, and getting rid of the farmers who employ them, in order to supply their place with small cultivators, we can look forward with certainty to an increased employment from my system of farming owing to land at present left in worthless pasture being again brought under the plough.

(*The Clifton Park System:* 138 - 42)

CAUSES OF YOUNG PASTURES FAILING

When they do, it is commonly attributed to want of sufficient food for the plants. I believe it is more often owing to defective soil conditions. Dr. Voelcker, chemist of the Royal Agricultural Society of England, tells me that he has often been consulted on the point, and on analysing the soil found that there was plenty of plant food in the land if the roots could only have freely travelled through the soil. I have the following reason for believing that the hard pan which sometimes exists just below the ploughing depth is often the cause of failure, partly because the roots of grasses and clovers cannot penetrate it, and partly because it checks the rise of water from the subsoil. The Longshot field - Crookhouse farm... is a case in point. When previously in ordinary arable cultivation, during about forty-five years, it never would grow grass. I laid it down twice to permanent pasture, and in the second case with an excellent mixture, but which did not contain any of the deep-rooting plants I now use. In both cases the pasture was a failure. In 1895 I again laid it down to permanent pasture. The field, now five years old, has been throughout a complete success. This I attribute to the deep-rooting plants used, and especially the chicory, which was a very large crop, and which... went straight down into the subsoil, after penetrating the very hard pan which lay below the ploughing depth. From the facts connected with this field previous to my occupation of it, and which I have personally ascertained from the former tenant, I have reason to surmise that the failure of land to grow grass and clover well, either when in rotation husbandry or being laid down to permanent pasture, must often be owing to hard pans below the ploughing depth, and this, of course makes it the more advisable that plants like chicory and burnet, which can penetrate the hardest pans... should be freely used. But besides the evils arising from hard pans, there is the fact that our soils are not kept sufficiently open owing to the deficiency of humus in the land, and hence the roots cannot readily traverse the soil, which, as Dr. Voelcker has shown, often contains enough plant food if it were fully available for the use of the plant. If, then, you do not give the plant a soil well opened up, and kept open by humus, you must spend more money in manure. In other words, as far as the plant is concerned, a small quantity of manure in an open soil is of more practical value than a much larger quantity of manure in a soil of inferior physical condition. There are three losses entailed by inferior physical conditions of soil: (1) that the plant is less able to contend with adverse seasons; (2) that the expense of manurial application must be greater; and (3) that much of the manure that is applied in excess of the requirements of the plants will be lost by waste or downward percolation, while much of it is liable to enter into insoluble compounds in the soil.

(The Clifton Park System: 170-1)

FINANCIAL BENEFITS OF THE CLIFTON PARK SYSTEM

I have been often asked to publish the accounts of my farm. As I have no desire to mislead the farmer (an evil that might often ensue, as was pointed out to me lately by a tenant farmer of great experience), I prefer not to do so.... I have given some general financial results regarding the system on which, I think, landlords should farm their own land. The object of my work is not to exhibit my skill as a stock farmer, or the want of it, as the case might be, but my skill in most economically producing cereals, potatoes, and food for stock - in other words, the introduction of an improved farming system which is calculated to attain these ends. To mix this up with the stock department of the farm would be to introduce an element of the greatest uncertainty, as it is an element which fluctuates all over these islands. Each farmer must observe what can be produced from the soil by my system of farming, and apply to the conditions of his own holding my principles and system, with whatever modifications may be suitable to his climate and present circumstances. All that the farmer requires to do is to visit one of our young grass fields, in which he will always find a large crop of clover and kidney vetch, which is the indispensable base of the system. The steward carries a crop book of each field for the last twenty years, so that the visitor can see exactly what the field has been doing, and how it has been treated. The steward also carries a seed book, showing cost of seeds and the mixtures used, and the visitor can learn from the shepherd what stock the field has kept. This year (1904), for instance, the Inner Kaimrig - twenty-five acres - has kept as much sheep stock or rather more than the grass fields aggregating eighty-seven acres of the adjacent farm which is much better land, by the way, but which is farmed on the old five-course system, and on which the generally used ryegrass and clover mixtures have been sown, and I have no doubt this is a difference that would pretty generally be found to prevail in Scotland. A reference to Rothamsted experimental field, devoted to the rotation of crops, will show him how all the subsequent crops are benefited by the manurial matter left behind from a large crop of the **Leguminosae**, and for evidence of this he can see the turnips, four years old grass of fine quality, cereals, and potatoes, and all grown without manure other than of the turf grown on the land, and only aided by the manure left by the sheep and the dung of lean cattle, which last is generally applied to the nearest fields to the steading, all the more distant fields having to depend solely on the turf grown on them. The quantity of cake used is so small that the farmer quoted in the preface considered it to be practically none. What the farmer could keep in the way of stock with the aid of such crops grown as cheaply as mine have been, and what he could make out of the cereals and potatoes, he must calculate for himself, with reference to his own surroundings, and no publication of all my profits could aid him, though it is just possible it might mislead him, seeing that, obviously, my results might be much worse or much better than a farmer could obtain who imitated my system. Confucius, the Chinese philosopher, once said: 'If I show one corner of a subject to a man, and he cannot see the other three corners for himself, then I can do nothing with him.' In the same way it is only necessary for the farmer to visit one of my young grass fields, which are always full of Leguminosae, and if, after going into the cost of production, he cannot see for himself all the consequential results which must arise from such a field, then I can do nothing with or for him.

But there is another and most important financial point to be considered. Farming, like every other business, consists of a capital account and the profits that may be made out of capital. It is of obvious importance that stock should be carefully taken of the latter - that it should be seen whether it is advancing, standing still, or declining. Landlords' capital mainly consists of soil, and the condition of the soil mainly depends on the amount of humus it contains. About 100 years ago Scottish agricultural capital was on a sound footing, because the system pursued maintained the humus of the soil... It is in an unsound condition now, because from continuous liming and the use of artificial manures the humus of the soil has immensely declined (hence the numerous complaints of the exhaustion of the soil), and is declining steadily except in those rare cases where enough farmyard manure can be obtained to keep up the supply of humus. The object of my farming system at Clifton-on-Bowmont is to show how Scottish agriculture may be restored to its originally sound position - not only to replace, but to steadily increase, the humus of the soil, and render the farmer, as he once was, independent of the use of artificial manures, though, as I have elsewhere pointed out, these may still be used under certain circumstances to a moderate extent. In other words, my farming system is directed to restoring the capital of the landlord to its originally sound and safe position, to lessen the expenditure at present required by the tenant, and place all his crops in a safe position for contending at once against foreign competition and vicissitudes of climate. How these ends may be achieved most economically has been shown at Clifton-on-Bowmont, and our agriculture never can be restored to a sound condition unless the principles carried out there - principles the soundness of which are admitted all the world over - are universally adopted in these islands.

(The Clifton Park System: 193-5)

THE NEED FOR ACTION

When visiting Clifton-on-Bowmont one day with an intelligent gardener, I remarked: 'Is it not wonderful to see such a fine crop grown on such poor soil?' He replied: 'Give me a good turf, and I don't care what the soil underneath it is' - a point he practically illustrated as to the value of turf by robbing my park of it whenever he could, though he had full command of all kinds of manures. I may remind the reader here of the quotation on the title-page, where it is declared that 'TO RAISE A THICK TURF ON A NAKED SOIL WOULD BE WORTH VOLUMES OF SYSTEMATIC KNOWLEDGE.' This is what has been done at Clifton-on-Bowmont. In little more than two years we can now raise a turf which, at a little distance, looks like old pasture, and on a close inspection might be taken for five-year old grass, while in five years we have grown pasture that no one could distinguish from old grass. I much regret not having kept note of the remarks made by agriculturists to the amount of one hundred a year - who have visited the farm. On remarking to a visitor that some of them had said that what they saw had been a revelation to them, he said: 'And it is a revelation to me too.' When lately showing an old agriculturist from East Lothian the Kaimrig field... he finally observed with a strange mixture of wonder and annoyance in his face: 'We have been like children.' In some instances we have certainly trebled the letting value of the land. Dr. Voelcker (chemist of the Royal Agricultural Society of England) remarked when visiting the farm in 1904 that I should have kept in each field an untouched patch to show what the land origin- ally was, for that it was now difficult to believe how bad it had been. What the tenant who had for long occupied the farm declared to be the worst field on it is now so changed that farmers will not believe in its ever having been bad land. But just as land of originally good quality, when mixed with a suitable proportion of vegetable matter, may be turned into the worst possible land when this necessary agent has been exhausted, so may the very worst land be raised to the value of good if you 'raise a thick turf on the naked soil', and if we keep on raising another before the preceding one has been exhausted we shall have done all we can to promote the fertility of the soil, and, there- fore, the condition of agriculture. I once said to an old tenant on the estate: 'How much more stock can you keep on your young grass fields since you have adopted my advice as to altering your grasses?' 'I can keep', he said, 'one-third more stock,' which, I need hardly say, doubles the value of the land. 'Now,' I said, 'I wish to ask you another question. Did you not at one time consider me to be (the fate of most innovators at first) a madman?' He laughed heartily, wagged his head from side to side, and said, 'Oh, no, no, no!' but in a tone which meant 'Yes, yes, yes!' It may not be uninteresting to mention that it was a remark made by this tenant which led to much of the valuable results we have arrived at. He once said to me, many years ago: 'What we want is something green and sappy to go with these grasses when they dry up in summer.' 'You want, then,' I remarked, 'something which corresponds to the dry grass as turnips do to hay.' 'That's just it,' he replied. I then sent to Mr. James Hunter, of Chester, for a list of all those plants which stock would eat, and which would not dry up in summer, and my subsequent study of the consequential results arising from their use showed me their immense value in at once tilling the soil, adding to our stores of reliable food for stock, deeply manuring the land, and improving the health of crops and stock.

One word more. There are large areas of land in these islands steadily going from bad to worse. They are not suitable for permanent pasture, and still less are they suited at present prices for profitable arable cultivation under the old system. Much of what is still kept in arable is steadily declining in value, and no wonder, for, to quote again my late friend, Mr. Faunce de Laune, 'farming, as it is prac- tised now, is more often the means of destroying natural fertility' - he means by running out all the vegetable matter in the soil - 'than adding to it, and it is therefore no wonder that the land becomes impoverished.' From the impoverishment of the soil, and large areas being allowed to what is called 'fall down' to profitless pasture, cottages are being rapidly emptied, and the whole conditions and prospects of our agriculture are most unsatisfactory. How this condi- tion of things may be ameliorated I have shown in these pages. It now only remains for the Government to propagate what I have eventu- ally, after many years of labour, proved to the hilt.

(*The Clifton Park System:* 199-200)

A chapter on Elliot's importance can be found in Soil and Sense *by Michael Graham (London, Faber, 1941), but the major tribute to him is* Thirty Years Farming on the Clifton Park System, *by William Lamin (London, Faber, 1944). Lamin subtitled his book 'How to Supply Humus, Texture, and Fertility by the Aid of Deep-Rooting Grasses', and described himself as 'a practical farmer'. The validity of that description is vouched for by Dr C.S. Orwin, who was Director of the Agricultural Economics Research Institute at Oxford, in his Fore- word. According to Orwin, Lamin had 'a triumphant success in handling some of the worst soil in cultivation in what is one of the poorer agricultural districts of the Midlands,* (Thirty Years Farming, *p.8).*

References

1   The Italians, in some cases, cut gorse and heather, and pile the cuttings between the rows of vines, and leave them (the gorse and heather) to decay, after which the decayed vegetable matter is dug in, in order to supply the soil with humus. It is interesting to observe how man everywhere found that this vegetable matter must be supplied, and that no chemical manures can take its place. This has been equally found by the Italian vine grower, the tea planter and coffee planter of India, and it must every day become more and more apparent to the cultivator of the humus-exhausted soils of Great Britain.

2   University of Illinois Agricultural Experimental Station. Bulletin No. 94, November 1905.

Sir Albert Howard

5

Maintaining Fertility (2):
The Indore Process

Sir Albert Howard

(1873-1947)

Sir Albert Howard is arguably the most influential of all the defenders of organic husbandry. Although he was caricatured as a superstitious believer in 'muck and magic', he was in fact a highly distinguished scientist - as indeed was his first wife, Gabrielle, who was regarded as playing Beatrice Webb to his Sidney for her importance to his work. Howard spent from 1905 to 1931 in India, and in 1926 was President of the Indian Science Congress. As Director of the Institute of Plant Industry, in the state of Indore, he developed the Indore Process - a means of applying modern scientific knowledege to ancient techniques of composting through the use of vegetable, animal and human waste. Howard returned to England after Gabrielle's death, married her sister Louise - who was another gifted botanist - and was thenceforth a tireless and highly uncompromising advocate of humus farming. He abhorred the work done at Rothamsted, was associated with the Kinship in Husbandry, and greatly influenced, among other people, Lady Eve Balfour (see chapter 6) and Friend Sykes (see chapter 7).

THE INDORE PROCESS IN PRACTICE AND THEORY

The restoration of soil fertility to a state approaching Nature's richness and with faithful regard to that all-important principle of an adequate storage of reserves of humus is the end to be kept in view. An imitation of natural methods of making this humus is therefore indicated. The practice of Oriental nations with their long and proved experience in maintaining their fields in a fertile condition will be a helpful guide. The "Indore Process", so named in honour of the Indian State of Indore whose Durbar generously contributed to the means which enabled the final experiments relating to this work to be carried out during the years 1924-31, is a working out of such proved practices. In addition, it claims the surety and detailed exactness which attaches to a method conforming to scientific principles. As an official of the Agricultural Department of the Government of India, the writer devoted many years of scientific investigation and much thought to perfecting the method and investigating the laws on which it is based not only at Indore but for a long period previously at the Imperial Experimental Station at Pusa, Bihar, and at Quetta in Baluchistan. A description of these investigations will be found in "The Waste Products of Agriculture: their Utilization as Humus" (Oxford University Press, 1931); the recent spread of the process to many parts of the world and the facts which have emerged in connection therewith are set forth in "An Agricultural Testament" (Oxford University Press) which appeared in the June of 1939.

The process reproduces, with a certain attention to human convenience, what takes place on the floor of the forest, where the making and storage of humus are carried out by nature in a way which can be observed with particular ease. The wastes which accumulate under the forest trees are mixed, being of both vegetable and animal origin - leaves, seeds and fruits, scales, needles, bark, twigs: excreta and wastes of mammals, reptiles, and insects and their bodies. They drop on the earth and mingle with it, and are exposed both to the rainfall - which reaches them finely divided into a gentle spray by the protecting leaf canopy - and also to the air.

The farmer and gardener must imitate all this. Firstly, he must collect his wastes, and they must be both vegetable and animal: it is a principle of the Indore system that some form of animal manure must be incorporated with the vegetable refuse. Secondly, these mixed wastes must come into contact with a thin layer of soil. Thirdly, they must be moistened. Fourthly, they must have air.

If these simple principles are followed, the result is bound to be some form of humus, the only questions arising being in the degree of breaking down achieved and in the rate at which this breaking down takes place.

The more perfect the degree of breaking down the better for the cultivator; his crops can then count on nourishment in the most assimilable state. Here Chinese practice is illuminating. The Chinese peasant has grasped the advantage of preparing the plant nutrients in the soil as one process and then feeding them to the plant as another. His supply of humus is manufactured not where his plants are growing but in a place apart, and then used on the crop areas as required. It will easily be seen that by this method much added wealth can be obtained: operations are going on at double speed, as it were. The waiting supply of finished plant food, always at hand to replace what has been used up, eliminates the necessity for any pause in the work of growing the crops, which follow each other with a speed and intensity not to be achieved by ordinary methods, presupposing, as they do, the need for renewing and even for resting the soil between the various sowings.

(Sir Albert Howard, 'Soil Fertility', in *England and the Farmer*, ed. H.J. Massingham, London, Batsford, 1941, pp. 38-40).

The heap must also include animal manure and earth. These cannot be omitted. In insisting that the contents of the heap be all-inclusive, we follow the absolutely primordial law which Nature has laid down - the law of the interdependence of all physical existences. Nature never separates her animal and her vegetable world: in their lives, as in their decay and deaths, beasts and plants are absolutely interlocked. She does not even recognize monoculture in her vegetable kingdom. Her sowings and harvests are mixed and intermingled to the last degree: the prairie, the forest, the moor, the marsh, the river, the lake, the ocean include in their several ways an interweaving of existences which is a dramatic lesson. If we Western nations feel ourselves obliged (Eastern nations do not) to adopt, for purposes of convenience, monoculture in our growing operations, we must at least make an effort to restore the balance by returning to the principle of admixture when we are trying to induce the process of decay.

A particularly erroneous point of view is to separate the animal from the vegetable. It is indeed astonishing that the faulty invention of the dung heap should have been for centuries so thoroughly welded into Western practice - it is unknown to primitive peoples or to Eastern civilization. The isolation of the manurial products of animals even for a short time is exceedingly wasteful. There is a great excess of nitrogen, which escapes to the atmosphere, and too little cellulose on which the fungi and bacteria can act. Nature is for ever telling us that this is all wrong: she warns us by strong odours and clouds of noxious flies. At the opposite end of the scale is the old-fashioned institution of the leaf-mould heap, exclusively vegetable wastes left to rot slowly without air. Both dung heap and leaf-mould heap eventually help fertility: in spite of the cardinal errors connected with their construction they do embody the principle of the return of wastes to the land. But they are a very inadequate application of natural laws, and should be replaced by the mixed heap, well aerated, odourless and flyless, rapid in decay and all-inclusive in its content.

(*England and the Farmer*: 43-44)

The Indore method of making compost may be regarded as a continuous one. Once more the cultivator does well to imitate Nature, who never ceases throughout the year to carry on the faultless methods she has devised for transforming wastes into something useful. Like Nature, the gardener or farmer has his heaps going all the time: certain seasonal accumulations are inevitable, and in this island the process is easier to manage in the warmer months than in the cold winter. But it is a great convenience that every scrap of waste in the garden or field can at once be got out of the way; moreover, on land accessory to habitations no item of household refuse should be allowed to escape the compost heap - such house-bin refuse, including vegetable peelings, tea-leaves, fats, etc., is a most valuable ingredient of the heap, and this is the only correct solution of the problem of disposing of this waste, which entirely loses its nuisance value the moment it is incorporated in the compost heap. The slightest tendency to smell or flies shows that the heap has not been properly made; it is possibly too wet, and had best have an extra turn at once; this corrects the error and restores hygienic conditions.

(*England and the Farmer*: 46-7)

Why are crops grown on fertile soil - one rich in humus - so superior to those raised by means of artificial manures? Has agricultural science omitted an essential factor when considering the nutrition of plants? Is there a want of correspondence between theory and practice? The answer to these questions will be found in a study of the manner in which a fertile soil and crop grown in it come into gear by means of the root system. In soils rich in humus the roots of the crop and the particles of soil come into contact in two ways: firstly, by means of the soil solution which contains, among other things, small quantities of nitrates, phosphates and potash salts; secondly, by means of the mycorrhizal association. This latter involves a partnership between the active cells of the absorbing portions of the roots and threads of fungous tissue (mycelium) which form a living bridge between the plant and the humus in the soil. The roots and the fungus grow together: the relation is one of symbiosis, the precise details of which have still to be investigated. Broadly speaking, a fungus living on the humus in the soil invades the cells of the active portions of the roots and lives therein, finally becoming digested. The products of the digestion of the carbohydrates and proteins contained in the fungous mycelium pass into the sap current and are carried to the green leaves where they act as essential factors in assimilation. The crop grown in a fertile soil, therefore, feeds in two ways - by means of the soil solution and by means of the digestion products of a soil fungus. It is only when the plant is nourished in this double fashion that we get disease resistance and high quality in our crops, our animals and in ourselves.

In marked contrast to this is the produce raised on infertile soil stimulated with the help of chemical manures. Here humus is in defect, the mycorrhizal association does not function effectively. The crops are only partially nourished. Their produce suffers in resistance to disease and in the development of quality. The animals and human beings who feed thereon suffer similar disadvantages. By failing to realize the dual nature of the nutrition of crops, agricultural science has been based on premises which are, to say the least of it, incomplete. The results have been disastrous. Undue emphasis has been laid on the maintenance of the soil solution and the use of artificial manures, which history will condemn as one of the greatest misfortunes which has befallen agriculture and mankind. We have now to retrace our steps, to jettison the theories and practice based on the work of the disciples of Liebig and of experiment stations like Rothamsted. We have to go back to Nature and to copy the methods to be seen in the forest and prairie. We must surely consider the possibility that the conception of the ceaseless circulation of organic matter in Nature through soil, plant and animal, back to soil, plant and animal, over and over again, endlessly and continuously, by processes which are throughout living processes, may be in its effects on our general outlook and on the shaping of our research work not unlike what Harvey's discovery of the circulation of the blood was for medicine...

(*England and the Farmer:* 48-50)

THE UTILIZATION OF TOWN WASTES

The human population, for the most part concentrated in towns and villages, is maintained almost exclusively by the land. Apart from the harvest of the sea, agriculture provides the food of the people and the requirements of vegetable and animal origin needed by the factories of the urban areas. It follows that a large portion of the waste products of farming must be found in the towns and away from the fields which produced them. One of the consequences, therefore, of the concentration of the human population in small areas has been to separate, often by considerable distances, an important portion of the wastes of agriculture from the land. These wastes fall into two distinct groups:

(a)   Town wastes consisting mainly of the contents of the dustbins, market, street, and trade wastes with a small amount of animal manure.

(b)   The urine and faeces of the population.

In practically all cases in this country both groups of waste materials are treated as something to be got rid of as quickly, as unostentatiously, and as cheaply as possible. In Great Britain most town wastes are either buried in a controlled tip or burnt in an incinerator. Practically none of our urban waste finds its way back to the land. The wastes of the population, in most Western countries, are first diluted with large volumes of water and then after varying amounts of purification, are discharged either into rivers or into the sea. Beyond a little of the resulting sewage sludge the residues of the population are entirely lost to agriculture.

From the point of view of farming the towns have become parasites. They will last under the present system only as long as the earth's fertility lasts. Then the whole fabric of our civilization must collapse.

In considering how this unsatisfactory state of affairs can be remedied and how the wastes of urban areas can be restored to the soil, the magnitude of the problem and the difficulties which have to be overcome must be realized from the outset. These difficulties are of two kinds: those which belong to the subject proper, and those inherent in ourselves. The present system of sewage disposal has been the growth of a hundred years; problem after problem has had to be solved as it arose from the sole point of view of what seemed best for the town at the moment; mother earth has had few or no representatives on municipal councils to plead her cause; the disposal of waste has always been looked upon as the sole business of the town rather than something which concerns the well-being of the nation as a whole. The fragmentation of the subject into its urban components - medical, engineering, administrative, and financial - has followed; direction has been lost. The piecemeal consideration of such a matter could only lead to failure.

Can anything be done at this late hour by way of reform? Can mother earth secure even a partial restitution of her manurial rights? If the easiest road is first taken a great deal can be accomplished in a few years. The problem of getting the town wastes back into the land is not difficult. The task of demonstrating a working alternative to water-borne sewage and getting it adopted in practice is, however, stupendous. At the moment it is altogether outside the bounds of practical politics. Some catastrophe, such as a universal shortage of food followed by famine, or the necessity of spreading the urban population about the country-side to safeguard it from direct and indirect damage by hostile aircraft, will have to be upon us before such a question can even be considered.

The effective disposal of town wastes is, however, far less difficult, as will be seen by what has already been accomplished in this country. Passing over the earlier experiments with town wastes... in which the dustbin refuse was used without modification, the recent results obtained with pulverized wastes, prepared by passing the sorted material (to remove tin cans, bottles, and other refractory objects) through a hammer mill, point clearly to the true role of this material in agriculture. Its value lies, not in its chemical composition, which is almost negligible, but in the fact that it is a perfect diluent for the manure heap, the weakest link in agriculture in many countries. The ordinary manure heap on a farm is biologically unbalanced and chemically unstable. It is unbalanced because the micro-organisms which are trying to synthesize humus have far too much urine and dung and far too little cellulose and lignin and insufficient air to begin with. It is unstable because it cannot hold itself together; the valuable nitrogen is lost either as ammonia or as free nitrogen; the micro-organisms cannot use up the urine fast enough before it runs to waste;

the proteins are used as a source of oxygen with the liberation of free nitrogen. The fungi and bacteria of the manure heap are working under impossible conditions. They live a life of constant frustration which can only be avoided by giving them a balanced ration. This can be achieved by diluting the existing manure heaps with three volumes of pulverized town wastes. The micro-organisms are then provided with all the cellulose and lignin they need. The dilution of the manure heap automatically improves the aeration. The volume of the resulting manure is multiplied by at least three; its efficiency is also increased.

Such a reform of the manure heap is practicable. Two examples may be quoted. At the large hop garden at Bodiam in Sussex, the property of Messrs. Arthur Guinness, Son & Co., Ltd., over 30 tons of pulverized town wastes from Southwark are used daily throughout the year for humus manufacture. This material is railed in 6-ton truck-loads to Bodiam, transferred to the hop gardens by lorry and then composted with all the wastes of the garden - hop bine, hop string, hedge and roadside trimmings, old straw, all the farm-yard manure which is available - and every other vegetable and animal waste that can be collected locally. The annual output of finished humus is over 10,000 tons, which is prepared at an all-in cost of 10s a ton, including spreading on the land. The Manager of this garden, Mr. L. P. Haynes, has worked out comparative figures of cost between nitrogen, phosphorus, and potash applied in the form of humus or artificials... There is therefore a distinct saving when humus is used. This, however, is only a minor item on the credit side. The texture of the soil is rapidly improving, soil fertility is being built up, the need for chemical manures and poison sprays to control pests is becoming less.

The manurial policy adopted on this hop garden has been confirmed in rather an interesting fashion. Before a serious attempt was made to prepare humus on the present scale, a small amount of pulverized Southwark refuse had been in use. The bulk of the manure used, however, was artificials supplemented by the various organic manures and fertilizers on the market. The labourers employed at Bodiam were therefore conversant with practically every type of inorganic and organic manure. One of their privileges is a supply of manure for their gardens. They have always selected pulverized town wastes because they consider this grows the best vegetables.

(*An Agricultural Testament*, London, Oxford University Press, 1940, pp. 104-7, reprinted by permission of Oxford University Press)

When it is remembered that the annual dustbin refuse in Great Britain is in the neighbourhood of 13,000,000 tons and that about half of this material can be used for making the most of the urine and dung of our live stock, it will be evident what enormous possibilities exist for raising the fertility of the zones of land within, say, fifty miles of the large cities and towns. A perusal of the Public Cleansing Return for the year ending March 31st, 1938, published by the Ministry of Health, shows that a certain proportion of this dustbin refuse is still burnt in incinerators. Once, however, the agricultural value of this material is realized by farmers and market gardeners it will not be long before incineration is given up and the whole of the organic matter in our town wastes finds its way into the manure heap. When this time comes the utilization of the enormous dumps of similar wastes, which accumulated before controlled tipping was adopted, can be taken in hand. These contain many more millions of tons of material which can be dealt with on Southwark lines. In this way the manure heaps of a very large portion of rural England can be reformed and the fertility of a considerable area restored. A good beginning will then have been made in the restitution of the manurial rights owing to the country-side. The towns will have begun to repay their debt to the soil.

Besides the wastes of the dustbins and the dumps there is another and even more important source of unused humus in the neighbour-hood of our cities and towns. This occurs in the controlled tips in which most of the dustbin refuse is now buried. In controlled tipping the town wastes are deposited in suitable areas near cities and sealed with a layer of clay, soil, or ashes so as to prevent nuisance generally and also the breeding of flies. The seal, however, permits sufficient aeration for the first stage in the conversion of most of the organic matter into humus. The result is that in a year or two the tip becomes a humus mine. The crude organic matter in these wastes is slowly trans-formed by means of fungi and bacteria into humus. All that is needed is to separate the finely divided humus from the refractory material and to apply it to the land.

(*An Agricultural Testament:* 108-9,
reprinted by permission of Oxford University Press)

In countries where there is no system of water-borne sewage there has been no difficulty in converting the wastes of the population into humus. The first trials of the Indore Process for this purpose were completed in Central India in 1933 by Messrs. Jackson and Wad at three centres near Indore - the Indore Residency, Indore City, and the Malwa Bhil Corps. Their results were soon taken up by a number of the Central India and Rajputana States and by some of the municipalities in India. Subsequent developments of this work, including working drawings and figures of cost, were summed up in a paper read to the Health Congress of the Royal Sanitary Institute held at Portsmouth in 1938... A perusal of this statement shows that human wastes are an even better activator than animal residues. All that is necessary is to provide for abundant aeration in the early stages and to see that the night soil is spread in a thin film over the town wastes and that no pockets or definite layers are left. Both of these interfere with aeration, produce smell, and attract flies. Smell and flies are therefore a very useful means of control. If the work is properly done there is no smell, and flies are not attracted because the intense oxidation processes involved in the early stages of the synthesis of humus are set in motion. It is only when the air supply is cut off at this stage that putrefactive. changes occur which produce nuisance and encourage flies...

A number of medical officers all over the world are trying out the composting of night soil on the lines suggested. In a few years a great deal of experience will be available, on which the projects of the future can be based.

As far as countries like Great Britain are concerned, the only openings for the composting of night soil occur in the countryside and in the outer urban zones where the houses are provided with kitchen gardens. In such areas the vast quantities of humus in the controlled tips can be used in earth-closets and the mixed night soil and humus can be lightly buried in the gardens on the lines so successfully carried out by the late Dr. Poore and described in his *Rural Hygiene,* the second edition of which was published in 1894.

Since Dr. Poore's work appeared a new development in housing has taken place in the garden cities and in colonies like those started by the Land Settlement Association. Here, although there is ample land for converting every possible waste into humus, the water-borne method of sewage disposal and the dust-carts of the crowded town have been slavishly copied. In an interesting paper published in the *British Medical Journal* of February 9th, 1924, Dr. L. J. Picton, then Medical Officer of Health of the Winsford Urban District, Cheshire, pointed out how easy it would be to apply Dr. Poore's principles to a garden city.

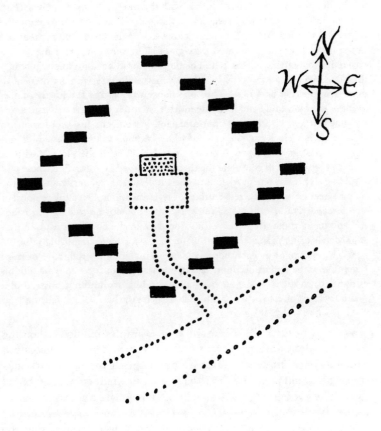

Fig. 1. A model layout for 20 cottages

'A plot of 4 acres should be taken on the outskirts of a town and twenty houses built upon it. Suppose the plot roughly square, and the road to skirt one corner of it. Then this corner alone will possess that valuable quality "frontage". Sacrifice this scrap of frontage by making a short gravelled drive through it, to end blindly in a "turn-round" in the middle of the plot. The houses should all face south - that is to say, all their living rooms should face south. They must therefore be oblong, with their long axes east and west (Fig. 1). The larder, the lobby, lavatory, staircase and landing will occupy the north side of each house. The earth closet is best detached but approached under cover - a cross-ventilated passage or short veranda, or, if upstairs, a covered bridge giving access to it. The houses should be set upon the plot in a diamond-shaped pattern, or in other words, a square with its corners to north, south, east and west. Thus one house will occupy the northernmost point of the plot, and from it, to the south-east and south-west, will run a row of some five or six houses a side, arranged in echelon. Just as platoons in echelon do not block each other's line of fire so houses thus arranged will not block each other's sunlight. A dozen more houses echeloned in a V with its apex to the south will complete the diamond-shaped lay-out. The whole plot would be treated as one garden, and one whole-time head gardener, with the help he needed, would be responsible for its cultivation. The daily removal of the closet earth and its use as manure - its immediate committal to the surface soil and its light covering therewith - would naturally be amongst his duties. A gardener using manure of great value, not a scavenger removing refuse; a "garden rate" paid by each householder, an investment productive of fresh vegetables to be had at his door, and in one way or another repaying him his outlay, not to speak of the amenity added to his surroundings, instead of a "sanitary rate" paid to be rid of rubbish - such are the bases of this scheme.'

What is needed are a few working examples of such a housing scheme and a published account of the results. These, if successful, would at once influence all future building schemes in country districts and would point the way to a considerable reduction in rents and rates. The garden-city and water-borne sewage are a contradiction in terms. Water-borne sewage has developed because of overcrowding and the absence of cultivated land. Remove overcrowding and the case for this wasteful system disappears. In the garden city there is no need to get rid of wastes by the expensive methods of the town. The soil will do it far more efficiently and at far less cost. At the same time the fertility of the garden city areas will be raised and large crops of fresh vegetables and fruit - one of the factors underlying health - will be automatically provided.

Such a reform in housing schemes will not stop at the outer fringes of our towns and cities. It will be certain to spread to the villages and to the country-side, where a few examples of cottage gardens, rendered fertile by the wastes of the inhabitants, are still to be found here and there. More are needed. More will arise the moment it is realized that the proper utilization of the wastes of the population depends on composting processes and the correct use of humus. All the trouble, all the expense, and all the difficulties in dealing with human wastes arise from following the wrong principle - water - and setting in motion a vast train of putrefactive processes. The principle that must be followed is abundant aeration at the beginning: the conversion of wastes into humus by the processes Nature employs in every wood and every forest.

(An Agricultural Testament: 112-15,
reprinted by permission of Oxford University Press)

THE POST-WAR TASK

The problem of disease and health took on a wider scope. In March 1939 new ground was broken. The Local Medical and Panel Committees of Cheshire, summing up their experience of the working of the National Health Insurance Act for over a quarter of a century in the county, did not hesitate to link up their judgment on the unsatisfactory state of health of the human population under their care with the problem of nutrition, tracing the line of fault right back to an impoverished soil and supporting their contentions by reference to the ideas which I had for some time been advocating. Their arguments were powerfully supported by the results obtained at the Peckham Health Centre and by the work, already published, of Sir Robert McCarrison, which latter told the story from the other side of the world and from a precisely opposite angle - he was able to instance an Eastern people, the Hunzas, who were the direct embodiment of an ideal of health and whose food was derived from soil kept in a state of the highest natural fertility.

By these contemporaneous pioneering efforts the way was blazed for treating the whole problem of health in soil, plant, animal, and man as one great subject, calling for a boldly revised point of view and entirely fresh investigations.

By this time sufficient evidence had accumulated for setting out the case for soil fertility in book form. This was published in June 1940 by the Oxford University Press under the title of *An Agricultural Test-ament*. This book, now in its fourth English and second American edition, set forth the whole gamut of connected problems as far as can at present be done - what wider revelations the future holds is not yet fully disclosed. In it I summed up my life's work and advanced the following views:

1. The birthright of all living things is health.

2. This law is true for soil, plant, animal, and man: the health of these four is one connected chain.

3. Any weakness or defect in the health of any earlier link in the chain is carried on to the next and succeeding links, until it reaches the last, namely, man.

4. The widespread vegetable and animal pests and diseases, which are such a bane to modern agriculture, are evidence of a great failure of health in the second (plant) and third (animal) links of the chain.

5. The impaired health of human populations (the fourth link) in modern civilized countries is a consequence of this failure in the second and third links.

6. This general failure in the last three links is to be attributed to failure in the first link, the soil: the undernourishment of the soil is at the root of all. The failure to maintain a healthy agri-culture has largely cancelled out all the advantages we have gained from our improvements in hygiene, in housing, and our medical discoveries.

7. To retrace our steps is not really difficult if once we set our minds to the problem. We have to bear in mind Nature's dic-tates, and we must conform to her imperious demand: (*a*) for the return of all wastes to the land; (*b*) for the mixture of the animal and vegetable existence; (*c*) for the maintaining of an adequate reserve system of feeding the plant, i.e. we must not interrupt the mycorrhizal association. If we are willing so far to conform to natural law, we shall rapidly reap our reward not only in a flourishing agriculture, but in the immense asset of an abounding health in ourselves and in our children's children.

These ideas, straightforward as they appear when set forth in the form given above, conflict with a number of vested interests. It has been my self-appointed task during the last few years of my life to join hands with those who are convinced of their truth to fight the forces impeding progress. So large has been the flow of evidence accumulat-

ing that in 1941 it was decided to publish a *News-Letter on Compost,*
embodying the most interesting of the facts and opinions reaching me
or others in the campaign. The *News-Letter,* which appears three
times a year under the aegis of the Cheshire Local Medical and Panel
Committees, has grown from eight to sixty-four pages and is daily
gaining new readers.

The general thesis that no one generation has a right to exhaust the
soil from which humanity must draw its sustenance has received
further powerful support from religious bodies. The clearest short ex-
position of this idea is contained in one of the five fundamental
principles adopted by the recent Malvern Conference of the Christian
Churches held with the support of the late Archbishop of Canterbury,
Dr. Temple. It is as follows: 'The resources of the earth should be used
as God's gifts to the whole human race and used with due consideration for the needs of the present and future generations.'

Food is the chief necessity of life. The plans for social security which
are now being discussed merely guarantee to the population a share in
a variable and, in present circumstances, an uncertain quantity of
food, most of it of very doubtful quality. Real security against want
and ill health can only be assured by an abundant supply of fresh food
properly grown in soil in good heart. *The first place in post-war plans
of reconstruction must be given to soil fertility in every part of the
world.* The land of this country and the Colonial Empire, which is the
direct responsibility of Parliament, must be raised to a higher level of
productivity by a rational system of farming which puts a stop to the
exploitation of land for the purpose of profit and takes into account
the importance of humus in producing food of good quality. The
electorate alone has the power of enforcing this and to do so it must
first realize the full implications of the problem.

They and they alone possess the power to insist that every boy and
every girl shall enter into their birthright - health, and that efficiency,
well-being, and contentment which depend thereon. One of the objects of this book is to show the man in the street how this England of
ours can be born again. He can help in this task, which depends at
least as much on the plain efforts of the plain man in his own farm,
garden, or allotment as on all the expensive paraphernalia,
apparatus, and elaboration of the modern scientist: more so in all probability, inasmuch as one small example always outweighs a ton of
theory. If this sort of effort can be made and the main outline of the
problems at stake are [[sic]] grasped, nothing can stop an immense

advance in the well-being of this island. A healthy population will be no mean achievement, for our greatest possession is ourselves.

The man in the street will have to do three things:

1. He must create in his own farm, garden, or allotment examples without end of what a fertile soil can do.

2. He must insist that the public meals in which he is directly interested, such as those served in boarding schools, in the canteens of day schools and of factories, in popular restaurants and tea shops, and at the seaside resorts at which he takes his holidays are composed of the fresh produce of fertile soil.

3. He must use his vote to compel his various representatives - municipal, county, and parliamentary - to see to it: (a) that the soil of this island is made fertile and maintained in this condition; (b) that the public health system of the future is based on the fresh produce of land in good heart.

This introduction started with the training of an agricultural investigator: it ends with the principles underlying the public health system of tomorrow. It has, therefore, covered much ground in describing what is nothing less than an adventure in scientific research. One lesson must be stressed. The difficulties met with and overcome in the official portion of this journey were not part of the subject investigated. They were man made and created by the research organization itself. More time and energy had to be expended in side-tracking the lets and hindrances freely strewn along the road by the various well-meaning agencies which controlled discovery than in conducting the investigations themselves. When the day of retirement came, all these obstacles vanished and the delights of complete freedom were enjoyed. Progress was instantly accelerated. Results were soon obtained throughout the length and breadth of the English-speaking world, which make crystal clear the great role which soil fertility must play in the future of mankind.

The real Arsenal of Democracy is a fertile soil, the fresh produce of which is the birthright of the nations.

(*Farming and Gardening for Health or Disease*,
London, Faber, 1945, pp.24-7)

Other works by Howard include The Waste Products of Agriculture: Their Utilization as Humus, *with co-author Yeshwant D. Wad (London, Oxford University Press, 1931); an Introduction to* Darwin on Humus and the Earthworm *(London, Faber, 1945); an Introduction to* Gardening With Compost, *by F.C. King (London, Faber, 1944); and a contribution to the symposium 'Crops Without Chemcals?' in* The Countryman *(Burford, Oxon, January 1940). His second wife, Louise Howard, wrote a very valuable account of his career abroad in* Sir Albert Howard in India *(London, Faber, 1953).*

A systematic presentation of the case for and against chemical fertilizers is given in Chemicals, Humus, and the Soil *by Donald Hopkins (London, Faber, 1945); a good deal of this book concerns Howard's ideas, though the author in the end considers them not proven.*

Howard was greatly influenced by Farmers of Forty Centuries, or Permanent Agriculture in China, Korea and Japan, *by F.H. King (London, Cape, 1927), which describes oriental methods of composting. A book which deals with making compost in the light of twentieth-century knowledge is F.H. Billington's* Compost for Garden Plot or Thousand-Acre Farm *(London, Faber, 1942). On the same subject are two books by Maye E. Bruce:* From Vegetable Waste to Fertile Soil *(London, Faber, 1943), and* Common-Sense Compost Making *(London, Faber, 1946).*

The use of town wastes for making compost is discussed in Soil Fertility and Sewage *by J. van Vuren (London, Faber, 1949), and in two books by J.C. Wylie:* Fertility From Town Wastes *(London, Faber, 1955), and* The Wastes of Civilization *(London, Faber, 1959).*

Your Daily Bread, by Doris Grant (London, Faber, 1944; revised edn., 1962), is dedicated to Howard, and deals with the relation between health and a fertile soil.

Other books about the soil, written from a point of view sympathetic to organic methods of cultivation, include Soil and Sense *by Michael Graham (London, Faber, 1941);* Charter for the Soil *by John Drummond (London, Faber, 1944); and* Soil Fertility, Renewal and Preservation *by Ehrenfried Pfeiffer (revised edn., London, Faber, 1947), which puts the case for the bio-dynamic approach to farming and gardening.*

Lady Balfour's work is dealt with in the following chapter.

Lady Eve Balfour

6

The Origins of the Soil Association

Lady Eve Balfour

(b.1898)

Lady Eve Balfour, niece of the Prime Minister Sir Arthur Balfour, decided at the age of twelve that she wanted to become a farmer, and took the Agricultural Diploma at Reading in 1917. Two years later she and her elder sister bought New Bells Farm at Haughley in Suffolk, and learnt about agriculture the hard way, during the depression of the 1920s and 1930s.

In 1938 Lady Eve read Lord Lymington's book Famine in England *(London, Witherby, 1938), which opened her eyes to the question of the relation between health, food, and the treatment of the soil; the same year, she met Sir Albert Howard (see chapter 5) and began reading everything she could find on the issues which Lymington and Howard discussed. As a result of knowing Howard she also came into contact with Dr L.J. Picton and Dr G.T. Wrench (see chapter 8). In her own words:*

> Nowhere had a long-term, comparative, controlled ecological experiment been undertaken to test the theories put forward, by Howard and others... I was deeply impressed with the urgent need for the establishment of some such test. [1]

The situation in 1939 was that Lady Eve farmed New Bells Farm as owner-occupier, and was also farming Walnut Tree Farm, the neighbouring land, as tenant. The owner of this land was Miss Alice Debenham, with whom Lady Eve discussed her desire to set up the experiment. Miss Debenham responded by establishing the Haughley Research Trust, and to this Trust she made a gift of her farm. Haughley Research Farms Ltd was registered shortly before she died. Miss Debenham's sister Agnes was acquainted with one of the directors of Faber and Faber, and Lady Eve thereby came to know Richard de la Mare, editor of Faber's agriculture list. The result of this meeting was

Lady Eve's book, The Living Soil *(London, Faber, 1943), which aroused such a response from other people thinking and working along the same lines that the establishment of a formal organization to pool their experience became inevitable.*

After much discussion the Soil Association was registered, and launched at a meeting in November 1946. Its aims were:

1.   *To bring together all those working for a fuller understanding of the vital relationships between soil, plant, animal and man.*

2.   *To initiate, co-ordinate and assist research in this field.*

3.   *To collect and distribute the knowledge gained so as to create a body of informed public opinion.* [2]

The following extracts are all taken from the third edition of The Living Soil, *which appeared in June 1944. They therefore predate the existence of the Soil Association, but give an idea of its genesis and philosophy.*

THE NEED FOR AN EXPERIMENT

The evidence... presents the case for a view on health that can be summed up under five propositions.

(1) The primary factor in health (or the lack of it) is nutrition.

(2) Fresh unprocessed natural whole foods (such as wholewheat bread, and raw vegetables and salads) have a greater nutritive value than the same foods when stale, or from which vital parts have been removed by processing, or have been destroyed by faulty preparation.

(3) Fresh foods are more health-promoting than preserved foods (dried, canned, or bottled).

(4) The nutritive value of food is vitally affected by the way in which it is grown.

(5) An essential link in the nutrition cycle is provided by the activities of soil fungi, and for this and other reasons the biological aspects of soil fertility are more important than the chemical.

My own view is that of these five premises, the first two have been pretty conclusively proved, but that the last three have still to be fully established. Nevertheless while admitting that critical scientific proof is at present lacking, I maintain that the indications in support of them are so strong, that it has become a matter of the utmost national urgency to submit them, without delay, to a final and conclusive test.

I now invite those of you who share this view to consider with me how this can best be done.

Lord Teviot recently put forward a suggestion in a vigorously worded letter to the *Farmers' Weekly* ⟦ 18th September 1942 ⟧. Here are some extracts from it:

'There has been a suggestion in various quarters that a "Nutrition Council" should be formed, to go into the question of food and food values, and I am most hopeful that this may happen. The necessity for it is obvious. ...I am convinced from my own studies of the experiments, tests, and experiences, of many learned men in medicine and agriculture, that the chief cause of disease in man, plant and animal, is due to their food, and undoubtedly there is outstanding evidence from distinguished men that food produced from soil deficient in rich healthy humus is a source of ill health.

'The tests which have been made demonstrate that food grown from fertile soil, rich in humus, means good health and happiness, while the same food produced from soil impregnated with chemical artificial fertilizers, causes bad health and sterility. ...Let the Government make a test; it is quite easy. Grow, say, a given number of acres of various crops on identical land in the same area, using compost or well-prepared organic manure, also in the same number of acres use artificial manure. Test various animals by feeding them on both: the result will become quickly evident.

'My reason for raising this question is my apprehension that owing to the increased use of artificials, the health of our people is being and will be further damaged....'

The opponents of these views, as well as the more cautious among their supporters, will at once say that he takes too much for granted, and claims as facts those things which are still only opinions. This same criticism is frequently levelled at Sir Albert Howard. Very possibly it is justified, but there is a significant point to be noted. The humus enthusiasts are invariably ready to have their theories put to the proof, whereas their critics, usually chemists, have discouraged all attempts to carry out such a test as Lord Teviot calls for. The inference is obvious - either the chemists are, at heart, not sure of their ground, or else, suspecting that they are wrong, they are fighting to preserve their vested interests at the possible expense of the national health. If it had not been for this obstruction, this vital question would surely have been answered long since. It may be asked, why have not some of the humus enthusiasts carried out such a test on their own initiative. One reason is, that few have been in a financial position to do so, all large scale experimental work is expensive, but I believe there is a deeper and more fundamental reason; a psychological one. In attempting to explain it, I must ask you to make allowances for the error inherent in all generalizations.

Broadly speaking then, the mentality of the large scale users of chemical fertilizers is, I think in the main a commercial mentality; the mentality that measures values in terms of money and is out for quick returns, whereas the 'composters', inevitably made alive all the time to the biological factors of soil, develop different standards. They are very much aware of their responsibility; their outlook is one of service to the soil, not exploitation; farming to them is a vocation, not a trade. When they become convinced that their biological approach to the soil is right in the interests of the soil itself, any soil treatment which runs counter to this, becomes such heresy to them that they cease to be capable of a detached and purely scientific attitude to the problems involved.

I am aware of this danger in myself, but I have been brought up with a sufficiently scientific background to be able to control it, in the interests of truth. For it is quite clear to me that if humus is indeed the basis of health, we shall get no further towards achieving health until evidence is provided of so conclusive a nature that scientists are ready to accept it as proof. Scientists are always slow to accept any new principle because scepticism is a necessary part of their make up. Without it they would not be scientists. This scepticism only ceases to be a virtue when suspicion of any new theory is carried to the length of obstructing work designed to provide proof. Unfortunately, the history of new scientific discoveries is interwoven with just such obstruction from the very people whom one would expect to welcome investigation...

Thus it seems to me that such a test as Lord Teviot suggests, if it were undertaken by the Government, could only succeed if a completely detached research scientist were put in charge of it, the practical work being carried out under his ultimate authority by two entirely separate staffs. The organic portion of the land should be managed by an expert cultivator of the compost school, assisted by a team of biologists and mycologists, and the chemical portion managed by agricultural chemists.

(*The Living Soil*: 159-61)

The new world (if such indeed it prove to be) which is appearing on the horizon as a result of the probable relationship between humus and health, has not lacked its Columbus, and it has had at least one Raleigh too, in the person of the late Alice Debenham. The tragedy is, that she died at the very outset of her great purpose, leaving to others the task of bringing to fruition the seed she sowed.

A practical farmer, trained in science and medicine, and during the latter years of her life an invalid, Alice Debenham saw very clearly the potential importance of the evidence concerning soil fertility and health. She saw equally clearly that this scattered evidence must be collected and reproduced under controlled conditions if it were to convince the scientific world, and that unless science is convinced, Governments will not act.

Outstandingly public spirited, she founded a Research Trust to carry out this work. As custodians of it, she appointed the East Suffolk County Council. By this means the Trust immediately obtained an official status that a purely private body would not have achieved, while, at the same time, the terms of the Trust gave it much greater freedom of action than would have been possible to a Government-run concern. To this Trust she presented, under a deed of gift, about eighty acres of farm land together with a limited number of farm buildings and an admirably modernized farm-house. This eighty acres marches with a 150-acre holding which I have been farming since 1919 and it was agreed between us that this land should be leased or sold to the Trust so that the total experimental area should not be less than two hundred acres. This was considered to be the minimum acreage needed for carrying out the experiment for which the Trust was chiefly formed.

(The Living Soil: 162)

First and foremost, it is necessary, as far as is humanly possible, so to control the conditions under which the experiment is carried out that the issue shall be quite clear cut. That is to say no loophole must be left, whereby any other explanation than that of the different soil treatments, can be held to explain any differences that may result, between the health of crops or stock in the two sections....

It is comparatively easy to achieve such control under laboratory conditions, but not at all easy under farm conditions. Among the obstacles to be overcome are the natural variations occurring in soil (there are few farms where this does not vary from field to field); differences in aspect (fields sloping north or south, for example, have an influence on crops); and weather variations (crops to be compared should be sown or planted at the same time, an operation not always easy to arrange). None of these difficulties is insurmountable but they increase the complexity and cost of field trials. This is no doubt one of the reasons why research workers, when undertaking field trials, usually adopt the procedure of small plot experiments. Unfortunately for such a test as we are considering this method would be useless. It has been clearly shown in this book that the factor to be determined hinges on the activity of soil organisms, not only such comparatively immobile things as fungi, but also motile pests, and such animals as earthworms and even moles. Largely because of this, the effects of the two types of soil treatment are cumulative. Constant applications of chemical fertilizers greatly discourage or inhibit, and finally destroy or banish, these organisms, while continued applications of properly prepared humus - and also to a lesser degree of farmyard manure - increase their numbers and activity. This fact should make it clear that small plots will not serve, for through the natural drainage system of soil, the chemical treatment in one plot would tend to influence organisms in the adjacent organic plot, and conversely, chemical plots would tend to become repopulated by such creatures as earthworms from neighbouring organic plots, so that the final result would be more or less to reproduce the conditions of ordinary mixed farming, where both muck and artificials are used.

Different types of organic treatment can be tried within the main organic area, so long as the plots are reasonably large (say, not less than an acre), and different chemical fertilizers in the same way within the chemical area, but the main issue, viz. inorganic plant nutrients plus raw organic matter of vegetable origin, versus humus composed of animal and vegetable wastes in due proportion and properly composted, can only be determined by large area tests. The area of any plot must in no case be less than a whole field; if we are to equalize natural variations in soil (and so eliminate that factor) several fields must be included in each trial, and each half of the total experimental area must follow the same rotation of crops. When all these considerations are taken into account, it becomes clear that at least one hundred acres are required for each half of the experiment.

Miss Debenham saw all this very clearly, and she was partly prompted to her generous gift because of the extreme suitability, for this experiment, of the proposed site at Haughley. Firstly, the area is about right, a total of 236 acres; secondly, the land is all flat, so that differences in aspect hardly arise; thirdly, the fields are all fairly small; and fourthly (because owing to their flatness the drainage system demands it), they are all surrounded by deep ditches, therefore any soil treatment applied to one field cannot possibly affect conditions in the next. Lastly, the character of the soil is fairly uniform - clay loam, on mixed clay and sand subsoil, overlying chalk. Such variations as do occur are distributed in such a way that all soil types can be represented on both halves of the area.

Conditions are also favourable for that part of the experiment dealing with livestock. The pasture on the two farms, about thirty acres, is well fenced and the various farm buildings can easily be adapted for the needs of different classes of livestock. Both farms are well watered by deep artesian bores and both are electrified by connection with the main grid system. Finally, the house which is included in the deed of gift is admirably suited for eventual conversion to laboratories.

At the time when the project was mooted, and the Haughley Research Trust was created, it was realized that the experiment must proceed by a series of definite stages. Stage 1, in order to create uniform conditions, must be to clean out all ditches, amounting on the two farms to a total of seven miles, and to drain any fields that required it. Also, where necessary, to carry out subsoiling operations so that, in so far as mechanical treatment could achieve it, the whole of the experimental area should be equally well drained and aerated. Stage 2 would consist of dividing the farms into two halves in such a way that every variation in soil type is represented on both halves, and then, having decided the rotation to be adopted, so to arrange the cropping that not only should each half carry that rotation as a complete and independent unit, but that in any given year a crop on the organic portion (Unit A) should be growing on the same type of soil as a similar crop on the chemical portion (Unit B). These two stages would be arrived at simultaneously, and it was considered that two years would be required to complete them. Stage 3 (though this also could start before Stage 2 was completed) would be to build up the fertility of Unit A with large dressings of organic matter, as much of it as possible in the form of compost. Since the sooner that this stage could be completed the sooner would it be possible to provide positive evidence by feeding tests, it was considered probable that at the outset external sources of organic matter would have to be obtained so that during the first two years really heavy applications of humus could be made, somewhere in the neighbourhood of thirty tons to the acre. It was considered that one possible source of this outside humus might be the Stowmarket Town 'tips', if investigation proved this to be suitable, and an option on it was obtained. Local dustbin and slaughter house refuse were considered as being further possible sources of supply. While this building-up process was being carried out on Unit A equally liberal dressings of complete artificial fertilizers were to be applied to Unit B. The chemical equivalent of Indore compost averages 1 per cent nitrogen, 1 per cent potash and 0.5 per cent phosphorus, so that the minimum requirements for Unit B would be approximately 224 lb. each of nitrogen and potash and 112 lb. of phosphorus for every ten tons of compost applied to Unit A, but since the comparison to be made is really one between two types of farming the actual quantities and proportions of fertilizers to be applied would be governed by the accepted standard of crop requirements as recommended by recognized agricultural experts. Organic matter would be supplied to Unit B by ploughing in straw and green crops. Both units would of course receive periodical dressings of chalk. It was considered that for this preparatory stage another two years would be required. Thereafter some 400 to 500 tons of compost per annum should be sufficient to maintain the fertility of Unit A, and for this quantity the farm should by then be self-supporting. Stage 4 would consist of growing crops for seed, the view being held that vigour and health (or the lack of it) start in the parent stock, so that although there might well be earlier indications, no real comparison between the health or quality of crops grown on the two units ought to be made with first generation plants. The crops to be tested must, if grown in humus be the offspring of humus grown plants, and the chemically grown crops the offspring of chemically grown plants.

Throughout these four stages careful records would be kept and frequent examinations made both as to soil conditions and as to root responses. The soil tests would include the usual chemical analyses for phosphorus, nitrogen, potash and lime, and also biological tests to determine the extent of fungal activity and, so far as possible, the behaviour of the soil population generally, including earthworms. Particular attention would be paid to mycorrhizal activity, and the relationship of this to the different soil treatments. All field tests would be supplemented wherever possible by pot experiments under laboratory conditions. These various tests would continue throughout the whole course of the experiment so that the results of them could later be correlated with any results obtained in feeding experiments.

(*The Living Soil*: 164-7)

...Stage 5 would carry the experiment into the animal kingdom. Here again recent experience suggests that early results of a kind, might be expected, but since the object of this experiment would be to provide proof rather than indications, once more, the verdict would be based only on results obtained with second generation stock. That is to say, the animals to be tested, whether fed on humus or chemically grown plants, must be the offspring of parents raised on a like diet.

The time taken for this stage would vary considerably according to the class of livestock undergoing comparative tests. These would range from laboratory animals such as rats, with which definite results should be obtained in a single year, to cattle which would require five to six years. For such animals as pigs and poultry two years would be needed. If the results of this fifth stage were promising, the sixth stage would consist of immunity tests. Groups of these second generation animals would be removed to special quarters and there, diseased animals imported from outside would be introduced among them. Each group would continue, of course, to be fed from the produce of their own unit, and careful records would be kept as to the extent to which individual members of each group succumbed to the infection with which they were in contact. Here again, the time required for the different classes of livestock would vary, so that Stages 5 and 6 would overlap. Stage 6 would be reached in the case of rats and pigs while cattle were still in Stage 5.

Throughout the whole course of the experiment the work would be under county control, and experts in the various fields of science involved in the experiment, would be appointed as consultants. It was considered by Miss Debenham, and those authorities whom she consulted, that such an experiment as I have outlined would provide conclusive proof, one way or the other, of the question at issue within a period of ten years. If the result were to establish beyond reasonable doubt, firstly that crops grown on properly prepared humus, were superior in quality, and more resistant to disease than identical crops grown with chemical fertilizers, and secondly, that animals fed on this humus-produced food were also healthier, and more disease resistant than those fed on the chemically grown food, then an attempt would be made to carry the experiment a stage further, into the human field. For this the co-operation of the medical profession would be sought, but it was considered to be too early at that time, to lay down any details as to how this stage should be carried out.

That was the plan as proposed by Miss Debenham, and for which the Haughley Research Trust came into being. It was realized, however, that the possibility of carrying it out would depend on the extent of financial support that could be obtained. The Trust was formed in 1939 and some of the consultants appointed. The proposed plans of operation, and the evidence which gave rise to them, were then printed in pamphlet form. In a preface to this pamphlet Sir Robert Hutchison [[President of the Royal College of Physicians]] wrote: 'It is highly important that the question should be settled without delay and the experiments planned to be carried out at Haughley are admirably calculated to determine the question at issue once and for all. For that reason they are deserving of every encouragement and support from the medical profession.' This pamphlet was privately circulated, with a view to obtaining other expert opinion, and the result was so encouraging that a campaign to raise funds was about to be launched when the war started. For the time being it seemed as though the project would have to be abandoned. Long-term research work seemed out of place, and in any case labour difficulties, and war-time control of agriculture would have made the experiment very difficult to carry out except as a Government project, and it was not long before the immediate urgency of national survival inevitably ousted from people's minds all thoughts of future national well-being. Yet in one sense, the experiment was made all the more necessary by the war, since it seemed probable that the country's very existence might come to depend on its own agriculture. The Haughley Research Trustees... therefore decided that although it must be recognized as impossible, at that time, to raise sufficient funds to enable them to carry out the scheme in full, they would nevertheless endeavour to carry out the first two, and possibly three, stages of it, so that when, later, money became available, all preliminary work would have been done, and the experiment proper could begin at once.

In the summer of 1940 Miss Debenham became gravely ill, but before she died in the October of that year she knew that the work her vision and enterprise had started was to continue. The trustees had formed a Holding Company (Haughley Research Farms Limited) partly financed at Miss Debenham's express wish, with certain funds left by her to the Trust. Most of the directors... of the company were appointed from among the trustees and the balance of the required capital was found by the issue of shares, taken up, some by the trustees themselves, and the rest by outside sympathizers who believed in the importance of the work.

This company then became tenants of all but twenty acres (which was already let separately) of the 236 acres which was to have formed the experimental area of the Trust. I was appointed resident farm manager. The company's farming operations began on 1st November 1940. Now, two years later, the first two stages, as described above, have been to all intents and purposes completed. The seven miles of ditches have been cleaned, the land drained where necessary, the division of the farms made (see Fig. 6), and a four course rotation brought into operation in both halves...

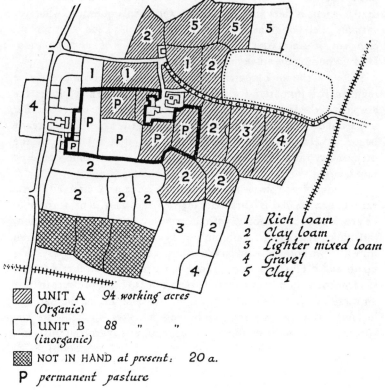

1 Rich loam
2 Clay loam
3 Lighter mixed loam
4 Gravel
5 Clay

UNIT A   *94 working acres*
(Organic)

UNIT B   88 "   "
(inorganic)

NOT IN HAND *at present:*   20 a.

P *permanent pasture*

Fig. 6 (1942 Division)

Now that the war situation allows the question of reconstruction, and post-war health and well-being, to come to the fore, this particular piece of research work is, in my view, and in that of many recognized authorities, one which the country can no longer afford to postpone, although slight changes in procedure may have to be made in view of the recently changed attitude to soil fertility. For example the idea, prevalent until a comparatively short time ago, that stockless farming could be undertaken without ill effects to the land, has been largely abandoned. The importance to soil fertility of mixed farming, as against specialization, has also become widely accepted. It might therefore be found desirable to rearrange the present divisions so as to include a third section to follow the practice of ordinary mixed farming, receiving both muck and artificials.... However this may be, the main issue will still remain to be determined. Is, or is not, the biological aspect of soil fertility in general, and fungal activity in particular, of vital importance to health? Since future correct soil management is dependent on an answer to this question, whatever variants of the original scheme are adopted, this issue must remain clear cut. It is a matter of urgency to all sections of the population. Delay in finding the answer may be disastrous.

So long as the work is carried out in a thorough and comprehensive manner, it is immaterial whether it is done at Haughley, under the auspices of the Haughley Research Trust, or elsewhere under another impartial body. The advantage in continuing the experiment already begun at Haughley, lies only in the fact that so much of the preparatory work having been done, much valuable time would be saved.

To those of you, who having read the evidence contained in the earlier chapters of this book share my view that, as citizens, we need to be provided once and for all with the true answer to this vital question, (affecting, as it may, not only our own health, but that of our children for whom we hope to build a better world), I have just this to say: 'It is up to you.' This is a democracy; you can demand that such an experiment be undertaken; it is in your power to bring pressure to bear on those to whom you have entrusted the spending of the national income - the money provided by you in taxes - to allocate the comparatively small sum that would be required to carry out this test.

(*The Living Soil*: 168-72)

HEALTH AND POST-WAR PLANNING

A short time ago Sir William Beveridge, broadcasting on his report for
social security, said that security against sickness was one of the two
factors of reconstruction that did not raise any big political issue, but
this would not be true if it were shown that the primary factor in the
prevention of sickness lay in soil management, for in that event, any
government, if it is to fulfil its duties of serving the common good,
would have to exercise a wide control, not only of land utilization and
management, but also over the whole range of subsidiary interests that
at present handle the production and distribution of the nation's food
supplies, as well as over the methods employed for disposing of
municipal wastes. Among those concerned in this wide range of
activities are some very powerful vested interests, and thus any
programme for the promotion of health that was based on soil fertility
would raise political issues of the first order.

I now ask you to face some of these issues squarely and see where they
lead us, because as citizens of a democracy, the matter will rest
ultimately in your own hands.

First and foremost would be the need for a complete revolution in
outlook. If the nation's health depends on the way its food is grown,
then agriculture must be looked upon as one of the health services, in
fact the primary health service...

Once agriculture came to be regarded as a health service the only
consideration in any matter concerning the production of food would
be: 'Is it necessary for the health of the people?' That of ordinary
economics would take a quite secondary place.

In deciding whether or not new medical clinics should be opened or
new schools built, we do not ask 'Will they pay?' but 'Are they needed?'
We regard them as necessary social services and as such the whole
community is expected, and in the main is willing, to pay for them.
The greatest social service of all is, or should be, the provision of the
people's food.

If fresh food is necessary to health in man and beast, then that food
must be provided not only from our own soil but as near as possible to
the sources of consumption... If this involves fewer imports and
consequent repercussions on exports, then it is industry that must be
readjusted to the needs of food.

If such readjustment involves decentralization of industry and the
reopening of local mills and slaughter-houses, then the health of the
nation is more important than any large combine. That the welfare of
the people as a whole must in future take precedence over all narrow

interests is a principle which has been accepted. This acceptance has been expressed by Lord Elton in the following words: 'What are the true objects of industry and commerce? Presumably they are the same as all activities within the state, the material and physical well-being of all its citizens.' [3]

If health demands adequate supplies of humus for the soil, then means must be found to provide it; if this involves, among other measures, the complete reorganization of existing sewage and town waste disposal plants, then local authorities must put the needs of the soil first. Actually the claims of the ratepayers coincide in this case with those of the soil, for this is a reform which would result in practically every case, in a reduction in rates... but even if it had the reverse effect, it would be better to receive health in return for rates, than to spend the money in a perpetuation of the present wasteful system.

If a big increase in livestock is another necessary measure for the preservation of soil fertility, then these must be kept, imports of meat being controlled to whatever extent is necessary. If this upsets the world of finance, and reduces dividends to investors whose capital is abroad, then still the nation's health is more important than dividends.

If further investigation should prove that certain chemicals injure the health-giving powers of the soil, then application of these chemicals must be forbidden. If this cuts across vested interests, then the nation's health is more important than any vested interest, and are we not fighting this war to end exploitation of all kinds? If, in order to serve the needs of the soil, and thereby serve every citizen of the land, instead of just a few, it becomes necessary to turn the whole organization of food production, preparation, and distribution, over to public ownership; if farmer, miller, butcher, baker - all of us concerned with food - have to be incorporated into one vast social service, decentralized, but nevertheless unified, equivalent to the proposed State Medical Service, then even so drastic a step as that must be taken, for *still* the nation's health comes first. These possibilities are an indication of what I mean by a revolution in outlook. Such a revolution may be the price of health, are we prepared to pay it?

If the purpose of the planners of the New Britain is genuinely to prevent in future the exploitation of the many by the few, then of all exploitations the most anti-social is surely exploitation of the national health. Thus the more the implications are considered, the more urgent does it become to provide a definite answer as to whether health *is* dependent on the activities of the soil population.

(*The Living Soil*: 173-5)

To sum up; first we must determine the factors governing healthy food, and having done so, no private interest must be allowed to prevent such food being made available to all sections of the public.

Secondly, our attitude must change towards refuse. It must no longer be considered as useless and objectionable rubbish, to be got rid of as cheaply as possible, but, on the contrary, as potential wealth.

Thirdly, we must educate our people to realize the interdependence of town and country, and that a nation's soil fertility is its most precious asset, and lastly, we must not overlook the implications of the definition of health arrived at as a result of the only scientific inquiry into the nature of Health in Man that has so far been made. [4]

The biologists who conducted this inquiry came to define health as 'mutual synthesis of organism and environment', implying that a 'self-sustaining ecological balance underlies health' and that 'unless both man and his environment are obeying the biological law of mutual synthesis, there can be no health'.

Such a definition means that everything implied by the word vitality is as much a property of the environment as of the organism, since a *two-way* flow between them must take place. Health, they claim, 'is not a state at all. It is a process'. [5] In other words, organism and environment, *both* living, must grow and develop together, *each* deriving its sustenance from the other. Thus to cultivate health one must first cultivate a vital environment.

In plant life, and to a lesser extent with animals, the organism's environment can be defined as the source of its food. Man's environment, however, 'is the source of his food *and* of his experience - mental, social, and spiritual'. [6] The biological law of mutual synthesis applies to his environment as a whole. The fruits of his experience enrich or impoverish the quality of the environment from which all his experience is drawn.

If one accepts this theory of mutual synthesis as a true definition of health - and these investigators offer cogent evidence in support of it - then it follows that any attempt to promote full health in the community must concern itself with maintaining the vitality of the *whole* of man's environment, from the soil in which his food is grown, to the 'soil' in which his spirit can expand. Success in such a venture cannot be achieved in a society dominated by the science of pathology, or the philosophy of materialism.

(*The Living Soil*: 191-2)

THE NEED FOR A NEW OUTLOOK

Man is born selfish, but in moments of great national crisis he is capable of sinking utterly his own interests for the good of the community. How often do we hear it said that if only we were prepared to put into the constructive arts of peace, the united effort in courage, sacrifice, labour and money, that we are prepared to exercise in the destructive art of war, we should be assured of our better world.

One reason why we can rise to such heights in war, seems to be that only when we are threatened by destruction from *outside* do we recognize that our own interests are ultimately bound up with those of our fellow countrymen, and thus a common danger brings unity of effort.

If it is a common danger that is needed to produce co-operation and unity, then the whole world shares a common danger in the disappearance of its soil. At present we are not awake to that danger. Our attitude to it is very reminiscent of our attitude to the Nazi menace in the pre-war and early war periods. It took the rape of Europe to make us fully alive to the Nazi menace. Must mankind wait until famine overruns a whole continent before he realizes the danger that threatens him from encroaching deserts? If so, our awakening will be an even ruder one than it was in 1940. Should this happen, peoples will be faced with two alternatives. Either there will be a scramble for what little remains of the habitable globe, or else once more, there will be a 'United Nations' - this time of the whole world - to work shoulder to shoulder to meet the common peril, in the labour and sweat of self-preservation.

(*The Living Soil*: 198-9)

When a new generation has arisen, taught to have a living faith in the Christian ideals, to value and conserve its soil, and to put service before comfort, then not only will our land have citizens worthy of it, but it will also be a land of happy contented people, for it is important to remember that happiness is a by-product. It is, moreover, a by-product of activity, not of ease. It cannot be found ready made. Nor can it be fashioned out of those things usually covered by the term 'a higher standard of living' - material comfort, more leisure, more money, more gadgets. Important as they are, these are static things. Happiness, which must not be confused with pleasure, results only from those activities which develop personality and character. It can be achieved in varying degree through the physical exertion of work or play, through the mental exertion of acquiring knowledge, through the spiritual exertion of creative effort, through the exercise of skill, through service; perhaps most of all through service. If we seek happiness as an end in itself, it will elude us; if we make service our aim, happiness will follow automatically. This is as true for a nation as for an individual. We shall never succeed in building a 'better and happier world' until we recognize it. When we do, we shall discover that we are on the high road to building a Christian society, for happiness through service is a creative force of unlimited power for good. In its atmosphere ecology - the most needed of all the sciences - could flourish, and could in time help us to become truly aware that everything in Heaven and earth is but part of a single whole. Then for the first time in many a century could we justifiably claim to be entering on an age of progress.

(*The Living Soil*: 201)

The Soil Association Ltd is now based at 86 Colston Street, Bristol, BS1 5BB, and published its Organic Manifesto *in February 1987.*

The guides to further reading at the end of chapters 5, on Howard, and 8, on Wrench and McCarrison, are both particularly relevant to the issues dealt with in The Living Soil.

References

1 Eve Balfour, 'The Soil Association', *Mother Earth: Journal of the Soil Association*, vol.6, no.3, July 1952, p.36.
2 Ibid., p.42.
3 *St. George or the Dragon* (Collins, 1940).
4 *The Peckham Experiment*, Pearse and Crocker (Allen and Unwin, 1943).
5 Ibid.
6 Ibid.

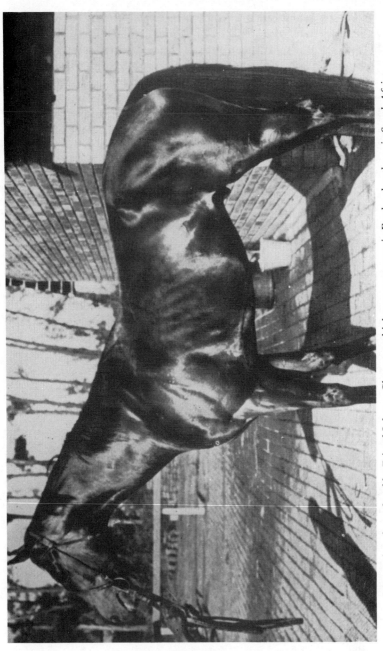

Matronic: a horse bred by Friend Sykes at Chantry, which won two races in England and two in South Africa

7

Humus Farming and Animal Breeding

Friend Sykes
(1888-1965)

Friend Sykes was a distinguished breeder of livestock and racehorses who bought the Chantry estate, near Andover, in 1936. It was poor land on the eastern escarpment of Salisbury Plain, being sold for only £4 per acre, but Sykes wanted the challenge of transforming its capacity for fertility without the use of artificials. With the support and encouragement of Sir Albert Howard he made Chantry a showpiece for the methods of humus farming, supplies of his organically-grown wheat being bought by, among other well-known figures, J.B. Priestley and Yehudi Menuhin. He was a founder member of the Soil Association, but not himself a practical farmer; essentially he was a man of ideas with a gift for communicating them. [1]

The passages which follow concentrate mainly on the economic aspects of farming, and on the breeding of animals; the latter serving to illustrate Sykes' belief that '50 per cent of the pedigree goes in at the mouth'. [2] *They are all taken from* Food, Farming and the Future *(London, Faber, 1951).*

ISSUES OF ECONOMICS

During the last fifty years, chemical plants for the production of sulphuric acid, together with the tonnage actually produced each year, have increased beyond belief. The country thus has to face the problem of disposing in peacetime of the accumulations of this product which is so essential for our possible wartime needs. The resourcefulness of the chemist has suggested, and manufacturers have adopted, the utilization of this sulphuric acid for the making of sulphate of ammonia and superphosphate. The sale of these fertilizers to the farmer, in huge quantities, has therefore become a prime object which *appears* to coincide with national necessity. This, doubtless, is one explanation for the flood of persuasive (and largely effective) propaganda put out by the manufacturers and government departments alike. The stuff was there, and the farmer had to be talked into buying it.

Quite apart, however, from anything that I may have said or written on the subject, discriminating farmers have observed that these fertilizers are by no means an unadulterated blessing. Practical tests conducted by myself, and many others, indicate that they make the crops or herbage to which they are applied unpalatable to livestock. If, for instance, stock are turned into a ten-acre field, five acres of which have been composted and the other five dressed with four hundredweight to the acre of sulphate of ammonia and superphosphate, they will show a marked preference for the composted portion and cannot be persuaded to touch the other unless forced to do so by hunger. Even then, they will eat the composted herbage right down to the crowns of the plants before they will resort to the artificially-dressed portion.

It has always been my contention that, in determining the merits of our husbandry, we should first consult the animal and carefully observe its preference. Having done this for many years, I have never, in a single instance, found stock show preference for grassland treated with artificials, especially with those manufactured by the use of sulphuric acid. If it is a reasonable deduction that whatever makes herbage unpalatable to stock is probably undesirable as a food and a life-sustainer, then the farmer, if he is wise, will sooner or later decline to use it.

(Food: 25-6)

True economy, basically conceived, is the accumulation of real wealth. All real wealth comes from the farmlands, the forests and the mines. There is no other wealth provided by nature. The only part that man performs in this scheme of things is to make use of the provision of nature in its many forms. These need to be organized and arranged equitably for the benefit of the whole community. There has never yet been created a system of economics that achieved this; but because we have failed so frequently, and booms and slumps have occurred so painfully often, there is no reason why we should not continue to strive for a better state of affairs.

It is here that I would call attention to the operation of nature herself. Her mineral deposits are a constant factor, but the growth of her agricultural lands and her forests is not. Here we are dealing with a living quantity. Here, we have production and reproduction. We are dealing with life, and life alone should be the basis of a controlled economy. Life creates life, and so long as the integrity of the cycle is maintained by the succession of birth, growth, maturity, death and decay, so that out of decay springs the resurrection of life, life can go on to the end of the world.

It is here that a basis of true economy can be found. We have the production of our farm crops and our grasslands and our forests. These are all living growths, and if these are adequately manured and fed we can create fertility; we can create life; we can reinforce fertility with renewed vigour; we can reinforce the stamina of life by providing food grown on fertile land. A virile soil is the birthright of the nation, and herein lies the epitome of a sound and practical economy.

No economy can be based upon a gold-standard, or a printing-press, or a controlled issue of paper pound notes. These are only the means by which trade and business can be the more easily negotiated, and have nothing to do with the basic principles of political economy. In every case, these devices need to be backed by goods or commodities of true value in terms of living; otherwise the paper note is useless, for it represents nothing and will buy nothing. But life can reproduce life, and can add to the world's potentialities, provided always that the cycle of life is adequately nurtured.

This brings us back to the basic theme which underlies this book, and to the criticism of present policy which should be replaced by a more enlightened system of organic husbandry. We seek to enlarge and increase our knowledge of organic life in all its aspects, and to learn how, with better attention, the land will not only yield more, but will supply its own micro-organic and bacterial life in increasing numbers. These organisms need to be increased if the minerals of the soil are to be made available for our use and living, but they cannot be increased or maintained in good health unless they are adequately fed with supplies of humus, provided by intelligent farming. In this way, more food will be made available; land will rise in fertility; disease will diminish; the peace of the world can be ensured, for contentment will follow the provision of adequate food.

Is it not possible for economists to try to understand that production is possible only so long as it is based on *re*production? The only instrument by which *re*production can be obtained is the *living* species. The machine *cannot* reproduce. It does not make two machines or fifty machines. It is only a drainpipe for production so long as it is fed by sufficient raw materials which it can transform into things of everyday usefulness. Life *can* produce, for it alone has the inherent capacity for *re*production.

Herein lies the true economy, for out of life alone can life be created, and only through the operation of life can all the material assets of the world be made available to man.

(*Food*: 72-4)

REGENERATION OF SEED BY HUMUS

A few years ago I was approached by an eminent firm of seedsmen with the following proposition:

'One of the most valuable strains of perennial ryegrass is Aberystwyth S.24. This grass is a special strain of great productivity. The seed for it has been grown for many years in the north of Ireland. The growers in that region have applied sulphate of ammonia in such heavy dressings that the seed has altered its character considerably. Whereas they used to harvest half a ton of seed to the acre, with a 97 per cent germination in fourteen days, and would add to this two tons of hay per acre, now, after several years of this forcing treatment, they have reduced the germination to about 55 per cent, and the hay yield has fallen to as low as fifteen hundredweights to the acre. With your organic methods of farming, we are wondering whether it would be possible for you to regenerate this seed, and to grow a large area, so proving the value of your theories.'

After some consideration, I agreed to try this experiment and promised to grow a hundred acres of this ryegrass for seed. Accordingly, it was sown. The first year, the crop did not come at all well. We cut and dropped it. The second growth was rather more pleasing, and this was heavily grazed with cattle. Their dung and urine fell on the previously dropped crop, and made a sheet of humus-forming material. During the winter, this sheet of humus decomposed, and in the second year we had the most successful crop of ryegrass that I have ever seen. The growth was phenomenal, and the quantity to the acre very unusual. We harvested this crop for seed, and in the best areas recovered fully half a ton of seed to the acre and two tons of hay. In due course, the seed was tested, and the results of the test showed 89 per cent germination in three days, and 98 per cent in fourteen days. This really startling change from low-germinating seed was achieved within two years, and is unmistakable evidence of the virility which an all-organic soil can produce.

We have tested our own seeds again and yet again in grass, chicory and cereal crops, as well as clovers; and we have never found any seed anywhere, from any seedsmen, which compares in germinating qualities and general vitality with that which we produce ourselves.

(*Food*: 123-4)

THE COSTS OF FARMING

I receive letters regularly from people who would return to the land. It might not be out of place to give at least one illustration of what may have to be faced by anyone who wishes to go farming. The case I propose to quote is one that can be repeated many times in my own knowledge.

I bought a property for clients, and appointed the staff. Similarly livestock and implements were subsequently accumulated. The area of the farm was about two hundred acres, and the price was in the neighbourhood of £10,000. Negotiations were difficult because competition was keen. In its then condition the farm had little to recommend it, especially judging from a critical pre-war standard. It consisted of about five to nine inches of sandy loam, overlying downlands of chalk. In its then condition it could not be described in other words than being practically derelict. The amount of produce that was cashed out of that farm was very low. It could not have been otherwise. The farm buildings were in considerable disrepair. The two cottages were not habitable and had to be repaired - almost rebuilt. The farmhouse itself needed a great deal of attention and had to receive its share of maintenance work and rebuilding. Three fields totalling fifty acres in all shared their water supplies from two troughs and water had to be taken to every other field on the farm. The farm was situated in the centre of a district where thousands of rabbits abounded. The fencing was not stock-proof and had to be renewed in its entirety everywhere, and we had to rabbit-wire the whole boundary.

When we came to the farm-land itself - that piece of material out of which the farmer has not only to make his living, but to provide food for a hungry nation - the picture was grim. There was little growing anywhere: and most of what was growing was couch. On many fields there was almost nothing to be seen.

It may well be asked, why start on a farm which was so seriously out of condition as this one certainly was? There are many answers to the question. In the first place, my client wished to be in that particular district, and there was no other property then available. From many other points of view, his family also wished to reside there.

With the aid of a resourceful architect, we were able to save the house itself from demolition. It was pulled about considerably and, after a great deal of effort, was made a very habitable and practical farmhouse, fit for anyone to live in. The cottages were repaired and partly rebuilt; additional housing had to be bought in the neighbourhood. As stated before, the entire property was fenced with wire and rabbit fencing. This was inevitably costly; but unless it was done, no farmer could ever hope to grow crops against the ravages of such a rabbit population. Internal fences had to be renewed; farm buildings were repaired or rebuilt. We set about the cultivation of the land and for a whole season had no livestock on the property. Our energies were devoted to cultivating again, and again, and yet again. We subsoiled, and after six months of hard and diligent work, we were able to apply half a ton of slag to the acre... by the end of June; to sow a crop of mustard on 125 acres of land; to plough in that mustard in about five or six weeks; and to sow two bushels to the acre of rye, accompanied by

5 lb. cocksfoot	1 lb. wild white clover
5 lb. perennial ryegrass	3 lb. late-flowering red clover
1 lb. Italian ryegrass	1 lb. alsike
3 lb. timothy	3 lb. lucerne
1 lb. crested dogstail	2 lb. American sweet clover
½ lb. rough-stalked meadow grass	10 lb. Hampshire common sainfoin
2 lb. chicory	

The remaining seventy-five acres had been put into spring corn.

The cultivations during that hot, dry summer killed the couch and turned it into humus. The phosphatic dressing in the slag secured a desirable take of plant, and we soon had evidence of a promising abundance of food. The necessity to buy livestock arose. Accordingly we bought thirty attested Ayrshires, dehorned, bred from thousand-gallon dams, with over 4 per cent butter-fat. These calved down. They were milked in a portable milking-bail adjoining an open stockyard, where we intended they should winter. The growth of the crops was considerable, and on the 6th of the following March we were actually grazing the rye.

There was ample food to keep the stock going, and the necessity arose to buy another twenty similar Ayrshires.

The figures available for one twenty-six-acre field show that between 6th March and 23rd September £1,197 worth of milk was exported, and twenty tons of hay at £10 per ton was made, while twenty growing Ayrshire yearlings were grazed 'on and off'. This is £54 per acre, with the grazing stock thrown in for nothing. This particular field previously was utterly unproductive and was regarded as the problem field of the farm.

What was the total cost of these farming operations up to date? By the time that everything was completed - the original cost of the farm; the restoration of farmhouse and cottages; the buying of additional accommodation; the rebuilding of farm buildings; the provision of water supplies; the erection of rabbit-proof fences, the purchase of live and dead stock, and the rest - no less than £35,000 of capital had been expended. In the first full year of operations on the farm it is entirely self-supporting, with home-grown food providing sustenance for forty-five to fifty milking cattle and their followers - some eighty to ninety animals in all. We are in no way yet at the peak of production; as the fertility rises the output will be further augmented. There may be - there probably will be - additional labour employed. Little objection can be taken to the employment of labour where every labourer is producing usefully more than his cost. I am not one of those economists who believe in the sacking of men as the only effective method by which costs may be reduced. I seek rather to increase output and thus employ more people. This has been my farming policy over a long time; and according to my experience it is sound and profitable.

Another recent example is a six-hundred-acre farm which cost £35,000. It was moderately well-equipped, but needed further capital expenditure to make it an efficient instrument of production. Its fertility was moderate. Under previous occupation, it may have been punished somewhat by the application of artifical fertilizers. The new owner was inevitably faced with a fertility-building-up process. The farmhouse needed expenditure. There were nine cottages, every one of which might have been demolished, if further more modern accommodation could have been made immediately available. There was no other accommodation available, and so they had to receive a measure of temporary renovation. The farm buildings called for repair. They were useful so far as they went, but they were out-of-date, and some approached a worn-out condition. Only about one-third of the farm was watered. Pipelines had to be laid for the remainder. Fencing was little in evidence, in most of the farm non-existent. New fencing had to be provided. Rabbits, again, existed in thousands on the adjoining estates. Rabbit-wire had to be bought and erected. Altogether, additional capital outlay was needed approximating to £15,000; and in round sums the figures then read:

	£
Cost of Farm	35,000
Rebuilding, fencing, water supplies, etc.	15,000
Live and dead stock, and working capital	30,000
	£80,000

These two farms, which are taken from a large list of similar experiences, are typical. Are there not certain lessons here for the reader to learn and to assimilate in all intensity? The first is that it does cost a lot of money to go farming in these days. The second is that unless there is a well-thought-out farming plan it is not likely that any farm can be made to pay.

Not every farm in England is a profit-making institution. It is important that a farm should be bought which, although perhaps derelict when acquired, has possibilities when reorganized, and when fertility-creation, rather than fertility-extraction, becomes the objective.

A non-fertile farm will bring everyone to bankruptcy. Only fertile land can produce prosperity. All land can be made fertile if farmed with humus; but even so, one needs good planning, good management, and the understanding of a highly technical, complicated job which, sad to say, few farmers possess. If, indeed, the standard of technique in farming is low, it will be evident, even to the uninitiated, what a serious gamble it will be to go farming without knowledge or the necessary skill and direction.

In the course of forty years' farming and professional life I have seen industrial magnates come into farming with determination to show the farming community what can be done with a farm, if only an industrial genius brings his profound intelligence to bear upon the simplicity of a farmer's problems. I have seen these same great men, one after the other, approach the farming altar, not with the humility that is called for, but with the lofty superiority that so often accompanies industrial success. I could name some of the most eminent people who have received a chastisement at the hands of the land which would make good and startling reading. They come in like a lion; they go out like a lamb, and with their tails well down, sometimes leaving behind tens of thousands of pounds. I know of no business anywhere in the world which calls for a higher standard of knowledge than does farming. A farm well-planned and efficiently managed is profit-earning. But to farm with meagre knowledge a farm which is badly-designed and ill-conceived is a problem calculated to break the stoutest heart.

This chapter, therefore, may be regarded as a word of encouragement to those determined to go farming, but also as a word of warning to all to proceed cautiously. It is no service to farming for people to come into it and lose money; they go out and give farming a bad name. It is preferable that people of the right sort should come into farming, make a job of it, and stay in it for all time.

Personally, I welcome the acquisition of some of these alert industrial brains by our farming community. I give them every word of encouragement so long as they are made of the right stuff. Far too many of that class left the farms during the days of industrial prosperity. I seek only that they should be reintroduced to the land of their birth with the fullest possible understanding of the magnitude and responsibilities of the task they may wish to reassume.

I will conclude this chapter with a brief answer to another economic question that I am frequently asked, namely the present and future costs of estate management. The figures which I will give refer to the typical rural property, no matter whether it is held by a large investment corporation which specializes in agricultural land ownership, or a privately-owned estate such as we are all familiar with in the older properties, some of which have been unfortunately broken up because of death duties.

I have gone into costs and expenses fairly thoroughly, and I am satisfied that there is little land in this country which costs much less than £2 per acre per annum for general estate management costs. If, therefore, a company or private owner wishes to let a farm, they cannot make any profit for themselves unless they charge a minimum of 50s. per acre per annum by way of rent. Compared with pre-war times, this figure is a considerable rise; but it must be remembered that the pound has a value far less than it had in pre-war days, and that the costs are comparable to the devaluation of the pound itself.

I mention this important economic fact because, whether one owns one's farm or rents it, it is right and proper to put down, as an annual charge for simple management costs alone, a figure that approximates to a minimum of 40s. per acre per annum, and it might be safer for book-keeping and accountancy purposes to reckon on 60s. per acre.

An item of interest that may well be added to this chapter is the following story.

A farm of reputation, which is under the technical guidance and direction of a famous agricultural college, has had the following experience.

In a field where hops had been grown for a number of years, it was decided to grub the plants and bring the land back to grass. Accordingly it was put into a ley. When the field was ready to graze, the shepherd was instructed to put his ewes into it. He was an old and wise man, with a long experience of his calling. He told the professors, 'If you put sheep into new grass after hops, the sheep will die.' In incredulous surprise, the professorial staff enquired, 'Why?' The shepherd, in his delightful simplicity, replied, 'I do not know why! I only know that sheep will die if they are grazed on grass which is grown immediately after hops.' The professors waved aside the shepherd's advice, and he was peremptorily told to put the sheep on the new ley. Twenty-four hours later thirty-six sheep were found dead, and the others were hastily removed. Motor lorries were running round that farm, even in the dead of night, collecting carcases which had fallen as a result of having grazed that field. Local gossip says that the sheep died from nitrate-poisoning. I do not pretend to know.

The moral I wish to convey from the recital of this story is simply this - that much of the knowledge which is often obtainable from very old servants of the land ought to be received with respect by all, even by the most advanced scientists who ever looked through a test-tube. These old men, very inarticulate at times, and sometimes unable to give good reasons for many acts of livestock husbandry which they perform, nevertheless often have a degree of wisdom, born of experience, that does not always become the possession of the scientist. We need a combination of science and practice; and we older farmers, who can look back over a long life associated with the soil, yearn to see the day when the practical farmer might be more scientific, and the scientist a little more practical.

(*Food*: 173-80)

THE DANGERS OF INDUSTRIAL METHODS

This chapter can fittingly be closed with an account of a conversation I had, a year or two ago, with an eminent engineer who is engaged in the designing and manufacture of agricultural tractors and implements. He is a man of outstanding ability, very enthusiastic about his work. Without giving offence to either his reputation or his achievements, I would say that he is imbued with the importance of his own mission in the world's economy. Certainly he gave me the impression that he considered he was making a very important contribution to the better structure of the world by his inventions and manufactures. He is, of course, a business man, seeking his due measure of profit as a result of his initiative and enterprise. But it was his imagined mission, and the important services he was rendering to mankind by making tractors and implements, and the number in which he is making them, that gave me occasion to enter into a discussion with him one day, in a most friendly spirit. I suggested that, instead of his being regarded as one of the world's great benefactors, through having invented and made so much agricultural machinery, he might be looked upon by the historians of the future as one of the greatest curses that had ever visited the earth.

The suggestion took his breath away. He had never for one moment considered the possibility of his doing other than serving mankind to the uttermost. But when I pointed out that his machinery provided more efficient methods by which fertility could be *extracted*, rather than fertility *created*, he began to see the force of my arguments and to realize, perhaps for the first time, that a tractor and all the equipment associated with it is not necessarily one of the world's greatest servants. In other words, unless humus farming, with all the complete understanding that goes with it, is practised side by side with the increasing use of the tractor in every country, there cannot be any other end to the soil than its complete exploitation and destruction.

It is a sad fact to have to record that, so far as concerns England, which claims to be the most highly mechanized country in the world's agriculture, that faithful servant, the horse, is threatened with extinction. At the time I now write (1950), it is predicted that the heavy horse, so commonplace in our farming landscapes for generations, promises to disappear within three, four or five years from now. This animal, which has served man so well and so faithfully, is no longer capable of working at the speed and with the pressure that modern life and farming require; and so the whole programme of farming implements and appointments has been redesigned for complete mechanization, eliminating the horse utterly.

It must be remembered that the horse did leave some fertility behind. It is true that he needed land upon which to grow the corn and hay that he consumed; but he did an efficient job. Because he was slower, it was actually for the most part better done. Ploughing was shallower, and fertility was better maintained. The tractor, with its speed, inevitably ploughs more deeply, and it certainly leaves no manure behind it for re-fertilization.

I am sufficiently sentimental and old-fashioned to deplore the passing of the horse; and when, if ever, the world runs short of oil supplies, I sometimes wonder if the generations then living will view with complacency the decision the present regime has taken in eliminating the horse. It will then be too late to retrace our steps, and our descendants may have to go back to the period before the horse, when the ox was the principal beast of burden, of the plough-team, and the heavy worker on the land, as it is in Portugal to-day.

(*Food*: 193-4)

Another interesting consultation comes from Sweden. For a very long time a large farming company, controlling over seven hundred thousand acres of land, have applied chemical fertilizers according to the modern orthodox teaching. After having read *Humus and the Farmer*, they made a special journey to Chantry to study our methods. Here they found evidence supporting all the claims which that book records. They, too, have decided to make humus farming the rule of their husbandry for the future; for they have been overtaken by almost every kind of disease in their livestock - sterility, barrenness, mastitis,

Johne's Disease, contagious abortion, tuberculosis, and the rest; and so insistent is the accumulation of these diseases, which veterinary science cannot explain, that they have at long last come to the conclusion that it is in the organic farming of the soil that their salvation lies.

These are world-wide indications of what is taking place as the result of chemical warfare in farming. Sir Stanton Hicks said, in his Sanderson Wells Lecture, that it has been estimated there are over forty tons of living organisms per acre, exclusive of earthworms and grubs. We know that the salts of superphosphate and sulphate of ammonia will poison the earthworm. We know equally well that if we, as another representation of living specie, were to swallow these salts ourselves, we should be lucky if we survived. Is it not fair to assume that this forty tons per acre of living micro-organic life and fungi similarly display a resentment to the application of dead salts which, if not thoroughly poisonous, cannot do them any good? The soil was made a living soil, and the life was introduced to the earth for functions to be performed. What right has man to destroy or impair that life, even if he might increase his farm cropping by so doing? But does he?

Is this good farming? The results are not impressive.

(Food: 206-7)

ANIMAL BREEDING

The pastures where my race-horses are reared are grazed by four different classes of livestock. Poultry find their place upon it, sheep, cattle, and, last of all, the horses. While the cream of the paddocks is retained for the horses, the number of horses kept is small. There would appear to be a bacterial balance in nature which stock of mixed species provide, and which keeps the various classes of stock in the enjoyment of a superlative standard of health. Contagious abortion, tuberculosis, Johne's disease, mastitis, and the other main troubles that can beset the livestock breeder, will be found to disappear entirely if a mixed system of husbandry is followed, rather than any specialized system of farming. There is nothing which cries out so loudly for condemnation as the small specialized stud farms. These exist in numbers all round Newmarket and in many parts of England. Their areas are often from forty to one hundred acres. Only too often are they literally saturated with a plethora of horse-stock; and although bullocks are sometimes run in the paddocks, there is no doubt about it, the horse population is far in excess of the land available.

The Equine Research Station of Newmarket is devoting immense scientific talent to the causes of many diseases, like strongyle-worm, ascaris-worm, and many other troubles to which the thoroughbred is heir. I do not wish to make any adverse comment on either the contemplated programme or the work that is being actually carried out, but I am going to make one interesting statement.

Last October, at the Sales, I had two fillies for sale, the property of Chute Farms, Ltd. One of the leading veterinary surgeons of the Equine Research Station at Newmarket was taken by a professional friend, an Irish vet, and he spent quite a long time looking over a filly, now known as Amy Leigh and in training with Mr. Fred Armstrong. This veterinary surgeon told me that he had never seen a more perfect or healthier specimen of thoroughbred in all his experience, and he said, 'Frankly, Mr. Sykes, how have you produced such a lovely animal? I am interested to know.' I told him it was not the product of internal dosings for parasitic worms. In fact, I am not at all sure whether this animal ever had any dosing of that kind. The many reports we had taken of examinations of her droppings all testified to the fact that no evidence was found of either strongyle-or ascaris-worms. My answer to this enquiry was 'Good farming'.

These two fillies were reared in company with cattle, sheep, and poultry on the chalk downs of Wiltshire, eight hundred feet above sea-level, where acts of goodhusbandry are the order of the day. We grow a four-year ley, and this consists, as my books written on the subject describe, of a mixture of grasses, leguminous plants and deep-rooting growths by which five, ten, or possibly fifteen feet of soil are explored by these botanical specimens in search of the minerals which they need. The subsoil is limestone (calcium carbonate) and into this the feelers from all these plants penetrate, and through their stems and leaves the deep-seated minerals collected pass into circulation in the top soils of our lands through the droppings of the animals and their urine. In this way, minerals and trace elements are increasingly added to the surface fertility of our lands. The four different classes of stock which get their living from our fields all add their own bacterial contribution to the general balance of living organisms which go to make a living soil.

The management of our fields is important. The first year we entirely graze; the second and third years the fields are hayed and grazed; and the fourth year entirely grazed. Such is the volume of organic matter which is introduced to our pastures by this management that we find it absolutely imperative that the fields be ploughed at the end of the four-year term and, without the use of any artificial fertilizers whatever, we then subject that land to an arable period of treatment, when cereal crops consisting of wheat, oats and barley are grown. In the fourth year of the arable break we devote the early spring to a period of summer tillage. This cleans the land of noxious weeds and stoloniferous growths like couch, and about the first week in June we sow twenty pounds of mustard to the acre. At the end of July the mustard is about two feet high. This green crop is cultivated into the top two inches of soil with a special implement, known as a Rotavator, making a mulch of the green material into the top two or three inches. About 1st August we sow two bushels to the acre of rye, together with the complicated seeds mixture recorded in *Humus and the Farmer*.

Within six to eight weeks, such is the growth that it is necessary to graze this sward heavily, and again before Christmas. The growth in the early spring is phenomenal. In the second or third week in March, even at this altitude above sea-level, the sward is ready to graze, and so we go on for the four years under grass; making a total rotation of eight years.

What has this done? Our stud of race-horses is very small now - only seven mares - and it is not part of my intention to boast about what we have done. We bred Statesman, who ran third in the Derby, and His Reverence, who won eight important races (although these two horses were not produced at Chantry). Since we came to Chantry, from the progeny of one mare, Dail (dam of Statesman and five other winners) we have bred our present stud of seven brood mares. They have all been entirely reared on the produce grown on this farm. Every animal bred and raced has won races, with the exception of three, all of which have been placed. One day, perhaps, we may have the good fortune to breed a Classic winner - that remains to be seen. But with access only to such stallions as we have found it possible to obtain nominations to (never stallions in the first flight) we have produced Chanter; one of the best milers of his year, who won eight races and was placed many times, invariably carrying top weight; Eastern View, who won sixteen races; Robin O'Chantry, winner of fourteen races and a champion hurdler; Matronic, the winner of the Johannesburg Christmas Handicap of £6,000 in 1949 and ran third in the Durban July

Handicap of £10,000 (1950), beaten only by one and three-quarter lengths, after having won two useful races in England before he was exported; Alirosa that won two races of £800; Amigo; Harum-Scarum; Madam Grey; Pheronica; Clyno; Milnchester; Hunza, etc. - these results are submitted with modesty. They are not in themselves startling; but they are results worthy of examination in so far as they are produced more from good food and good farming than from aristrocratic breeding, so far as the sires are concerned, and, above all, note should be made that there are no duds. This is the whole point of this article. However important the lineage may be, it is of little avail unless it is accompanied by all the acts associated with good food production that such aristrocratic breeding is entitled to.

But the horses are not the whole story. We have bred a herd of a hundred and sixty Guernsey cattle, also a herd of thirty Galloway beef-cattle. They are free from disease. They are, near enough, 100 per cent regular breeders. Barrenness is nearly unknown. This in itself is a sign of health. For some time now, our dairy herd has been under the scientific surveillance of a well-known public independent authority, and whilst their complete investigations cannot yet be made known, some of their findings can be briefly stated.

They discover that our milk contains over 20 per cent more protein than the average for the country. Our butter-fat is phenomenally high, whilst the non-fatty-solids (most important of all) is higher still than the average. Analysis of all our foods shews a percentage of protein seldom met with, and every food a *whole* food and in perfect balance. They describe their investigations as startling and of far-reaching scientific value, which may result in widespread agricultural reform.

Now all this is plain, simple, unassailable evidence of good farming, which produces life-sustaining food that really sustains life and builds robust stock which are disease-resistant.

It is my opinion that if man and beast were adequately fed on truly life-sustaining foods, neither would have much need of medical or veterinary assistance to keep them in good health. Surely there is something wrong with our system of farming (which produces the foods upon which we live) if we need all the artifical aids invented by these two eminent professions to keep us going. It is not so much a reflection on the inability of these two professions that disease still defies us, but rather that our farming is thoroughly bad in its fundamentals. In my respectful submission as a farmer over a long period of time, it is to farming that we should look if we would regenerate the well-being of either livestock or mankind. Furthermore, small specialist studs are a mistake, and a menace to bloodstock.

(*Food*: 232-6)

A description of Chantry during its days as a showpiece can be found in H.J. Massingham's The Wisdom of the Fields *(London, Collins, 1945, pp. 173-6).*

The Discipline of Peace *by K.E. Barlow (London, Faber, 1942) contains a chapter on the place of animals in the pattern of nature.*

Other books on humus farming which would serve as good introductions to the problems and successes of this approach are Organic Farming *by Hugh Corley (London, Faber, 1957);* Fertility Farming *by Newman Turner (London, Faber, 1951); and* The Farming Ladder *by G. Henderson (London, Faber, 1944).*

References

1   I am indebted to Mrs Julia Sykes, wife of Friend Sykes' godson Michael, for the above information.
2   *Humus and the Farmer* (London, Faber, 1946), p.2.

Major-General Sir Robert McCarrison

8

Healthy Soil and a Whole Diet

G.T. Wrench and Sir Robert McCarrison
(d. 1954)   (1878 - 1960)

Dr Guy Theodore Wrench was granted full registration with the General Medical Council in 1902, and subsequently spent time in India. His book, The Wheel of Health, (London, C.W. Daniel, 1938; New York, Schocken Books, 1972) deals with the relation between methods of cultivation, diet, and human nutrition, and gives a detailed account of the experiments on diet undertaken in India by Robert - later Major-General Sir Robert - McCarrison.

McCarrison joined the Indian Medical Service in 1901 and soon began to investigate the incidence of goitre, cretinism, and deficiency diseases - researches for which he was to achieve international recognition, as well as the First Class Kaiser-i-Hind Gold Medal for public service in India. He founded the Nutrition Research Laboratories at Coonoor and was their first Director, ensuring that the laboratory investigations were combined with field observation. McCarrison won innumerable prizes for his work, and from 1945 to 1955 was Director of Post-Graduate Medical Education at Oxford. His interest in nutrition stemmed from his encounter with the remarkably healthy Hunza tribesmen of the North-West Frontier. Wrench's book tells the story of this encounter and the research which followed it, and goes on to deal with the wider implications of that research.

THE HUNZA PEOPLE

Hunza... is in the main a stretch of intense cultivation, extending some seven to eight miles along the northern bank of the Hunza river. It is a place of brilliant beauty. Facing it to the south is the great white cloud of Rakaposhi, 25,550 feet high, rising some 18,000 feet above the valley itself and dominating it, though on a vaster scale, as Mont Blanc dominates the valley of Chamonix. Between the valley and the snows are huge barren precipices, except where the slopes allow of terraced vegetation. These terraces in summer are bands of brilliant green or golden corn from the river bank almost up to the verge of the snows. In the autumn the green of the abundant fruit trees change [sic] to scarlet and gold and vermilion and even bright pink, so that Mr. Skrine in *Chinese Central Asia* (1926), on his way through Hunza, wonders that no artist has made his name "world-famous" by transferring to his canvas something of the incomparable brilliancy of the multi-coloured valley, with its tremendous frame of grim, rocky walls, above which are the immeasurable snows.

Here dwell the Hunza, whose numbers Major Biddulph in *Tribes of the Hindoo Koosh* (1880) roughly calculated as 6,000 people, but who have, since the census was instituted about 1911, it seems increased, to their detriment, to 14,000.

Their occupation has been and is agricultural, but to this they added, before coming under the British suzerainty, a little banditry. They were not cruel; indeed, they seem to have regarded the looting of fat Turkis on their way to Mecca or the Khergiz of the Pamirs in part as a sport. But it was a sport that often ended in failure and a long journey home without food.

As brigands they showed their wonderful powers of endurance, travelling for miles along cruel precipices and crossing turbulent rivers at a speed none other could accomplish. They were, of course, much feared, and in 1891, Colonel Durand led an expedition to stop their practices. It seems that they were not unwilling to stop. Durand (*The Making of a Frontier*, 1894) discovered that they did not care to neglect their fields for banditry. Agriculture was their real desire, and true agriculturists are not military. "As brigands," says Durand, "they appear to have acted always on the orders of their chief, and the admirable culture of their ground, the immense and persistent labour spent on their irrigation channels, and on the retaining walls of their terraced fields," showed him clearly where their interests as a people lay.

Since brigandage has had to be abandoned as an extra source of income by the chiefs, its place has been taken by the profit received from the hire of porterage by travellers and mountaineers. The Hunza are quite exceptional porters. All mountaineers are agreed on this point. Two quotations from Volume 71 (1928) of the Journal of the Royal Geographical Society are examples of the general testimony.

General Bruce, of Mount Everest fame, recounted in 1928 at the Royal Geographical Society, how, in 1894, he had to call up the one-time Hunza Rifles; how they left their flocks away up in the mountains, collected their kit, and "went to Gilgit in one march of sixty-five miles of very bad country indeed... I found the Hunza people most charming and perfectly companionable. They are as active as any people can possibly be... and as slab climbers nobody in the world can beat the Hunza men. For very hard work in the mountains, if we had a trained body, they would not prove inferior to our best Sherpa porters," who have so nobly assisted our Everest climbers almost to the top of the world, but not quite.

The second testimony is that of Captain C.Y. Morris, who explored the Hunza side valleys and glaciers in 1927. "These men were with us for just on two months," he said at the same meeting of the Royal Geographical Society in 1928. "During this time they were continuously on the move and over what is probably some of the worst country in the world for laden men. Always ready to turn their hand to anything, they were, I think, the most cheerful and willing set of men with whom I have ever travelled... At the worst part of all we halted in order to help the porters across. They disdained our proffered assistance, however, and came over, climbing like cats, and with never a murmur at the hardships of this day's work."

If there is anything to try the nerves in these parts and give the equivalent of neurasthenia, it must be the danger and the exhausting work of porterage. Other porters give up, as the readers of the tales of recent expeditions... know. Not so the Hunza. They know neither the fear nor the weariness which spoils the will.

Far from being nervous or morose, nearly every visitor testifies to their freedom from quarrels and exceptional cheerfulness. This cheerfulness, one notes, seems to be a characteristic of the little Tibetans of Baltistan, Tibetans, Chinese, Koreans, and Japanese, all of whom, we shall see, follow certain similar principles of agriculture.

The Hunza originally were brought into contact with the British power owing to their interference with trade, which was by the same British converted from a hindrance to an assistance. But no people, of course, can exist upon banditry or porterage. "Far from being mere robber tribes," wrote Biddulph in 1880, of the Hunza, "they are settled agricultural communities."

Here also, as might be expected, they excel. They are admirable cultivators, far famed as such and "conspicuously ahead of all their neighbours in brain and sinew," stated Schomberg. Their big irrigation conduit, the Berber, is "famous everywhere in Central Asia."

They are also what really follows from being capable agriculturalists, namely, good craftsmen. Amongst the peoples of the Agency not only are they "as tillers of the soil quite in a class apart," writes Schomberg, "they alone - and this always strikes me as truly remarkable - are good craftsmen. As carpenters and masons, as gunsmiths, ironworkers, or even as goldsmiths, as engineers for roads, bridges or canals, the Hunza men are outstanding."

Lastly, as Mr. C.P. Skrine notes in *Chinese Central Asia* (1926), as dancers "they are incomparably finer than the well-known Cuttack dancing of the North-West Frontier."

As to food, owing to their excellent agriculture they have enough to eat, except the few weeks preceding the summer harvest. They have wheaten bread, barley and millet, a variety of vegetables and fruits. They have milk, buttermilk, clarified butter, and curd-cheese. They have occasional meat. They rarely have any fish or game. They take wine, mostly about the time of Christmas. They used to make spirits, but this has been forbidden.

(*The Wheel of Health*, 1972: 16-19)

The Hunza people... are something very old, an erratic block of an ancient world, still perhaps with its peculiar knowledge and traditions, and preserved in that profound cleft of theirs from the decay of time... All one can say is that this people of Hunza, so unique amongst peoples, is no less unique in its racial characters. Everything suggests that in its remoteness it may preserve from the distant past, things that the modern world has forgotten and does not any longer understand. And amongst those things are perfect physique and health.

(*The Wheel of Health*, 1972: 22)

McCARRISON AND THE WHOLISTIC APPROACH

It is clear in this article of 1925 upon "The Relationship of Diet to the Physical Efficiency of Indian Races" that McCarrison's review of the fighting races had removed him from the conventional attitude of medical research to an over-riding interest in healthy peoples. The question that now presented itself to his mind was: "How is it that man can be such a magnificent physical creature as the Hunza, the Sikh, or the Pathan?"

Health is wholeness. The careful reader of McCarrison's *Studies in Deficiency Diseases* will note that wholeness lay in the very texture of his mind. The work reveals an intellectual passion for wholeness. Up to that time... research workers in malnutrition had studied the effects of faulty food upon the nerves, the eyes, the bones and so on. They fragmented the subject. He was the first "to survey the whole realm of the body by microscopic means." He had to see wholly. One can, indeed, watch this sense of wholeness increasing in his work, until it shaped itself in the whole view of health.

(*The Wheel of Health,* 1972: 30)

A WHOLE-DIET EXPERIMENT

A striking whole-diet experiment was carried out in Denmark in the last year of the War.

The blockade, following the entry of the U.S.A. into the war, put the Danes in a very serious position. Professor Mikkel Hindhede, Superintendent of the State Institute of Food Research, was made Food Adviser to the Danish Government to deal with it.

The problem that faced him was this: Denmark had a population of 3,500,000 human beings and 5,000,000 domestic animals. She was accustomed to import grains from the United States for both. There was now a shortage of grain foods.

The pigs had provided hams and bacon for the English as well as for Danes. In the crisis the question arose: Would it be wise to get rid of the pigs and let men eat the food which otherwise the pigs would eat? Hindhede decided it would be wise, so some four-fifths of the pigs were killed and about one-sixth of the cattle. Their grain food was given to the Danes, and it was given, not in the exact form in which it was given to the pigs - not as bran mash, for instance - but as wholemeal bread with the extra coarse bran that is not put into ordinary wholemeal bread incorporated.

In addition to this bread... which was made official for the whole country, the Danes ate porridge, green vegetables, potatoes and other root vegetables, milk, butter, and fruit. No grain or potatoes were allowed for the distillation of spirits, so there were no spirits. Half the previous quantity of beer was permitted.

As some pigs were left, the people on the farms got meat; the people in the cities - 40 per cent of the population - got very little meat. Only the rich could afford beef.

The food regulations were begun in March 1917 and were made stringent from October 1917 to October 1918.

The result of this enforced national diet was a remarkable lowering of the death-rate. The death-rate, which had been 12.5 in 1913, 1914, now fell to 10.4 per thousand, "which is the lowest mortality figure that has been registered in any European country at any time." (Hindhede).

Hindhede puts this impressive result in another way. Taking the average from 1900 to 1916 as 160, in the October to October year it was 66. Even in men over sixty-five the figure fell to 76.

Hindhede attributes this extraordinary rapid and marked change to two things: (1) less meat, (2) less alcohol. He regards the bran as having largely filled the gap of the scanty or absent meat, bran having a good proportion of vegetable meat or protein. He regards the experiment as a triumph for his previous teaching. "The reader knows," he writes in the *Deutsche Medizinische Wochenschrift* of March 1920, "how sharply I have emphasised the advantages of a lacto-vegetarian diet. I am not in principle a vegetarian, but I believe I have shown that a diet containing a large amount of meat and eggs is dangerous to the health."

Now, when the Americans exported wheat and barley from the virgin soil of the prairies, about 1870-1880, and drove European farmers to despair by their low prices, the shrewd Danes quickly changed their agricultural methods. They bred pigs and cattle and poultry, and sent bacon and eggs and butter to England. They also became big eaters of meat and eggs themselves. The war forced them to go back to the foods they used to eat before the invasion of American wheat - foods which their forefathers had eaten for centuries. Especially was this the case with bread.

Hindhede lays much emphasis on the change in bread. Before his fiat the Danes ate fine meal bread and wholemeal bread. He made them eat only wholemeal bread with extra bran. Its proportion he gives as 67 per cent rye, 21 per cent oats, and 12 per cent bran.

Except for the bran, which added vegetable meat for those who were animally meatless or meat short, the bread was the good baked bread which "has been the national bread of Denmark for centuries. For ages it was the only bread procurable in the country and even now it is the common form." (Hindhede).

This was the whole diet of the Danes, which in such a short time had such admirable results: wholemeal bread with added bran, green vegetables, potatoes, other root vegetables, fruit, milk and butter; meat variable, but always less than before and in towns scanty; less alcohol.

There is no doubt that Hindhede is justified in claiming that this proved an excellent diet, producing as it did the record low European death-rate in so short a time. He does not make the inference that it was the commercialism of Americans called forth by western needs that first spoilt this diet about half a century ago and that it was only when the war shut out this American commercialism that it was able to reappear.

If looked at carefully, it will be seen that the foods more closely resemble the Hunza and Sikh foods than those of any modern European diet. The Hunza and Sikh eat wholemeal grains, vegetables, fruit, plenty of milk, butter, and not much meat or alcohol.

(*The Wheel of Health*, 1972: 56-9)

ILL-HEALTH CAUSED BY ABANDONMENT OF DIET

There have been... many experiments on human beings the reverse of the above, namely, of ill-health due to the abandonment of a previous and the enforcement of a new diet. These have been unintentional and undesired by those who cause their enforcement and by those who suffer it... I will take but one... It is given in these words by McCollum and Simmonds:

"There is no better illustration of the soundness of the views regarding the types of diet which succeed in inducing good nutrition than the experience of the non-citizen Indian of the United States. All who observed the Indians in their primitive state agree that most of them were exceptional specimens of physical development. With few exceptions, however, during two generations they have deteriorated physically. The reason for this is apparently brought to light by a consideration of the kind of food to which they have restricted themselves since they have lived on reservations.

"There is no group of people with a higher incidence of tuberculosis than the non-citizen Indian. As wards of the Government they have been provided with money and land, but have in general shown little interest in agriculture. They have lived in idleness and have derived their food supplies from the agency stores. In addition to muscle cuts of meat they have, therefore, taken large amounts of milled cereal products, syrup, molasses, sugar and canned foods, such as peas, corn, and tomatoes. In other words, they have come to subsist essentially upon a milled cereal, sugar, tuber, and meat diet. On such a regimen their teeth have rapidly become inferior and are badly decayed. They suffer much from rheumatism and other troubles which result from local infections. Faulty dietary habits are, in great measure, to be incriminated for their susceptibility to tuberculosis.

"Other classes of Indians, who have become successful farmers, have not deteriorated as a result of contact with civilization, except in so far as they have suffered from alcohol and venereal infections. The non-citizen Indian has suffered, not because of contact with civilization, but because he has been forced into dietary habits which are faulty."

(*The Wheel of Health*, 1972: 62-3)

THE HUNZA FOOD AND ITS CULTIVATION

Plant life is by its nature less mobile than man's. Movement is only by winged or carried seed, and is limited. Therefore one would expect the making of plant-life in man's image would have a far more serious effect on plants than on man. Indeed, I sometimes marvel that plants have survived some of the great disturbances to which they have been subjected. It argues much for the scientific skill of man that he should have been able to bring about so many changes at all. But, nevertheless, nature hits back, and she hits back with disease.

From these changes, except for the introduction of the potato in about 1892, the plant-life of Hunza has been exempt.

The unchanged conditions include one of supreme importance,

that of food for the plant. This has continued century after century with the utmost constancy.

The chief factors of plant-food have been two.

Firstly, there is the continuous slight renewal of the soil by a sprinkling of the black glacier-ground sand, which is brought to the fields by the aqueducts.

Secondly, there is the direct preparation by man of food for the plants, given in the form of manure.

The Hunza, in their manuring, use everything that they can return to the soil. They carefully collect the cattle manure and store it in the byres. They collect all vegetable parts and pieces that will not serve as food either to man or beast, including such fallen leaves as the cattle will not eat, and mix them with dung and urine in the byres. They use the human sewage after keeping it for six months. They take silt from special recesses built in their irrigating channels. They collect the ashes of their fires. All these they mix together and make into a compost. They also spread alkaline earth from the hills on their vegetable fields on days when the fields are watered.

The act of manuring is so important in its bearing upon agriculture that the subject needs elaboration. As its classical representatives are the Chinese, it will be their method we will now study. It is to be noted that the Hunza claim to have received culture from Baltistan, the inhabitants of which are Tibetans.

The Chinese have pursued their method of manuring for a period of time which makes modern progress appear an infant, a period which permits the late Professor F.H. King to call his classic of description and understanding by the really stupendous title of *Farmers of Forty Centuries*.

The principle of the method is that of the forest and prairie. It is that everything that comes from the soil, whether it passes through animals or not, is returned to the soil. Nothing is lost, all is preserved. Nothing foreign is intruded, but day by day, year by year, century by century, there is the local transference of death to life again. At one time each piece of matter is dead, but its death is but the awaiting of the time when it will be restored to the living by way of plant food.

The Chinese manure or compost is made of everything that can be collected which once got its life from the soil, directly or indirectly. They are mixed together until they form a black friable substance which is readily spread upon the fields. King describes a number of different processes he saw in different parts of China. One he describes as being carried out in compost pits at the edge of a canal, a process entailing "tremendous labour of body and amount of forethought." Four months before his visit men had brought waste from the stables of Shanghai, a distance of fifteen miles by water. This they had deposited upon the canal bank between layers of thin mud dipped from the canal, corresponding to silt collected in and taken from the recesses in the Hunza aqueducts, and left to ferment. The eight men at King's visit had nearly filled the compost pit with this stable refuse and canal silt. The pit was in a field in which clover, with its peculiar power of taking nitrogen from the air, was in blossom. This was to be cut and piled to a height of five to eight feet upon the compost in the pit, and also saturated layer by layer with canal mud. It would then be allowed to ferment twenty to thirty days, until the juices set free had been absorbed by the winter compost beneath and until the time that the adjacent land had been made ready for the coming crop. The compost would then be distributed by the men over the field.

At another time he saw a compost pit within a village in which had been placed all the manure and waste of the households and streets, all stubble and waste roughage of the fields, all ashes not to be applied directly, mixed up with some soil. Sufficient water was added to keep the contents of the pit saturated and to promote their fermentation. All fibres of organic material have to be broken down, which may require working and re-working, with frequent additions of water and stirring for aeration. Finally the mixture becomes a rich complete fertiliser. It is then allowed to dry and is finely pulverised before it is spread upon the land.

Every foot of land, says King, is made to provide food, fuel, or fabric. "The wastes of the body, of fuel and fabric, are taken back to the field; before doing so they are housed against waste from weather, intelligently compounded and patiently worked at through one, three or even six months, in order to bring them into the most efficient form to serve as manure for the soil or as feed for the crop."

There is no human waste. "While the ultra-civilized Western elaborates destructors for burning garbage at a financial loss and turns sewage into the sea, the Chinese uses both for manure," reported Dr. Arthur Stanley, Health Officer of Shanghai in 1899, and quoted by King. "He wastes nothing while the sacred duty of agriculture is uppermost in his mind. And in reality recent bacterial work has shown that faecal matter and house refuse" (prepared as it usually is in China in hard-burned glazed terra-cotta urns and in Japan in sheltered cement-lined pits) "are best destroyed by returning them to clean soil, where natural purification takes place. The question of destroying garbage can, I think, under present conditions in Shanghai, be answered in a decided negative. While, to adopt the water-carriage system for sewage and turn it into the river would be an act of sanitary suicide."

(*The Wheel of Health*, 1972: 118-21)

That which is of the soil is best returned to the soil by spreading it as evenly as possible. This was done by the ancient Peruvians, is done by the Hunza, is done by the Chinese and Japanese. All these have great engineering works of irrigation and canalisation. The Chinese spread "the enormous volumes of silt" of their rivers and canals over the land directly as well as a part of their compost. Their huge rivers, as great almost as the Mississippi, sometimes overwhelm them with flood and destruction, but this checks, it never stops, their tireless efforts. Silt and compost must be evenly spread, and so these people take infinite pains to make their land into a series of flat surfaces, "the careful and extensive fitting of fields so largely practised, which both lessens soil erosion and permits a large amount of soluble and suspended matter in the run off to be applied to the fields.... If the total area of fields graded practically to a water level in Japan aggregates 11,000 square miles, the total area thus surface-fitted in China must be eight to tenfold this amount. Such enormous field erosion as is tolerated at the present time in our southern and south Atlantic States is permitted nowhere in the Far East, so far as we have observed; not even where the topography is much steeper" (King).

No, nor in Peru nor Hunza, where the topography is of the steepest.

In China, Japan, ancient Peru, Dutch Java, Hunza and other countries, agriculture is a gardening, a care of the soil, a repayment of the soil, carried on by many men and women with never-ending industry.

It is a gardening in which everything that has once had life, even ash and rag, offal and refuse, is brought back to life by the resurrecting power of the soil. The Chinese and Japanese, in following this great principle, prepare and use human excreta, thereby preventing a loss of phosphates alone which King calculates "could not be replaced by 1,295,000 tons of rock phosphate, 75 per cent pure." "The men of Hunza, the most careful and painstaking husbandmen of Asia" (Schomberg), follow the Chinese custom. They have flat fields. They spread out the compost evenly like butter upon bread. They follow, in a word, the garden culture of the immemorial East, and, according to that which Vavilov has found and may yet find, it may perhaps be that it was in their country of the lofty hills that in the distant past this form of compost-culture first came into being in Asia.

It is possible also that in this form of culture there is an excellence of vegetable health which can be obtained by no other means - in Hunza, for example, there is that excellence, and plant disease is insignificant. It is possible that by full repayment to the soil we alone get a full return. It is known that our own agriculture is rather a loan from the soil, for we never repay it in full. We have worked our agriculture on the capital of the soil, and in virgin land we have raided the soil. When the soil sickens we restore it or strive to restore it by scientific doctoring; we return to it in the way of tonics the nitrogen, calcium, phosphorus, of which we have robbed it. Thus disease is patched and mended, but not abolished. The impoverishment of the soil remains our chiefest ill.

(*The Wheel of Health*, 1972: 122-3)

THE SECRETS OF HEALTH

The prevention and banishment of disease are primarily matters of food; secondarily, of suitable conditions of environment. Antiseptics, medicaments, inoculations, and extirpating operations evade the real problem. Disease is the censor pointing out the humans, animals and plants, who are imperfectly nourished. Its continuance and its increase are proofs that the methods used obscure, they do not attack, the radical problem.

(*The Wheel of Health*, 1972: 130)

Transference, transference, transference - three transferences, that is the secret of health. These three transferences - soil to vegetable, vegetable to animal, animal and vegetable back to the soil - form the eternal wheel of health.

(*The Wheel of Health*, 1972: 131)

... if individually we wish to get some extra health and physique like that of the Hunza, we should remember the following twelve points:

1. See that the vegetables eaten have the repute of healthiness; do not skin them and waste the skins, and do not throw away the juices and water in which they are cooked. (79 per cent of the green vegetables and 99 per cent of the potatoes eaten in Britain are home-grown).

2. Eat garden vegetables and fruit, if procurable, as soon as possible after gathering them, so as to get the peculiar value of freshness.

3. Eat salads and palatable well-stored raw root vegetables.

4. Drink more milk, buttermilk, skimmed milk, and, if palatable, sour milk. (The fresh milk drunk in Britain is exclusively home-produced).

5. Eat less meat, if grain, vegetables, milk, and cheese are taken; eat animal organs and skin as well as the flesh.

6. Eat plenty of fresh fruit when in season.

7. At other times, take dried fruits, preferably sun-dried.

8. Take germinated gram, grain, or beans, especially in winter and early spring.

9. Eat wholemeal bread; to get the *health* of a food, eat the *whole* of it as far as possible.

10. Eat butter and cheese.

11. Drink fresh wine when there is opportunity, or old English ale, if procurable.

12. Do not eat too many different foods or dishes at one meal; simplify.

From these twelve maxims one may choose as the central essentials: wholemeal bread, sprouted gram in the winter and spring, milk products freely, green-leafed and root vegetables, plenty of fruit, and not much meat. That which divides modern people from them is chiefly one thing - ignorance. They do not know that wholemeal bread is so much more healthful than white bread, yet they are anxious for health. They do not know that sprouted gram is one of the most widespread foods in the world in the winter and early spring, the chief period of sickness, yet they are anxious for health. They do not know the great additional health which can be procured by the free use of milk and its products. They still go on with a little milk in their tea. Yet they are anxious for health. They do not know that there is a good protein in wheat, milk, cheese and vegetables, and that meat is not its only source. They hold, by tradition, that meat is the essential food for strength, and they believe eating it in plenty is a part of human wisdom. For they are anxious for health.

Valuable as these deductions from the Hunza are, they are nevertheless fragmentary. The *whole* meaning of this people is something much greater. It is none less than that the perfect physique and health, which we have grown accustomed to regard as the privilege of the wild, and, with rare exceptions, beyond the attainment of civilized man, is not unattainable. It is attainable, if we give the same devoted service to our soil, its health and the health of its production, as for centuries this remarkable people have given to theirs.

(*The Wheel of Health*, 1972: 141-2)

G.T. Wrench also wrote The Restoration of the Peasantries *(London, C.W. Daniel, 1939) and* Reconstruction by Way of the Soil *(London, Faber, 1946), both of which deal with the social and economic implications of different methods of cultivation.*

An introduction to McCarrison's ideas can be found in Nutrition and Health *(London, Faber, 1936; 3rd edn 1961), which has a postscript by H.M. Sinclair, who was Director of the Laboratory of Human Nutrition in the University of Oxford. Sinclair edited* The Work of Sir Robert McCarrison *(London, Faber, 1953), of which section 6 - 'Researches on Human Diets in Relation to Health and Disease' - is the most relevant to this chapter. The McCarrison Society, founded 1968, can be contacted at 5, Derby Road, Caversham, Reading RG4 0HF.*

Questions of health and diet are discussed by some of the other writers included in this anthology: for example, Friend Sykes, in Food, Farming and the Future *(London, Faber, 1951); Lady Balfour in* The Living Soil *(London, Faber, 1943); and Sir Albert Howard in* Farming and Gardening for Health or Disease *(London, Faber, 1945).*

A major work on this topic is Thoughts on Feeding *by L.J. Picton (London, Faber, 1946); Picton also contributed the chapter 'Diet and Farming' to* England and the Farmer, *edited by H.J. Massingham (London, Batsford, 1941).*

A book to which one finds a number of references is The Peckham Experiment: A Study in the Living Structure of Society, *by I.H. Pearse and L.H. Crocker (London, Allen and Unwin, 1943), which gives an account of the Pioneer Health Centre established in South London between the wars.*

Other works which can be consulted are Your Daily Bread, *by Doris Grant (London, Faber, 1944; revised edn, 1962), which contains a very detailed bibliography; and* The Stuff Man's Made Of *by Jorian Jenks (London, Faber, 1959).*

Reference

1   I regret that I have been unable to discover the year of birth of Dr Wrench, but presumably it would have been around the late 1870s.

Sir George Stapledon

9

The Importance of Variety

Sir George Stapledon

(1882-1960)

R.G. Stapledon, knighted in 1939 for his research on the improvement of grasslands, which won him an international reputation, worked from 1910 until 1940 at the University College of Wales, Aberystwyth. He was appointed as lecturer in Agricultural Botany, later becoming Professor, and from 1919 to 1925 was Director of the Welsh Plant Breeding Station. From 1940 until his retirement in 1945 he was Director of the Grassland Improvement Station at Drayton in Warwickshire. His experiences working at Suez in 1904-5 for the family business convinced him that England's dependence on overseas trade and neglect of her agriculture were dangerous folly, and the aim of much of his later career was to demonstrate that apparently useless land could in fact be made fertile. In this he was influenced by the ideas of R.H. Elliot (see chapter 4).

Although not committed to the humus school of farming to the extent that, for example, Howard was - though he shared Howard's dislike of the 'laboratory hermit' - Stapledon was closely associated with the Kinship in Husbandry, and opposed the increasing trend towards specialization and monoculture. His doubts about such changes stemmed from an outlook which had been developed by his wide reading in literature, history and philosophy, and which questioned the tendency of scientific research to seek strict classification rather than to study the way a pattern of stability is affected by the complex influences of innumerable external factors.

STAPLEDON'S EXPERIMENTS

... These ecotypes are discernible in the wild. His ⟦ Stapledon's ⟧ first experiments at the W.P.B.S. ⟦ Welsh Plant Breeding Station ⟧ were designed to demonstrate this. He grew plants of the same type from different localities in groups of five hundred. Distinctly different varieties emerged. In a sense every single plant interested him in view of the possibility that its progeny might create a variety of value to the farmer. That the plant must be judged by its progeny is the principle of plant breeding, and the exception to type may be the most significant plant.

Stapledon raised these discoveries, as was his wont, to a philosophic as well as a practical level. He quoted Blake in support: 'Without contraries is no progression.' Within the apparently uniform races of plants and men, if one looks closely enough, there are immense differences, even contraries, and it is the inter-breeding and interfusion of all these differences that provide the breeder of plants and animals (including man) with endless cause for excitement and anticipation. The unknown, that which is not yet created or not yet found, may solve the problem that baffles us today; or it may transcend the problem and show a new way altogether. If Nature can produce something that is needed, then a way of deliberately reproducing it must be found.

'A hundred years after Blake,' Stapledon pointed out to his students, 'our great geneticist William Bateson was urging his students to hunt the exception.'

(Robert Waller, *Prophet of the New Age*,
London, Faber, 1962, pp.127-8)

His mind was always roving backward and forward from the trial plot to the actual conditions of Nature and the farm. 'In the study of grassland, it is interactions that must be investigated and therefore an over-isolation of factors and an over-simplification of experiments, although giving results which so far as they go are supremely accurate, may lead to erroneous conclusions. Interactions, such as those between single plants and groups of plants, or between animals and plants, can only be studied by setting up innumerable experiments.'

(Waller, *Prophet*: 133)

... though the climate cannot be altered, vegetation can. The tyranny of climate can be reduced with new tactics, and freedom - that is, the scope - of management enlarged. Stapledon now had good evidence that the fertility of the land could be raised by the herbage. The land of the Cahn Hill Improvement Scheme (hereafter referred to as Cahn Hill) was generally regarded as worthless by reason of its climate, soil and geographical position, so Stapledon determined to use it as a shop window for the W.P.B.S., an exhibition of what could be done by combining the new varieties with techniques of reclamation and ley farming methods.

The experiments undertaken with Captain Bennett-Evans had already proved that climate was not the overruling factor. The 'sweet' patches that Stapledon, as a young surveyor, had first observed on the hills were now created at will by heavy manuring with artificials supported by more intense, controlled grazing. In this way a sward of the purple moor-grass was rapidly transformed into one consisting mainly of *Agrostis*. This showed to everybody who cared to come and look that the climate could not suppress better grassland once fertility had been raised. The next stage had been to sow wild white clover on these areas and in a short time a fine clovery sward had developed.

(Waller, *Prophet:* 172)

Stapledon could not fail to appreciate that the small hill farm was an uneconomic unit, and he foresaw with misgivings that the commercial company was only too likely to invade agriculture and organize farming estates on the industrial model. Although this would have the obvious advantage of bringing much needed capital into farming he regarded it with horror. The manner in which society was solving its economic problems seemed to him to be turning England into a nation in which everyone obeyed orders; the spirit of independence was being sacrificed to false ideas of economic efficiency and everyone seemed to be absolutely convinced that there was no alternative except bankruptcy. Stapledon held the opposite view, that there were alternatives, and that we were making the wrong choice. The strength of a nation depends on the character of its people.

(Waller, *Prophet:* 215)

〖 Captain Bennett-Evans recalls...〗 'Stapledon's great idea was to scratch, scratch and scratch: lime and phosphate, and oversow. This scratching business was rather slow and tedious and I'm a bit of an impatient chap. Trefor Thomas was excellent; he followed out his instructions to the last word. But I said to him one day: "Look here, Trefor, if you think this going up and down this hill is economic, I don't. We've got no tilth at the end of it all" (the mat of old herbage on that area was about three inches thick). We were using a New Zealand harrow, a pretty drastic one, it certainly did a bit of ripping, but it was bouncing about too much. I got tired of watching it, so I said: "Look here, I'm going to buy a plough." When I told Stapledon, he said: "Oh, are you? Well, ploughing is completely out of date. But it's your land, you carry on if you want to and I'll lend you all the help I can, but I'm against it." I said: "Very well, I'll plough alongside your scratchings and I'll do it in plots, controlled, and all the rest of it, and then we can compare which is the better." He went off shaking his head: but I did buy a plough, a three-furrow disc plough, and I ploughed very carefully by the side of his scratchings. We let a winter pass to break the furrow down and then we disced it and harrowed it and Trefor put down his plots. And in a very short time the ploughed area was a beautiful emerald green. *Stapledon was delighted.* He brought the world and his wife to see it - Lloyd George and the Minister of Agriculture (Walter Elliot) were ordered down to see it; Lord De La Warr and the Master of Sempill flew to see it.'

'Mind you,' said Bennett-Evans, taking out his snuff box reminiscently, 'the scratchings did well too, they came on later. The fact is that improvement is not so complete under the plough, but it's quicker, and you can't wait for ever for your returns. It takes as long as ten years to get a good sward by that method. Stapledon was right. I've given up ploughing now and have gone back to scratching. But that ploughing was a damn good advert for him: the scratching doesn't produce such a nice emerald green. The scratching method brings in white clover, the foundations of fertility, the mother of milk. I've got a sward like that 1,760 feet up equal to anything in Gloucestershire: and I'll bring it up to 2,000 feet some day. You can tell that this scratching/discing method works because of the increase of worms and moles; they do a lot of the cultivating for you. Two years before he died he wrote to me about my surface regenerations. I don't know where he got his ideas from but he was undoubtedly right. He was right too about sending in the cattle before the sheep as their hoof cultivation breaks up the sod and they don't graze the young grass so heavily as sheep, so that when the sheep come along there's a new growth of grass for them. The cattle prepare the way for the sheep. Sheep all the time and the land reverts.'

There is a touching tribute to Bennett-Evans written by Stapledon during the war: 'I remember motoring into Aberystwyth from Stratford-on-Avon on a dull and cold winter morning and suddenly being roused from my apathy by the sight of Bennett-Evans's green patches vibrant against the lowering background of dark and forbidding hills, the first vivid green to meet my eyes since I had bundled myself into my car early that morning. I wondered rather morosely as I drove on , who cared? Who of the thousands who passed over that road on a normal summer gave those patches a moment's thought, or even noticed them. Were there any who had been suddenly thrilled? Who wished to know what like of man lived in that bleak isolated spot in that strange home built of stone and railway carriages. What sort of man was this who single-handed and of his own initiative was waging war against the elements and the Forestry Commission? On the one side of the road trees, trees, thousands of trees planted at the public expense, on the other turnips and grass, the raw material of food brought into being by the sweat and faith and enterprise of a private individual - of a farmer, of a man who lived on his hill and loved it. Who cared?'

(Waller, *Prophet*: 166-8)

ROTATION AND VARIETY

I am forced to the conclusion that underlying all our farm practices, even those which we may conceive to be wholly admirable and equally in the byre and on the field, there lurks an evil genius born of standardization. We may not in the least suspect the presence of this evil genius and have no conception of its infinite ways of working, but there it is, the ever-present enemy alike of the good farmer and the bad, on rich soils and poor. By ceaseless labouring, and perhaps almost incredibly slowly, it relentlessly toils to undermine our endeavours and eventually may be to render them well-nigh nugatory. There is, I am convinced, but one method of keeping the evil genius inherent in all our farm practices in subjection, and in subjection for all time, and that is *change,* and the avoidance at all costs of too rigid adherence to narrow standards of evaluation, and shunning the adoption of restricted practices over long periods of time.

There remain further incompatibilities to be discussed, incompatibilities which have an influence on the ration that can be made available to the animal and on the character of the sward and therefore upon the ultimate manurial value of the sod.

Early spring growth is incompatible with late autumn and winter grazing. We can, however, go much further than this and say that in order to get maximum nutritive growth at any particular date range of the year the sward should have been rested at an earlier and appropriate date range. We can go further still and say that maximum growth at any particular time of the year cannot be obtained year after year at that particular time on one and the same sward. The reason being that as a result of the heavy grazing applied during the process of conversion the particular species best able to provide the grass to suit the programme will be excessively harshly treated relative to those species contributing but little. The productivity of the appropriate species at the required time will therefore grow progressively less and less as the years advance.

This is a situation which has to be met both in the case of permanent grass, and of the longer duration leys. The plan to adopt is to arrange to obtain maximum spring growth or maximum growth at other set periods from different fields in different years, that is to say, the seasonal periods of maximum use must as such be rotated around all the older duration swards of the farm. The situation can also be met by employing a variety of different short duration leys each designed primarily to cater for a definite date range within the grazing season. It is this latter and very important need, amongst other cogent reasons, that makes it imperatively necessary to use several different rotations of crops on one and the same farm.

To sum up what we have here said about the animal-plant complex: we have endeavoured to show that a rotational system of grazing in order to conform to the canons of scientific practice must be such as to distribute all round the farm and on a proper date schedule all the various and different procedures that are severally applicable to meet the separate and special-purpose demands that will be made on sward and sod. We shall have to rotate the procedures as such around the farm, and on each field conduct the treatment that is appropriate to it in any particular year and in the various seasons of the year.

The same necessity applies to the rotation of crops. The various rotations adopted must be taken around the whole farm, while on the several fields individually the rotation in operation in each case will have to be gone through during the years duly allocated to it.

The arguments we have here developed apply in their greatest force to grass-arable rotations, though I am very far indeed from thinking that in principle they do not also apply to more orthodox arable farming. I indeed believe that no farming whatsoever should be conducted on the basis of a single crop rotation per farm. On scientific grounds all the arguments are against it; against it on the score of maximum elimination of weeds, maximum elimination of diseases of all kinds, and on the score of the creation and maintenance of maximum fertility.

(Sir George Stapledon, *The Way of the Land*,
London, Faber, 1943, pp. 230-2)

In view of the immense amount that has been published during the present century it is not without significance that the leading agricultural journals contain but few articles dealing primarily, or even remotely with the rotation, and next to nothing relative to the basal philosophy of the rotation. The truth is that agricultural thought in recent decades has turned ever more exclusively towards the narrow, too narrow as I think, path of commodities, each considered as such. Excessive concentration on commodities leads inevitably towards mono-culture, and to what we too lightly please to call specialization, and leads away from the rotation and ultimately to disaster. Greatly daring, then, I have set myself to combat this modern fetish of over-concentration on commodities, a fetish that has revealed itself not only in the trends of agricultural science, but in a very great deal of what the State has endeavoured to achieve for agriculture and which daily reveals itself in the actions and utterances of the leaders of the agricultural industry.

(Stapledon, *The Way of the Land:* 181)

AGRICULTURAL POLICY

This is a small island with a large population, and that alone should be a sufficient reason for always maintaining a fully productive home agriculture. Apart from war, to be dependent to an exaggerated and wholly unnecessary extent on imported food for ourselves, and feeding-stuffs for our livestock, is gratuitously to court unwarrantable risks.

(Stapledon, 'The Reclamation of Grasslands', in *England and the Farmer*, (ed.) H.J. Massingham, London, Batsford, 1941; p. 131)

... in matters agricultural satisfactory adjustments at short notice are impossible, and a nation which invites the necessity of attempting such adjustments does so at the peril of jeopardizing its greatness, or even its very existence.

(Stapledon, *England and the Farmer*: 132)

... ever since the last war all world changes have been combining with relentless and steady pressure to undermine the position which had made it possible for us so long and with such impunity to neglect our home agriculture.

(Stapledon, *England and the Farmer*: 132)

This country is no longer the workshop of the world; after the war it will no longer be the workshop of the British Empire. This I conceive to be all to the good, for some reorientation in population, in industrialization and in authority throughout the British Commonwealth of nations would almost certainly be exhilarating and inspiring to the British peoples as a whole. The mother country should be rather the spiritual pulse of the Empire than the hub around which all major financial, material and political activities and actions revolve. These changes sooner or later inevitably will react sharply and decisively on the economic and social life of this country. A fully productive home agriculture on this account alone will therefore become essential. It will be necessary alike to help give employment to our peoples and to afford additional markets for our industries.

(Stapledon, *England and the Farmer*: 134)

Parallel with the over-industrialization of certain countries and regions has gone the thoughtless ravaging of the soil of others, till at last senseless systems of monoculture designed to produce food and other crops at the cheapest possible cost have rendered waste literally millions of acres of once fertile or potentially fertile country. These pre-war influences of the industrial era add weight to the shattering blows of the war, blows that will drive home with great force on a country such as ours which will have seriously to strain its financial resources, and has a huge population in relation to its land surface.

(Stapledon, *England and the Farmer*: 134-5)

A fully productive agriculture, first and foremost, must be such that it uses every available acre to the best advantage; gives the maximum amount of well-paid employment on the land, and such as is based on systems of husbandry which lead to a progressive and all-round increase in soil fertility - systems which ever build fertility and never exploit reserves. Further than that, a fully productive agriculture must as far as possible be self-sufficient and self-assured, and only dependent within reasonable limits on imported feeding-stuffs.

(Stapledon, *England and the Farmer*: 137)

I am concerned with a long-term agricultural policy, the kind of policy that would take at least ten years to put into full operation, and consequently we have to consider not so much immediate war danger as war danger as such, a danger that owing to our island position would seem to be something from which it is now hard to see how we shall ever escape. I believe the extent of the influences of soil erosion and depletion is not even yet fully realized. All methods of countering this must in the last resort react against the British housewife, and must tend to increase the cost of overseas production, while taking soil erosion, soil depletion and land deterioration together a vaster area of the globe is undoubtedly affected than is generally supposed.

Our own rough and hill grazings have manifestly deteriorated: witness the spread of bracken, to quote only the most obvious but by no means the most serious example. They have become increasingly depleted of lime and phosphates in recent decades, and the same thing must be happening to a greater or lesser extent - and sometimes accompanied by actual erosion - in all the great ranching areas of the world. In framing our own long-term agricultural policy heed must be taken of every shred of evidence on land deterioration that is available all the world over, for it is patent that when the sum is totted up the total will far exceed what is already only glaringly manifest.

The immediate, and on all hands generally admitted, need of our peoples is an abundance of fresh food. An abundance of fresh food is not compatible with a superabundance of permanent grass.

I make no apology for this somewhat long, and in a sense non-agricultural and at all events non-technical introduction, for it seems to me imperative to stress our national needs, for it is these needs which should govern our whole agricultural outlook and, therefore, should determine all our systems of farming. To sum up so far, and on the strength of the various considerations I have brought forward, I would say this. What is demanded of our agriculture is, *firstly,* to maintain as large a rural population as possible, for probably on a large and contented rural population depends to a marked degree the increase of our population as a whole. *Secondly,* to maintain as large an acreage as possible in a highly fertile and always ploughable condition, and *thirdly,* so to conduct our farming as to allow at all times, and in all places, for the absolute maximum of flexibility in commodity production.

(Stapledon, *The Way of the Land:* 182-3)

THE DANGERS OF SCIENTIFIC KNOWLEDGE

Stapledon was worried by the feeling that he had himself contributed unwittingly to man's conceit in his own knowledge and his technological control over Nature: and he was haunted by the possibility - at times he felt certainty - that Nature would revenge herself upon man for his 'ignorant assurance'. With his scientific mind, Stapledon began to work on this idea as if it were in fact a law of Nature: that ignorance was an operative force that could acquire more power than knowledge, if we did not take it into account in our knowledge. In other words, whenever we make new attempts to control Nature, we set in action all kinds of repercussions of which we are entirely ignorant: it is these repercussions that finally dominate the situation, not man's scientific control. This intuition acted upon Stapledon as an inhibiting force because he felt it was positively dangerous to add to human knowledge until man was emotionally guided by the feeling that 'he is drest in a little brief authority and most ignorant of what he's most assured'.

The criminal lack of moral restraint in contemporary society with regard to scientific research, commercial expansion and popular entertainment, gave him an ever stronger sense of impending disaster. It was these emotions that dominated the end of his life and drove him into a despair that at times over-mastered his optimism and contributed to the breakdown of his health. Nevertheless by freely exploring his strongest feelings he had regained his soul and put the seal of fulfilment on his search.

From time to time his agony of spirit was made public, as when he sent a message to the Grassland Society summer meeting at Hereford in 1956. He was the founder, but was too ill to attend, so the message was read for him by Dr. Tom Evans, who had been a student at Aberystwyth. Evans has a deep philosophical appreciation of Stapledon and it was this in part perhaps that persuaded Stapledon to bare his thoughts and feelings, though aware that they must give offence to many scientists.

I reproduce this address in full because it traces in his own words the changes that took place within him during the last years of his life when, although dying he was 'wondrously renovated'. It was because he had nothing further to live for but a deeper insight into truth that he made the most concentrated expression of his philosophy: he had no 'other consequences' to restrict the freeplay of his mind:

A Message from our Founder President
to Members attending the 1956 Summer Meeting
at Hereford

To you of our Society, including not only my old friends of the grassland world, but also, and in some ways even more particularly, those of you of the newer generations (who will be destined to carry - I bet - terrifying responsibilities) I send my sincere and humble greetings.

I look back rather wistfully over the life-range of our Society, which as near as no matter has covered the same run of years as my own retirement from active participation in grassland research and from energetic and carefree mingling with farmers and agronomists in the best of all good places - on the farm. I can't decide which has changed the most, the whole farming scene, including the attitude of farmers and scientists alike, or myself. For the moment to go right back to, say, 1919 when facilities first came my way: I was then dismayed at the apathy of everybody - yes, everybody, not just the farmers - and I was all agog to acquire new knowledge and to establish new schemes of farming and new techniques. Knowledge was the need, the only need and to hell with *IGNORANCE* - as such ignore it. That was my motto and I expect the motto of every budding technologist of those remote times.

Today technology has begun to run riot and amazingly enough perhaps nowhere more so than on the most progressive farms. The red lights, if as yet only on the sub-threshold, are there for those who can to discern them.

I make bold to assert that, if not today, anyway in the very near future, in so far as the human situation is concerned, and the human situation of course covers the farming-agricultural situation: 'It is not so much the acquisition of new knowledge that matters; but what chiefly matters, and will increasingly matter is our attitude towards ignorance.' With science delving into ever more abstruse fields, and in proportion to the glitter of the prizes it wins; so necessarily will the danger of the hitherto unexpected ignorances newly brought to bear on our human affairs and techniques be increasingly threatening. My own belief is that these dangers will become, and very soon become, of much greater significance in the biological fields than even in those of physics and engineering.

This is a huge subject and one demanding several *ad hoc* chairs of research devoted to it. Years ago it was lightly touched upon by Eddington but I doubt if even yet it enters into the syllabus of a single university or technical college. Well - and it may amuse you all to know it - that is me today. I think and talk about nothing else but what I please to call the law of operative ignorance. It is ignorance in all its hidden fury that now terrifies me and no longer new knowledge that delights me. The truth is - and whether all the young research technologists of today and of the future like it or not - 'Probably, it will not be the incidence of new knowledge that will rule the world or dominate agricultural practice but the ruler or dominator will be the manner in which we contrive to regulate and hold in check the incidence of such new ignorance as will be continuously laid open and rendered operative by each and all of the increments of new knowledge.'

A last word: It is my view that science will never brave up to this uncomfortable situation unless or until it has vastly broadened the base of its outlook and totally revised the basis of a very great number of its techniques.

In my own case - and this may mean something - I now know what I know; or perhaps I should say see what I see because I no longer study science or adopt the techniques of science. But and this is the point: against the background of a life devoted to science, I have plunged headlong into history, literature and poetry. The result is that for the first time in my life I have been forced to realize to the depth of my being that facts and factors as such (either singly or in small groups) in the affairs of life (including of course agriculture) mean precisely nothing; it is their mass inter-relationships and interactions - and these for all practical purposes are infinite - that mean everything. In my view a first-class historian or a first-class literary critic tends to knock spots out of a scientist of equal calibre when it comes to a critical consideration of the all-pervading amplitudes of interactions and inter-relationships.

This is a quite ridiculous message to send you. It can do justice neither to my idea, to myself, to your chairman my friend Professor Sanders, to your host my friend Dr. Evans, to lovely Herefordshire or to all of you. Unfortunately (for I wanted to say something more than just Hullo, chaps!) it was this or nothing, for I regret to say I cannot begin to contemplate either preparing, or coming to your London meeting to read, a considered paper supported by an adequacy of historical, literary, poetical and scientific evidence - but when and where and by whom I wonder will such a paper be read. The answer is that today no man exists who could read the paper I want - and least of all myself. Man in putting all his money on narrow specialization and on the newly dawned age of technology has backed a wild horse which given its head is bound to get out of control. No, what man should have done, was to have backed learning and scholarship in the true meaning of those great words and then soon he would have realized that the most devastating of all the contraries is knowledge: ignorance, then before putting his last farthing on the acquisition of new and separate parcels of material knowledge he would have tried to understand and come to terms with the innate interdependence between knowledge and ignorance.

GOOD LUCK TO ALL OF YOU ALWAYS,
R. GEORGE STAPLEDON

July 9th, 1956

(Waller, *Prophet*: 274-8)

Now the facts and assumptions of biology cannot with safety be left to stand alone. To date most of these facts and assumptions have resulted from the well-tried method of fragmentation. Life is, however, maintained by the delicate interaction of myriads of factors: it follows, therefore, that results arrived at by the study of factors *in vacuo* (or, for that matter, *in vitro*) may not be entirely applicable to life in action. It is the intricate interplay between thousands, nay millions, of factors operating under the totality of the conditions in which each individual organism has its being that makes it difficult to arrive at a reliable technique for biology and which, failing such a technique, renders suspect so many of its facts, findings, and assumptions. Adequately to study the natural interplay of factors under normal conditions, and by accepted scientific methods which demand control and counter-observations, may not prove to be possible. It is, therefore, scarcely thinkable that man will ever be able to devise sufficiently reliable experiments *accurately* to study the interplay between *all* factors under *all* conditions. There is hard irony in this: for it is only by a full knowledge of the interaction of all factors that man can reach safe conclusions about the control of environments most favourable to his animals and crop plants. Such favourable environments are necessary to promote his own health and the unfolding of his potentialities in directions advantageous to his progress - to his stability as a species or a race and to his wholeness as an individual in a society of individuals. There can be no escaping the fact that there are latent in all the facts and assumptions of biology (and in all biology it is far more difficult to prove the correctness of a 'fact' or an assumption than in the physical sciences) seeds of lethal consequences to mankind and man's domesticated animals and plants. Further than this, lethal consequences are all too likely to follow from the unguarded and wholesale application of the most tried and trusted facts of biology to man and the higher organisms generally, unless we are prepared to pay great deference to what we do not know. We must freely admit, however, when we aspire to know all about the complicated actions and interactions that constantly operate within the flux of which man is a part, that we are today only at the threshold. Such lethal consequences as may lie latent in some of the current facts and assumptions of biology are likely to act rapidly, but if false facts and assumptions are long retained as authoritative biological dicta and generally acted upon, then the consequences might well be lethal in the extreme, and culminate in the premature extinction of man, or of his domestic animals and plants, or of all three together. Reasoning of this general character animates the work and utterances of those who go the whole way, or even most of the way, with Sir Albert Howard in their strenuous advocacy of natural manures and of composting and in their abhorrence of chemical fertilizers. They are on the soundest of biological grounds in so far as they make generous allowances for what we do not know; but unfortunately their admirable enthusiasms [[sic]] carries them far beyond their facts. It is anathema to the scientific mind to make too sweeping allowances for what we do not know: but in the eyes of the scientist it is a crime of the first magnitude to accept as fact that which has not been well and truly proven by *current* scientific methods. It has *not* been well and truly proven that chemical fertilizers properly used have any short-term or long-term lethal action on plant growth or human life, *nor* has it been proved beyond all shadow of doubt that lethal properties do *not* lurk in some of them. We should exercise great care and be on the alert; that is as far as it is reasonable to go at present. The compost case is merely mentioned as a good example of the *dilemmas* in which biology cannot escape from being involved and because it is a live issue today.

(Stapledon, *Human Ecology,* Revised 2nd edn, London, Charles Knight, 1971; pp. 55-7)

... despite his wisest resolutions, man's creativeness will manufacture, if unconsciously, lethal as well as beneficial stimuli. Knowledge, as knowledge, has, inevitably, a lethal streak in it. This must be clearly recognized. Man organizes his individual, his social, his national and his international life, or, at least, he makes an effort to do so, on the basis of the sum of his knowledge; but this fund of knowledge can never be complete, and the use of incomplete knowledge is a dangerous weapon when dealing with life. The great danger is that the more man knows, the more he is tempted to act on the basis of his facts and to make decreasing allowance for what he does not know. If a man plays a highly complicated game without knowing all the rules, he will be 'offside' more often than a man who knows all the rules. This is our position today, greatly aggravated as it is by the dominance of science. Scientific knowledge carries a heavier and more vicious load of the lethal in its satchel than does any other type of knowledge. This must be recognized, recognized everywhere and recognized at once. We are on the threshold of tremendous advances in biology, in medicine and in biochemistry: and it is essential that wehave the courage to invite these advances. But let these advances only become as spectacular and far-reaching as the recent advances in the physical sciences, and there will be no end to the mischief man can do to himself: and he will have greatly to mend his ways if the good is to outweigh the mischief. Already we know that drugs can do the strangest of things with men's brains; and that hormones, which can now be used medicinally, in certain cases have remarkable influences on the personality. Advances in these and similar directions put responsibilities on man which, grave as they are, are as nothing compared to those which discoveries in genetics and nutrition have placed, and will increasingly place, upon his shoulders.

(*Human Ecology*: 83-4)

Other writings by Stapledon in addition to those quoted from above include The Land: Now and Tomorrow *(London, Faber, 1935);* Make Fruitful the Land! *(London, Kegan Paul, 1941); and* Disraeli and the New Age *(London, Faber, 1943). The Summer 1946 edition of* The Countryman *(Burford, Oxon) contains an autobiographical article by him entitled 'From Cotswolds to Wales and Back'. A personal reminiscence of Stapledon is given in Frances Donaldson's* Approach to Farming *(London, Faber, 1941).*

As mentioned in the introductory note to chapter 4, Stapledon wrote the Introduction to the edition of Elliot's The Clifton Park System of Farming, *issued in 1943 by Faber.*

Also worth referring to is Professor G.W. Robinson's book, Mother Earth *(London, Murby & Co., 1937), subtitled* Letters on Soil, Addressed to Prof. R.G. Stapledon.

A further book on grassland is Back to Better Grass, *by I.G. Lewis (London, Faber, 1942).*

H.J. Massingham with his wife Penelope and his sheepdog Friday

10

Reverence for God's Laws

H.J. Massingham

(1888-1952)

*Harold John Massingham - son of the great editor H.W. Massingham,
and sometimes confused with his brother Hugh, the journalist - was a
prolific writer of books and articles on ornithology, topography,
agriculture, gardening, and the arts. In his autobiography
Remembrance (London, Batsford, 1942) he describes how his love for
the landscape of the British Isles, and particularly for places with
Celtic associations, led him to turn his back on what he saw as the
falseness of the London literary scene and live in the country, thereby
learning to appreciate the values of regionalism, craftsmanship, and
traditional methods of agriculture. He became closely associated with
the Kinship in Husbandry, and his rejection of the assumptions on
which industrial society is based led him to join the Catholic Church.*

*In the books and articles which he wrote during the 1940s nearly all
the major ideas of the organic movement can be found, albeit
unsystematically presented. Although he was far from sharing the
pro-Nazi sympathies of men like Lymington and Gardiner, he would
have to be classed as a 'reactionary' in his social outlook, but it is a
paradox of the organic philosophy that so many of his views now
appear very far-sighted. This rebel against Victorian ideas of
'Progress' helped point the way towards the only sort of developments
which can enable the world to have a future at all.*

ECONOMIC IMPERIALISM AND FOOD

Any informed person who read the Commons debate on food on July
1st 〚 1948〛 must have put his paper down with a feeling of despair.

Many causes have been assigned for the downfall of the civilizations of
the past, but it is probable that the cause underlying all of them was a
complete sense of unreality. The morass of unreality in which the
debaters floundered about on July 1st was so devoid of a single dry and
solid foothold that I, for one, hardly know how or where to describe it.
There was, for instance, the ridiculous controversy between the two
Parties about the quantities of calories consumed now and earlier.
Does anybody know what calories really are? You might just as well
argue about how many letters there are in one line of Shakespeare as
compared with another and assume that the line with the most letters
in it was a better one than the line with the least. Nutrition, by the very
meaning of the word, is a qualitative datum, and the pseudo-scientific
nonsense about calories is simply a statistical gadget which has no
bearing whatever upon actual nourishment. It should be obvious to
the meanest capacity that food imported from abroad and processed
by the ingenious trickery of modern "science" has incomparably less
value as food that nourishes than fresh food grown on our own soils
and not subjected to various chemical dodges.

Far more serious was the attitude of mind ingrained in the
Government but hardly less so in the Opposition. That is, that the
supply of food which people need to live on is purely a matter of
successful trading and bargaining with foreign countries. Mr
Strachey's speech was almost entirely occupied with this point of view.
We had made an agreement with the Dutch to export eggs, bacon and
"milk products". We might be able to do a deal with Hungary for
bacon, eggs, poultry, lard and vegetable oil; there was the chance of a
good haggle with Eire for more bacon, eggs, butter "and other
things"; a bargain was in the offing with Yugoslavia; there were
possibilities in the Middle East and Southern Rhodesia; there might be
a trade agreement with Indonesia; Polish eggs and poultry had been
negotiated. It is perfectly clear from these naive utterances that, so far
as the fundamentals of life are concerned, the whole of the globe
outside the British Isles is regarded purely and simply as a gigantic
grocer's shop from which you can buy anything you like merely by
rustling paper (which may or may not be bank-notes) and bargaining
over the counter.

This is the attitude of the conjurer who by clever manipulation will
produce a card down his sleeve or a rabbit out of his hat. Even from the
commercial point of view (which is the only one ever considered), it is
as well, don't you think, to be sure of your bargaining capacity as a

means of inducing the grocer to hand over the stuff. If, to put it vulgarly, the supply of food depends on nothing more than making the oof-bird twitter properly, it is as well that the bird should be in your possession rather than the grocer's. Nobody dreamed, in imbibing the soothing syrup of these commercial transactions during the debate, of introducing the cold, cruel facts that in the first place there are precious few groceries behind the counter to sell and in the second that we owe money to the global grocer rather than *vice versa*.

A more sinister element emerged in *The Times* comment upon this debate. It spoke of the influence of the Overseas Food Corporation "in introducing new and progressive methods of cultivation in the standards of life of the poorest of the world's peoples".

When newspapers speak of the poor countries they invariably mean the peasant countries, for to modern civilization the self-supporting peasant is a poor creature, indeed, hardly more than an inferior beast of burden. The "new and progressive methods" which put 250,000,000 acres of the fertile land of North America out of cultivation would induce these wretched peasants to break their obsolete mixed husbandry and export what they grow to us in exchange for typewriters and gramophone records.

How nice and enlightening for them! They, too, will learn that to buy butter from some other country rather than make their own is civilization as contrasted with barbarism; they, too, will leave their lands for the cities, since food is a commodity to be bought, not a crop to be grown; they, too, will discard the spade for the tin-opener. For it obviously never so much as occurs to the modern legislator that the production of food has anything to do with such base matters as soil and plants and animals.

(*The Faith of a Fieldsman*, London, Museum Press, 1951; pp. 195-7)

THE FLOUR-MILLS DESTROYED

On his father's side he came of a line of landowner-farmers, seamen and parsons. It was from his mother's side that the milling tradition was inherited. Her father had plied his own steamboat with its brass funnel on the same Cornish river in whose crook stood the parental farm. It carried the wheats which were loaded from the boat for the mill on horse-waggons and in those spacious days there were 17 of them. This countryman too lived beyond the three-score years and ten, and rode his horse up to a few days before his death. His son, the brother of Hosking's mother, maintained the family vigour and independence as well as the milling business. He had three mills, was four times mayor of his town and had insisted on addressing a hostile mob from his steam-waggon.

But in the middle of the nineteen twenties, both the Devonshire mill and the two family country mills in Cornwall, were bought out by the milling combine, then in the thick of its campaign for putting the country stone-grinding mills out of action and so striking a mortal blow at the heart of the localised rural community. It was abetted by Government who passed the paralyzing law to veto the local farmer from selling bread-corn to the local miller. It was not because these local mills were "uneconomic," that they were struck down. The costs were as low as the combine's. But the stone-mills were smothered by the underselling of surpluses and the erection of temporary plant in the district. Long before the twenties, his uncle had migrated into Devonshire. There the nephew after his war-service joined him in the milling of flour and grist, in the merchanting of seeds, wool and fertilizer and in the farming of some 300 acres on the edge of Dartmoor.

So short a step, so minute a change - from Cornwall to Devon, from father to uncle, from a farm that was just a farm to a farm with a mill. Actually, it was a giant stride from world to world, the stride of one century that our nation took after the Industrial Revolution from a rural civilisation into industrialism. For Hosking passed at one bound from self-subsistent production to mercantilism, from growing and conserving things to buying and selling them. The wrench was self-confessed in his telling me that he used to drive 65 miles from Okehampton to the Cornish farm but stopped four miles away from it. He knew that, if he had added this fraction to his mileage, he would not have been able to return. It was not home-sickness after four years' absence at the war; it was the pull of the land from which he had been uprooted. He put the meaning of the change himself in saying that the people who walk on pavements have lost the sense of heaven and earth. Of earth *and* heaven.

The economy of his father's farm had depended like the self-renewal of the animal organism upon its own powers and processes of self-maintenance; now he found himself buying wool from farmers in Devon and Cornwall, seeds from London, from Timbuctoo, from anywhere. And selling them again, trafficking in them. The buying and selling in Cornwall had been incidental to the farm, but now it was the farm that had become incidental to the exchange from without of farm-products. So with wool. How little, he said, does the wearer of wool realise how much the weather, the soil and the nutrition of the animal affects the quality of what he is wearing! Seed, as he said himself, now represented so many lbs. at such and such a price; he was no longer seeing it from the cradle, watching its potentialities and assessing its quality. It was in his blood to note what the seed could make of itself and what he could do to induce it to make the best of itself; it had become his profession tomake what he could out of it. The sense of what seeds were and could be in themselves is stronger in him than in any man I have known, and the puzzled way he spoke of having looked at them from a totally different point of view was even more revealing than his tale.

Then there was the mill. This was a steel roller-mill, not the stone-grinding one his uncle had been forced to let go. The difference here was as great as that between growing seeds and only profiting by them. The stone-miller of course made his profit, but his primary purpose was to grind grain into flour. The primary purpose of the roller-miller is reversed; his rollers extract the wheat-germ because it is profitable to do so. Hosking was in no doubt at all about this. Long before the days of the breakfast-food firms buying the wheat-germ, he took it home with him for his porridge and his biscuits. To-day on his table he has the best whole-grain bread I have ever tasted, baked by his wife. The good miller, he said, milled the whole grain palatably, hygienically and digestibly from fresh wheat locally grown. But it would not keep (good things to eat seldom do). The modernised millers imported the dry Canadian wheats which will store and travel, standardised the moisture content and extracted the offals with the germ to be resold. Big business sprang out of lifeless bread. Because of their high moisture content, our home-grown wheats, superior in quality to any wheat in the world, cannot be stored for a prolonged period.

Both uncle and nephew were perfectly well aware that the whole-grain flour of the home-wheat had a dietetic value to which the imported wheats could not be compared. But by the irony of progress they found themselves buying wheats from all over the world at the expense not only of the old family business of watermilling, selling the flour locally and grinding it whole but of that very self-sufficiency of which the parental farm in Cornwall had been a shining example. At the expense too of nutrition. How important is this? We do not yet know. But we do know that when unpolished rice was stripped of its skin, beri-beri swept not only many a native population but our troops at Gallipoli. As soon as the whole rice-grain was issued to the troops, they recovered. The germ of the wheat lies close to the skin of the berry: both rice and wheat are cereals and the process of removing the life-force is much the same in both. The life-cell of any cereal is as the hearth to the house.

The pair bought Manitoba wheat for the good reason that it is a strong wheat with a high percentage of gluten, and gluten swells up the grain to make bigger loaves. And there were the "improvers" which made the grains blow up the more and like the soft wheats gave more loaves to the sack. They could bleach them to give that whiteness which had become the hallmark of suburban gentility. The germ, the real nutrient, went into the middlings or sharps for the cattle - that part of it that did not go into Hosking's porridge. Later, it was to make milling yet more profitable by being sold for proprietary breakfast foods and the like. An advertisement for one of these foods in an American magazine runs as follows: "Wheat germ is the golden heart of wheat that's added in extra amounts to natural whole wheat... 2½ times richer than the whole wheat in wheat germ." A few pages away is another advertisement, this time for the bereaved bread, which says: "It is enriched with thiamin, niacin, riboflavin and iron." In such ways commercialism replaces nature. As Hosking put it succinctly, he and his uncle had to make a profit for services not rendered but surrendered.

(*The Wisdom of the Fields*, London, Collins, 1945, pp. 215-18)

THE VALUE OF WEEDS

Weeding considered *per se* as a pursuit has little to recommend it. Yet weed you must. Charlock is the host of the flea-beetle and cruciferous weeds are of the slime fungus that brings club-root to cabbages. Weeds compete with food-plants and flowers for the supply of nutrients, especially nitrogen, and no gardener worthy the name can bear to look upon

> "an unweeded garden
> That grows to seed; things rank and gross in nature
> Possess it merely."

To an authentic owner nothing is more unpleasing than a dirty bed. But if the weeds go to the compost heap, the process of getting them there acquires a new significance, both practical and psychological. The weeder is acting one of the rhythms of nature but at the same time controlling it. And as he weeds he educates himself. For weeds are indications of soil deficiencies, and by a curious paradox - and life is a perpetual paradox - weeds in a garden are rich in the particular minerals that the soil lacks. The more vigorous certain types grow in a particular area of soil, the more lacking that soil is in those needs. Bad drainage, for instance, is betrayed by marestail, ranunculus, mosses, meadow sweet and other plants. Acidity is advertised by dandelion, plantain, daisy, dock, self-heal, bents, sorrel and others. Nitrogen deficiency is registered by the presence of the nitrogen-fixers - clovers and vetches. It is an interesting fact that nitrogen-fixing legumes like clover, if artificially overfed with nitrogen fertilisers, become consumers instead of producers of nitrogen. If the weeder glances at the nodules on their root-hairs, he can tell by their presence or absence whether his soil is rich or poor in nitrogen.

Thus, the weed extracts from the soil exactly what the soil needs, and the prevalence of one type of weed over another is a pointer to reading the soil like a manuscript. The absence of boron, cobalt, manganese, potassium, sulphur, phosphoric acid, sodium, zinc, iodine, silicon, copper, iron, or some other essential or trace-element in minute quantities becomes a language to be deciphered. The profound error of modern science has been in separating minerals and vitamins *from the plant,* whether in health as food for beasts and men or in decay as food for the soil. This is the root of the matter.

But let not the student be dismayed. The compost heap shoulders all the burden and he can lean back on nature's erudition. She is the librarian. Trundling his barrow filled with weeds, the weeder flings the whole bundle on to the stack. In time the fungi and bacteria, on whose activities the whole sensible world depends, reduce them to mould which in the spring or autumn is forked into the soil or laid on as a top dressing. Thus are restored those very elements whose shortage of supply was announced by the living weeds... The compost heap is the most precise of chemists and its prescriptions are impeccable. How then can the weeder regard his task any more with distaste and weariness? Bent to his toil, he is also the student bent to his book. He bows his head to the wisdom and economy of nature, and, acquiring this knowledge, perhaps offers a silent prayer to the Creator both of nature and himself. For the compost heap corrects the fallibility of his judgment and redeems a prosaic task of its pedantry and tedium. It gives him learning without tears.

(*This Plot of Earth,* London, Collins, 1944, pp. 107-8)

THE NEED FOR A PEASANTRY

There has reached me out of the blue a journal published by the *Société Française d'Equipement Rural,* and, turning over the pages in curiosity, I found some remarks by M. André Birre which reveal in unequivocal fashion how our own agricultural misdeeds are coming home to roost. M. Birre leads off with an account of a conference in which it was pointed out that the numbers of germs in pasteurized milk had been found to have increased from 30,000 to 500,000, a large quantity of which were pathogenic. When we remember the professorial rages that erupted when any criticism of the pasteurization nostrum was whispered, this news is decidedly entertaining. I often wonder myself what on earth is the use of T.T. herds when good milk is mixed with bad and the whole has the life boiled out of it. It appears, however, that life is getting its own back by replacing healthy with unhealthy bacteria.

Be this as it may, M. Birre goes on to suggest that the deterioration of milk is to be correlated with a biological disequilibrium in the soil, and that this lack of balance is the consequence of *"une agriculture abusivement technocratique"*, introducing the most important of all problems, how to replace this bad system with an agriculture of quality. He quotes Dr Carrel to the effect that mass production of crops and the techniques of commercialism have lowered the quality of all forms of produce, a devitalization generating in its wake (according to Dr Albreth of Missouri University) a *faim cachée* or hidden hunger in the peoples who believe themselves well nourished. So they eat more and more, in order to compensate for this qualitative deficiency in their food.

M. Birre then asks: What is the first cause of this loss of quality? It is, he says, the loss of vitality in the soil, and the main reason for this loss is the disuse of organic methods caused by a shallow assimilation of the practices advocated (and, I might add, virtually enforced) by an industrialized science. Thus, a tension has been set up between the responsible farmer guided by the need of replenishing his land and the industrials whose methods have nothing to do with biological processes.

What is of the first importance, continues M. Birre, is a conscience enlightened by the plenitude of life, grounded in the ways of nature and directed by an intelligence at once meditative and constantly alert. What is needed is exactly that which the world is applying itself to destroy, namely a peasantry, a body of men, that is to say, rooted in its own country, integrated in its own life, penetrated with the rhythms and harmonies of nature, sufficiently free and solidly established to have the power to create and continually recreate the world about them, a world from which emanate the sources of life. What primarily counts (I am still paraphrasing M. Birre) in a renaissance of agriculture devoted to restoring vitality in order to recover quality is not, except in a minor degree, technical progress, but the nursing of a society of master-peasants which will restore the losses of quality and health which have resulted from the blind idolatry of industrial techniques.

Then come these significant words - we (that is to say M. Birre's countrymen) believe that this indispensable renaissance is possible because we already possess a peasantry which, in spite of all, has kept intact in the depths of its conscience a sense of traditional values. So, we shall renew ourselves at the sources of life.

Fine, but what are we English going to do about it? By what is probably the supreme blunder of all our history (a bottomless stupidity which is still hailed by officials and professors as a glory of progress), we swept our peasantry away by the Enclosures of the nineteenth century. And now we are feeling the icy draught of retribution for our own folly. Well, I believe that M. Birre is talking like a wise man and that, if bad quality, plant-sickness and soil-depletion are not to be the end of us, we shall have to build up a new peasantry. And how is a new peasantry to be created? Only by fostering the small holder and small owner, by opening up new opportunities for them, by offering them just prices and priority for their produce and imports, and by training them in organic and biological methods.

(*The Faith of a Fieldsman:* 166-8)

EXAMPLES OF A SURVIVING PEASANTRY

Fleet the basketer is the liveliest of these descendants of the Makers of

England, but he is of Breton ancestry, and still wears his Celtic badge in his name, William Youens. When the stock came to England it was before the Huguenots, and as, according to Fleet, his people have never been other than basket-makers, perhaps he is descended from the wattle-weavers of the Glastonbury Lake Village, who were notable craftsmen. But the England of the twentieth century stopped the contemporary Fleet from making baskets, and he had to put his vegetables into foreign ones instead. He had to go on producing, that being his nature, so he set up a greengrocer's shop and sold in it the produce of his garden at back.

It was a raw, oozing, fog-bound day at the beginning of December when I last went to see him. It was like a legend that I found him making a Christmas Crib, the idea of which originated with St. Francis. A basket-maker come down from countless generations of basket-makers working on the happy idea of St. Francis, and since basketry is certainly as old as growing crops, using much the same methods in the making as the first colonizers of England. Whether St. Francis made his symbolic cradle out of withies like a creel or of thin pegged planks with panelled sides, hoods and rocking posts like the mediaeval cradles, yet the sight of him weaving his crib was the epitome and emblem of Christmas. The greengrocer who grew his own greenstuff to sell in his shop, making a Christmas crib in the small market town that had only changed in our own century - was not this an act of unconscious homage to the principle underlying the Story of the Manger, where all is native, of the country, of the soil and the immemorial peasantry? The Eastern Star shone over the byre, not the palace of Herod; the Magi came to a farmyard and a craftsman's workshop, not to the Temple-Bank of Jewry. The Christ of the Trades, of the farm, the workshop, the peasant household, of the integrated, self-sufficient life on the land, it was to him that wisdom and monarchy made pilgrimage, acknowledging the glorification not only of humility but of the roots of all civilization and of the loving intercourse between man and earth. All the implications of the craftsman's trade, livelihood and associations, its continuity, its virtue embedded in the soil, the family and the home, its natural goodwill towards man and nature, its modest but perpetual creation, these are all stressed, irradiated and transfigured by the place and scene and narrative and circumstances of the Incarnation. So, in watching my basketer making his Christmas crib, I was looking into a sacred picture as rich in symbolism and ultimate meaning as a Giotto or a Fra Angelico.

Nor could the continuity of creation have been more faithfully represented. The discarding of old truths as out-of-date is certainly not applicable to basket-making. There is one way of making one kind of basket, another way for another kind, just as there is one glory of the sun and one glory of the moon. There is no other way except by factory-basketing, and the difference there is not between one kind and another, nor between old and new, but between good and bad.

(*Men of Earth*, London, Chapman and Hall, 1943; pp. 88-90)

Only a few days ago, I spent the afternoon with Samuel Rockall in his workshop looking out on the common zoned in beech-woods. Both he and his son were hard at work on the chair-legs; the one at his chopping-block, the other astride the draw-shave horse. Busy and yet in deep repose, occupied in a score of jobs and yet a multiplicity in unity, such is the life of Samuel. In seeking him out I pass not merely from one place to another, even from one world to another, even from discord to order and from confusion to cohesion. In some mysterious way I pass out from the hallucinations of world-sickness into a speck of reality which is so extraordinarily stable as to defeat even time. I do not mean that Summer Heath will always have its Samuel -in a few years it may well be a bungalow village or a wilderness. What I mean is that the man's organic relation to his natural environment seems to me to be final. Given those woods and that heath - Samuel's life in them and work from them are what theology used to call "the will of God" or "the word made flesh". The natural scene as particularised at Summer Heath was waiting for its Samuel, its king and servant. He arrived, and there he is, the predestined, the meaning of the place, its human expression, its being made manifest in the man. I do not know how else to put it.

Samuel produced a shovel. Forty years ago he had bought it from a travelling tinker for fourpence. Every day for year after year he had gone out on the common with it to pick up what casual offerings from pony, cart-horse, sheep or goat he could find. This promptly went into the compost pit of his garden. In time, the shovel became worn to two-thirds of its original length and Samuel found a bit of metal off a telegraph post blown down by a gale. He hammered and riveted it to the shovel, and the very next day, while he was shovelling the sawdust of his garden-path for fuel, he found a sixpenny piece under it. This, as the Suffolk yokels say, "wholly" pleased him; now his shovel had not only paid for itself but at compound interest. It seemed to me that the fairies, approving of Samuel, must have slipped that sixpence under the sawdust. "I wouldn't", beamed Samuel, "sell this shovel for half-a-crown." Of course not: it was more worth to him than if it had been made of gold. There, in terms of a plain shovel, is the peasant notion of possessions. He makes everything he has go ten times further than another man would do with things ten times the value. Everything the peasant possesses is also ten times itself because of the wealth of associations gathered round it.

We went into the garden. There was a marrow bed which was non-pareil. Samuel expounded the mystery. The roots of the seedlings had been planted on the lip of the compost pit, while a small channel had been dug at the side to let off the liquid manure from the household slops. This vitalised the rest of the garden while the marrows luxuriated in the pit. A few steps away was a specimen of his grafting, a bulge of mud painted black - all Samuel's apples originated from crab-tree stock. This reminded him of the fourteen pounds of blackberry-and-apple jam he had just made in the cottage, and that in turn sent him off to fetch a tobacco jar of wild cherry wood and perfect workmanship he had cut and turned for a customer whom I had unwittingly brought him by my former chronicles of the deeds of Samuel. We returned to the workshop, he to his axe and his lathe, I to the Windsor chair he had fitted up from an 18th century design.

I have known Samuel for years, and yet he has always something new to tell and show me. Except in the felling season, he never leaves his cottage, but out of frugality come riches, and out of simplicity flowers novelty without end. Nothing is wasted; everything turns into something else. Just as nothing is lost in Nature, so with Samuel. The trees he has axed come from the wood; they make multiform objects of use and beauty, while the shavings feed the hearth of the home and the fertility of the garden. The transformations both of garden and wild maintain his family and preserve his independence. Trade, family, economy, livelihood, work, utility, ornament, all are parts of one organic whole. Independence and interdependence are woven into a fabric of wholeness and integrity bears its double meaning. Nature is the source of his industry and each gains by the enrichment of the other. The great primaries of life - Nature, the home, the family, the craft, the land - share an intimate and mutual relation without losing their separate identities. Each is seen to be necessary to the other in the fulfilment of an integrated life. Use and beauty here have no quarrel any more than the wild with the domestic. The cottage and the workshop front the heath and the woods, and this is a symbolic presentation of an inward truth that rules and fructifies the daily humdrum life of Samuel the Bodger. But a life thus creative from dung-heap to flower is homespun rather than humdrum when grace lies within its modesty and wealth within its limitations. All men desire the good life: in the agony of frustration they invent grandiose and visionary Utopias. But on Summer Heath it is embodied like a work of art.

(*Remembrance*, London, Batsford, 1942, pp. 134-5)

[Massingham discusses a letter written by Samuel Rockall]... If an "educationalist" should happen to read this letter, which is hardly likely, it is easy to imagine the pained uplift of his eyebrows as Samuel's words come tumbling forth like tin soldiers out of a box with little or no punctuation to restrain them. But would he know how to fell trees, saw, split or chop logs, drawshave them, turn them, make chairs and stools, grow and bottle fruit, make jam, tend a garden, sweep chimneys, grind tools, solder, repair, graft trees, build walls out of shavings, make tobacco boxes, cart timber and perform a great many other useful and skilled activities not mentioned in his own inventory, not to mention keeping a wife and family before the war on thirty shillings a week? But to do these things and others like them is no longer considered as part of education. If a young hopeful leaves school remembering the date of the Battle of Hastings, the multiplication table, the number of rivers in Europe, the principal exports of Peru, the name of the capital of Turkey and how to read the captions of a film-sheet and the headlines in the Sunday paper, he will pass, he is educated. For it has now passed out of the national consciousness that an illiterate man can be much better educated than one who knows how to read and write, nor does compulsory literacy seem to have produced a people that can discriminate between goodness and trash or can look after its own affairs or even find out how to feed itself. As Cobbett once said, it looks out of the window for the rest of the world to bring it its food and drink. But if education has anything to do with helping a man to stand on his own feet, regard the world with a steady eye and choose from it what is excellent in itself and serviceable to others, then I fancy that Samuel for all his high-handedness with stops and commas may qualify to be an educated man.

Though it is doubtful whether he has been off the Chilterns since he left the army, I have never yet paid him a visit without discovering some fresh aspect of his being or his labour. It might be puzzling to account for this inexhaustibility of the man, were it not for the fact that he is, as I have said, the complete peasant and therefore to our generation as strange and foreign a creature as was the first wild Indian brought back to Europe from the Americas by the first voyagers in uncharted seas. The modern English peasant is not only as rare as a raven, but his ways, his doings, his attitude to life and unexpressed philosophy about it are so unfamiliar to us that a curiosity almost amounting to excitement gathers about the least of his seasonal activities. It becomes excitement itself when it is realized that he is the living representative of nine-tenths of the English nation as it once was. In his part of the world, Samuel is the sole survivor of that village community that chamfered the waggons, carved the string-courses of the parish church, adjudicated on the administration of the local husbandry, brewed the beer, baked the bread, went a-summering on St. John's Eve, acted the Mystery Plays, made simples out of wayside herbs, plaited symbolic figures out of the last harvest sheaves, composed and sang ballads, worshipped the rural Christ, cultivated without exhausting the same soil for a thousand years, had a bottomless folk-memory, possessed a more democratic constitution than we so much as know the meaning of, and captured London in a few days in the Great Revolt of 1381.

(*Men of Earth:* 140-1)

THE RELIGION OF HUSBANDRY

It will thus be seen how inevitably my studies in craftsmanship led me on to husbandry. Husbandry *is* craftsmanship, the sum of all craftsmanship, and to try and turn it into something else, a business among businesses, is the way to utter disaster. Farming is essentially a handcraft, as all crafts are, and that is why extreme mechanisation and standardisation lead only to the literal desert. A craft is always flexible, varied, individual, like life, and the self-sufficiency of mixed farming with all its subtle and delicate inter-relations gives the utmost scope to craftsmanship. The machine, as a farmer once said to me, "takes the song out of the job".

The attempt has been made and is being made to turn farm into factory with the added disqualification to the farmer that his craft is being commercialised without the financial bolstering... accorded to other businesses. Without, too, the expert staff of the business firm, since the better accountant and industrialist the farmer becomes, the worse is his husbandry. The more he tries to adapt himself to an artificial economics, the worse is his violation of biological law. The greater his speed, the more broken is his rhythm. The closer he specialises, the more dislocated are his balances between arable, livestock and grass-ley and the poorer his crops. The more he confuses production with fertility, the sooner he loses the latter. The more he absorbs the urban mentality, the less countryman he. The more up-to-date he becomes, the more down-at-heels are his fields. Land is potential life, not raw material to be manufactured, and the poet's vision of it is far more real and practical than the business man's attitude to it as industrial plant. But the husbandman's treatment of it is the most realistic of all because it is based on an intuitive grasp of biological principles, tested by the experience of many generations.

The judgement of the earth is plain. It will have craftsmanship or nothing and to the predatory man it will refuse its fruits. Its udder will turn sour and then flaccid and sterile. The modern economic system is rejected of the earth because it is false. The earth's answer to it is unequivocal: it is soil-sickness, beast-sickness, man-sickness. A banker's earth is sick at heart. And is there no causation in this triple sickness of soil, beast, man? Vast moneys spent on scientific research and public health have not removed this sickness; they have not even discovered its cause, they have not gathered the three sicknesses into one sickness, which is the sickness of the earth.

But health-wholeness-holiness, only the very rarest man of science is aware of this trinity, a three-in-one. Average science will not stop men from preying on the soil as the plumage-traders preyed on birds in the breeding season for the milliners. An acquisitive society is responsible for the sickness of earth, beasts, plants and men. Nature and the spirit are at one in repudiating an acquisitive society, and such is the answer to Darwinian and company promoter alike. But the relation of the Hunza people (whom I referred to in the tenth chapter as the healthiest in the world) to nature is not acquisitive but, in Lord Northbourne's admirable term, "symbiotic", just as the craftsman's relation to nature is symbiotic. So the wheel comes full circle and it is possible to claim with some confidence that the human approach to the earth the earth most favours is the craftsman's.

Our modern food is bad because it is denatured out of its wholeness - it is, as we say without knowing what we mean, unwholesome. The profit-making motive is uncraftsmanly because it is unbalanced, hoisting the part at the expense of the whole. The primary question the craftsman-producer wants to know about an article is: "Is it good in itself?" not "Does it pay?" or "Will it sell?" Our subsidies on certain crops are unwholesome because the parts of a farm interlock to make the whole greater than the sum of its parts. Our artificials only restore to the soil part of what is taken out of it, and that the non-living part, whereas the "rule of return" restores all the waste as the potential of a new and vigorous life. There is a scientific term, "fractionation", which is beyond me, but, if it means "broken into fractions or fragments" admirably describes the scientific mind. A self-supporting husbandry as opposed to the parasitic reliance upon cheap, stale and imported foods produced by monoculture and exploitation is the true aim and the most practical because it represents the concept of an integer. Cut the physical element out of the cultivation of the soil by substituting machinery for human sweat and experience is halved and stunted. Cut the spiritual element out of it, and the heart of the whole is gone. The farmer is speaking in more than quantitative terms when he says that his land is "in good heart".

This new concept was revealed to me partly by intensive reading of farming literature, partly by the acute realisation of what the loss of a limb and a half actually means. It gathered up and bound together the distinct and separate strands of my previous experience. Thus it was exceeding bitter to me and is now that I could not put the concept into practice by balancing pen with plough. That was for ever denied me because the sense of this final integration, final for me, I mean, had come too late.

It is true that I have my garden in which year by year the linnets breed, always lining their nests with the hair of my sheepdog, Friday, to me a union by grace of the wild with the domestic. I see a symbol too in the wren's nest in the crotch of two rafters of my "Hermitage". And I try to handle my garden, only an acre as it is, but with many trees and an orchard in it that in time past I have planted, as a single organism, less the livestock, though now I have a pig and two geese. Once, it was a bare slope; now it is a grown-up garden, but, I am happy to say, it has not parted company with the fields, hedgerows, coppice and range of distant downs of which it was originally an integral portion. I have not dismembered it from them. The garden melts into fields, wood, hills in barely perceptible gradations and yet remains a garden. This principle I have tried to embody in detail as well as in general effect. So the hybrid tea-roses do not have it all their own way; they are preluded and accompanied by many Chinese, Tuscany, musk, damask and species roses that are either countrified or traditional. The rockery is built on broad low walls of stone that lead somewhere and according to nature's way. An irrelevant rockery can ruin a whole garden. The snapdragons appear in drifts after snowflakes that are hardly distinguishable from their wild brethren. The terrace, on the other hand, being immediately outside the house-walls, is of severely rectangular blocks, but draped with sun-roses of divers hues as the walls themselves are crowded with clematis, vine, fig, Cydonia, roses and other climbers that clamber almost at their will. There are three lawns, in size like the three bears in the story, and this triplicity illustrates the layout of the garden as a whole, wild farthest from the house, semi-domesticated between that and the house, and nearest the house itself, more formalised and geometrical. So the blend of colours is a study in itself in which my blundering is not for want of it. All on quite a small scale, of course, but a garden, however modest, can and should articulate in its own medium the intercourse between man and nature in as subtle and intricate a series of variations as its form and area permit. It is kept in balance by a proper rotational system and in fertility by a system of composting which I learned from the Indore Process of Sir Albert Howard. By putting fertility or quality first and production or quantity second, I have been rewarded by yearly increases both in excellence and mass of fresh food. Surely quantity, like speed, its other face, has been the evil genius of the modern world.

I can sense the mystery - time, the seasons, nature, death and life wheeling like the figures of a dance in the work of transmutation. I can grasp the immensity of Sir Albert Howard's conception of the endless circulation of organic matter through soil, plant and animal and back again in the reverse movement - a continuous chain of interwoven living processes - as of no less importance than, as he himself has suggested, Harvey's discovery of the circulation of the blood in medicine. And I can perceive that this discovery has much more vital implications than Harvey's, involving as it does a total revaluation of all our methods and transactions with the soil, with nature, and with our own lives. So, knowing that it is health rather than disease which medicine has missed, it is sorrowful to me that I cannot participate except through my mind in this music of earth which reflects a something beyond "the sphere of our sorrow."

(*Remembrance:* 135-8)

Now that I come to review the past of my own life with all its errors, vanities and delusions offset by but one validity, persistence of quest, I take one thing that has been granted me as its crown - the perception that the law of nature, be it truly interpreted, expounds the divine law. A divine law enfolding the infernal chaos of our times. But we who have made the chaos, we too are part of nature and of the divine law which is the projection into nature of the Eternal Mind. We see into nature through our experience of that law. Nature was God's idea, and we are enabled to perceive the idea through our own mental and personal experience of nature's reality. We cannot perceive beauty in nature without also being aware of truth and goodness, since they are not separable, and in the same way we see nature neither objectively nor subjectively alone but both in one and both are true. It is when man interacts with nature, searching her laws with his brain, gathering their rhythms into his being and translating them into his work, that his spirit can touch the eternal. The poet divines and the craftsman acts the whole in the part, while the part which is the place or region or work is a whole in itself that reflects a larger whole, outside of time and independent of matter.

So I have come to perceive that the love and understanding of nature are the only practical means to living at all, and everything I have seen, thought and read confirms me. "Nature", wrote Lord Northbourne, "is only terrible and squalid to those who do not understand her, and when misunderstanding has upset her balance. She is imbued above all with the power of love, by love she can after all be conquered, but in no other way. That has not been our way." The poet has expressed the same thought for all time: "Lady, we receive but what we give." In that faith I rest.

(*Remembrance:* 146-7)

Chapter 12 of The Rural Tradition *by W.J. Keith (Harvester Press, Hassocks; University of Toronto Press, Toronto, 1975) gives a summary of Massingham's life and work; the* Ecologist, *Vol.6, No.4*

REVERENCE FOR GOD'S LAWS   221

(May 1976) contains an article on Massingham by Nicholas Gould, "A Eulogist of Traditional Husbandry".

In addition to the books from which extracts are taken, the following works by Massingham also contain valuable material on topics connected with the organic outlook: The English Countryman *(London, Batsford, 1942);* Field Fellowship *(London, Chapman and Hall, 1942);* The Tree of Life *(London, Chapman and Hall, 1943);* An Englishman's Year *(London, Collins, 1948);* The Curious Traveller *(London, Collins, 1950); with Edward Hyams (see chapter 1)* Prophecy of Famine *(London, Thames and Hudson, 1953). Massingham edited the following books on husbandry:* England and the Farmer *(London, Batsford, 1941);* The Natural Order *(London, Dent, 1945);* The Small Farmer *(London, Collins, 1947).*

Massingham also wrote the Introduction to From the Ground Up, *by Jorian Jenks (London, Hollis and Carter, 1950), which gives an account of the economic and political forces behind changes in agricultural practice.*

NAME INDEX